Making Model

STEAM

BOATS

Making Model
STEAM BOATS

Stephen Bodiley

✳ THE CROWOOD PRESS

First published in 2022 by
The Crowood Press Ltd
Ramsbury, Marlborough
Wiltshire SN8 2HR

enquiries@crowood.com

www.crowood.com

British Library Cataloguing-in-Publication Data
A catalogue record for this book is available from the British Library.

ISBN 978 0 7198 4131 6

Disclaimer
Safety is of the utmost importance in every aspect of metalworking and model engineering.
When using tools, always follow closely the manufacturer's recommended procedures. However,
the author and publisher cannot accept responsibility for any accident or injury caused by
following the advice given in this book.

Typeset by Jean Cussons Typesetting, Diss, Norfolk
Cover design by Sergey Tsvetkov
Printed and bound in India by Parksons Graphics

CONTENTS

PREFACE AND ACKNOWLEDGEMENTS

Looking back, it was clear at an early age that I was interested in mechanical things. Childhood memories include taking mechanical clocks apart to see how they worked, and fixing the family car with my father. Christmas lists included Meccano, LEGO Technic, model steam engines and, one year, a radio-controlled car.

Later I studied mechanical engineering at college, and when we bought our first house, not only was there a single garage, but also a small square of land behind it, which was turned into a workshop space. Precious funds were put towards a Myford lathe – and a long period of self-teaching and learning was under way.

Many years later the workshop still holds my interest. It is used to keep a classic car and motorbike on the road, as well as doing jobs for neighbours and friends, and of course for model engineering.

Model engineering provides an interesting mix of mechanical principles and practical skills that come together to form a creative and rewarding hobby. Steam engines have long been a favourite model engineering topic, and model boats are particularly suited to steam propulsion, as even the simplest of engines can be made to move a model boat, so modest are the power requirements.

When I was asked to write a book on model boats, the aim was twofold. First, to present some model boat designs fully explained and with clear drawings, to enable builders of all abilities to make them; and second, to include information on the design aspects of steam engines and boats such that readers can create their own designs and experiment.

For me, workshop time is about learning new skills, self-improvement and enjoyment. With this in mind, here are some live steam model boats of my own design, which I hope people will enjoy building and sailing.

ACKNOWLEDGEMENTS

Much gratitude goes to the following people who have contributed to the writing of this book:

Alan Fisher
Alison Brown
Arthur Ganson
Chris Lloyd – Nexus Special Interest Model Books
Eric Baird – Brighton Toy and Model Museum
John Bodiley
Marvin Klotz
Mohammud Hanif Dewan
Odilon Marcenaro
Stan Bray
Tubal Cain

INTRODUCTION AND UNITS

This book contains the plans and building instructions for three live steam model boats.

The first is the simplest, quickest build and is reminiscent of the toys from the 1920s and 1930s. Companies such as Bowman, Mamod and Bassett-Lowke all produced similar designs. This first model is a good introduction to making a live steamboat, and uses a number of purchased parts to assist further the build process. It is fired by solid fuel tablets, and the engine is a typical oscillating cylinder model powered by a boiler with the minimum of fittings. The hull is flat bottomed to simplify manufacture and to ensure that the final result is stable at sea. This model is the smallest of the three and is designed to be a free steamer, the rudder being set to sail a course, alone on the water.

The second model is the 'Feature Build' and provides a step up in skills and complexity. The model is designed to be interesting to build without being overly difficult. The engine is of a rotary valve design, the steam and exhaust controlled by ports on the main axle. The boiler has the essential fittings of a safety valve and steam take-off, but also an extra bush for filling either manually or from a pump, and a superheater and lubricator are included. The smokestack acts as an exhaust and also a condenser, to catch any oil in the steam and prevent it entering the lake. This time the hull has a more complex profile, and there is room to add radio control to the rudder for more adventurous navigation.

Included within the Feature Build chapters are some rudimentary calculations and considerations to allow builders to adapt the model to their own design. This includes some safety points regarding boilers, boat theory including water displacement, centre of gravity and hydrodynamics for the hull, and some information on measuring engine performance.

The third model is a paddle steamer. This uses the boiler from the Harbour Pilot, coupled to a twin-cylinder oscillating engine, and uses a reduction gear to power the paddles. The hull uses a different construction process, and once again there is the option to use radio control.

As model engineering projects there is an expectation that some workshop facilities are available. Both engines involve machining and require some accuracy in the moving parts to get a working result. Where possible, a number of different approaches to a particular build step are described, as options will depend on the equipment available; and an attempt has been made to keep tooling to a minimum.

The boilers, although not complex, require some copper smithing and sheet metal work. The pressure vessels are of silver-soldered construction as is proper these days to ensure a safe outcome, and they should be pressure tested before steaming.

Finally, the hulls are woodwork projects. A bandsaw and sanding disc help make this part of the project easier, but hand tools will also do the job.

Altogether, the variety of skills is what makes live steam boats interesting. For newcomers to the hobby the build instructions are described step by step, and for experienced modellers the chapters on designs and theory should expand on practical skills and enable creativity.

For inspiration, Fig. 1.1 is a picture of a finished model out on the water. It is to be hoped that

Fig. 1.1   The Harbour Pilot maiden voyage at The Lake Grounds.

building and sailing your home-built model will give you many hours of enjoyment.

UNITS

Metric units are used wherever possible in this book. Being based on the number ten, they hold a certain logic and there is less of a requirement to know how many of one unit go into another; the answer is usually ten or one thousand.

Compare this to the imperial system, which has, over centuries, evolved to be quite complex. Length for example can be in 'thou', which is 1/1000th of an inch but is sometimes also (confusingly) called 'a mil'. There are 333¹/₃ thou in a Barleycorn, and three Barleycorns to the inch; 12in to the foot, and 6.0761ft in a fathom. It is not a particularly straightforward system.

However, steam engines come from a time when imperial units were the norm. Many of the books, and much of the wisdom on steam engines and boilers, is therefore in old units. Sometimes a metric conversion still makes sense, but there are other units, pressure for example, where pounds per square inch (psi) is more common and easier to relate to, than the metric equivalent. So apologies in advance in the use of mixed units throughout the book, but an effort has been made always to pick the most logical and straightforward units for a particular task or calculation.

The drawings in this book are in metric for the most part, but again, some imperial sizes are used where necessary. Copper pipe, for example, is usually sold in imperial units, so steam unions must be drilled to suit. You will also see bar stock sizes specified in imperial sizes, as this is what most model engineering suppliers stock.

The same mixture occurs with threads. Threads are a combination of British Association (BA) and Mechanical Engineering (ME) pitch. BA is, in fact, a metric standard and has its origins in the world of horology and scientific instrumentation. As a result, many small fasteners particularly suited to model engineering are sold in BA sizes.

ME threads are imperial but are classified by their pitch. So all the diameters have the same pitch, which is very useful for steam fittings where a large diameter fine pitch thread is called for.

To try to keep tooling investment to a minimum, the variety of thread sizes has been kept to the smallest range possible.

Finally, on the subject of units: the book sometimes talks about microns, which have the Greek symbol 'Mu' written as µ. This is 1000th of a millimetre, or 0.001mm. So 0.06mm can be written as 60µm, which means 60 microns.

CHAPTER ONE

WORKSHOP EQUIPMENT AND SAFETY

Every machine tool involves sharp edges or heat (or both), and as such it is impossible to write down every hazard. Machinists should get to know their tools and how to operate them safely so as to avoid injury. However, there are a few safety essentials, described below, that go a long way to ensuring you enjoy your workshop time.

Safety glasses: If you only follow one safety rule it should be this one: find some safety glasses that are comfortable, and wear them. You can get prescription ones if you need them, and once you have the habit of wearing them, it will feel wrong without.

Shoes: There is no need for safety boots, but avoid slippers and flip-flops.

Chuck keys: Don't leave the chuck key in any chuck. As you release the chuck and walk away, take the chuck key with you.

Tidiness: It is important to make sure the floor is free of trip hazards, particularly cables. Keeping the floor swept also makes it possible to find small parts when you drop them.

Brazing/silver-soldering: Brazing work is hot – very hot. Keep a bucket of water to hand, and always be aware how you pick up the hot work, such that if you drop it, it doesn't land on your arm or foot.

Pickling: Avoid serious acids such as hydrochloric or sulphuric, and work with citric acid crystals from a brewery shop. These are safe to work with and easy to dispose of.

Gloves: Gloves can be useful when brazing or pickling, but they have no place near machine tools, where they can snag and do more harm than good. Thin Nitrile or latex gloves are fine as they will tear if they get caught.

Hair: Long hair should be tied up or kept under a hat.

Ties: If you wear a tie, make it a safety tie, which will unclip if it gets caught.

WORKSHOP REQUIREMENTS

An effort has been made to keep the builds as uncomplicated as possible to enable more people to build them. However, as model engineering projects there is an expectation that some machine tools are available. As a minimum, a small lathe with a vertical slide is needed to produce the engine, and a drill press greatly helps speed things up when it comes to drilling and countersinking. A milling machine is not essential but is used in the book as a first choice for some of the operations, as it was available. Where possible, alternative methods such as using a D-bit instead of a reamer are suggested, to give the builder more options.

Taps and dies are needed – specifically, 8BA, $5/_{16}$in × 32tpi, $1/_4$in × 32tpi, and $3/_{16}$in × 32tpi ME threads. The metric M4 thread is also used.

Silver-soldering equipment is required to build the boiler. A gas torch, along with Silver-Flo rod and Tenacity 5 flux, is recommended.

The completed pressure vessel needs to be hydraulically tested to twice the working pressure, and a method is described to approximate this without building a pump, but a pressure gauge is necessary. Similarly, the safety valve tension must be set for it to be effective.

For the hull, only hand tools are needed, but shapes can be cut on a bandsaw if one is available. Sanding is quicker with a power sander, but hand sanding will suffice, especially if the timber is soft.

As a shopping list, some of the more specialized parts needed are these:

8BA hex-head steel bolts
8BA C/sunk steel screws
8BA grub screws
M4 grub screws
Copper pipe $5/_{32}$in diameter
Copper pipe $1/_8$in diameter
$5/_{32}$in nuts and cones to make steam unions
$3/_{16}$in bronze balls
Stainless spring length $3/_{26}$in OD, with a wire gauge of $1/_{32}$in
1¾in copper tube 20 or 22 gauge
Propeller shaft and propeller
Loctite 638 or similar, such as Truloc 268

A good model engineering supplier should be able to provide most of these parts, aside from the propeller and shaft, which are best sourced from a model shop.

Hex-head BA screws are sometimes available with a smaller head. This is a good option to take as they will suit the small scale of the engines in this book.

Also consider getting a box wrench for the hex

Fig. 1.2 The author's workshop with a Myford lathe as the centrepiece. Out of shot are a Dore-Westbury milling machine and bench grinder.

screws and a small 0.9mm hex key for the 8BA grub screws.

LATHES

A lathe is one of the most useful engineering tools. It can make a multitude of cylindrical components such as axles, wheels, pulleys, bushes, washers and spacers. Less obvious is that you can also turn castings and odd-shaped components with the four-jaw chuck, and even create square components using facing operations on a workpiece. With additional attachments you can turn tapers, spheres, cut slots, hob gears and cut threads. For the models in this book only a simple lathe is needed, and in case the reader is in the process of sourcing a machine, the following considerations should be borne in mind:

Speeds: High speeds are the realm of woodworking; for metalworking, being able to turn at a slower speed is more useful. A lathe with a range of 25rpm to 750rpm will be more useful for metalwork than one that runs at 3,000rpm but only goes down to 500rpm. Some lathes advertise variable speed control, which sounds nice, but the lower speeds are also lower power. More useful is a lathe with a 'back gear', which is a reduction gear that not only reduces speeds, but increases torque, which is very useful for large parts.

Thread cutting: The back gear is also desirable for thread cutting, where the tool will move relatively quickly towards the chuck – if the chuck speed is really fast you won't be able to stop it at the correct point every time.

Gearboxes: Gearboxes are useful if you do a lot of thread cutting, but other than that, they are quite a luxury. Thread cutting is still possible by using change wheels – not as convenient, but perfectly workable with a little patience.

Capacity: The size of the lathe is defined by the length and swing over the bed. The length is the distance between the chuck and tailstock (known as the 'length between centres'), and the 'swing' is the maximum radius/diameter that will fit over the bed. However, be aware that diameter over the cross-slide will be much less and is a more useful number to reference.

Overall, the size you need will be dictated by the size of the projects you are interested in making. Some lathes have a gap in the bed, which is a taller area near the headstock that can be used to turn large diameter items that are not too long. This is a useful feature.

Accessories: The list of accessories available for a good lathe is almost limitless, but a lot can be done with a three-jaw chuck, a four-jaw chuck, a vertical slide, a few tools and a set of drills. Other fixtures and fittings can be sourced as needed, or often made to some of the many plans published by other engineers.

Having said all this, any lathe is better than no lathe, and the budget might mean that a small hobby machine is the order of the day, in which case, so be it. It will have limitations, but also massive possibilities and many uses.

Finally, it should be said that not everyone has a large, dedicated workspace. This is always nice, because you don't have to tidy up at the end of the day, but plenty of people work in the garden shed or spare room – I have even seen plans for a small workshop situated in a reading desk. My first workshop was in the attic of our house, with dim light, low headroom and cobwebs in every corner, but it was a workshop nonetheless and was enough to produce some successful working models.

TOOLS, TIPS AND TECHNIQUES

Whole books can be written on the vast number of set-ups and machining operations that can be done in the home workshop, but a few tips and techniques that are relevant to steam launch builds are described here.

USING A LATHE

To get the best from any lathe there are some guiding principles that are worth thinking about. Rigidity is one of the main concerns. The more rigid the set-up, the better the results. You should get an improved surface finish, less noise, less tool chatter and better accuracy because there will be less springing of the tool and workpiece.

With this in mind, try to minimize tool overhang, minimize workpiece protrusion from the chuck, and ensure that the lathe slideways are smooth with no free play. If the tool is chattering, try slowing the spindle speed and/or adding some light oil or cutting fluid to the cut.

If the workpiece is long and thin, then use the tailstock to support the far end.

If the tool requires a high cutting force or is rubbing, check that the tool is sharp and on centre height; and check the tool geometry for the material you are cutting.

MARKING OUT

Marking out is an important step to ensure work is produced to the required accuracy. A selection of marking-out tools is shown in Fig. 1.3. It is not necessary to have all of these, but a steel rule, a small square, some dividers, a scriber and a centre punch are the minimum requirements. A protractor has its uses, and layout fluid greatly improves visibility of the markings.

Odd-leg or Jenny calipers are useful. Unlike normal calipers, these have one sharp point and one contact edge, which can be used to mark out lines parallel to the edge of the workpiece. Many drawings reference dimensions from the edge of the part, so these calipers can be used to transfer such dimensions directly. Jenny calipers can be accurately set against a steel rule by placing the blunt leg on the end of the rule and then 'feeling' the point drop into the correct graduation on the scale. Similarly, the points on standard dividers can locate on the rule markings, but it is easier not to start from the zero. For example, to set the

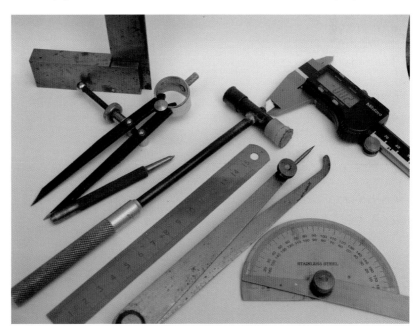

Fig. 1.3 A selection of marking-out tools. Digital calipers are sometimes (unfairly) called 'guessing sticks', but they are quick to use and provide internal, external and depth measurements. They are accurate enough for most model engineering purposes.

dividers to 20mm, put one point on 10mm and adjust until the other point drops into 30mm. This is more accurate than having one point on the zero, which is off the end of the rule.

A centre punch is vital to locate holes with any accuracy. A good technique is to lightly punch the hole location and then inspect it: if it is slightly out of place then a second tap (a little harder this time) with the punch at an angle, can be used to move the first mark across.

MEASURING

A digital caliper is one of the most useful measuring tools in the workshop. It is easy and quick to use, and gives enough accuracy for most model engineering jobs. It also has the ability to

Fig. 1.4   Edge-finder start position. A slow spindle speed (~250rpm) is best.

measure inside, outside and depth dimensions, typically up to 150mm.

EDGE FINDING

An edge finder (sometimes called a wobbler) is useful when milling, to find the edge of the workpiece from which holes or other edges can then be placed. The edge finder is a mechanical tool placed in the chuck of the mill (or lathe with the vertical slide); it uses simple physics to highlight when the edge of the work has been found. Before using the tool it is first necessary to know the tip diameter.

To use the tool, it is placed in the chuck and turned at a moderately slow speed. The quill is adjusted and locked to set the ball of the tool level with the edge. The tool will waggle around wildly at the start but as the edge of the workpiece contacts it, the edge finder will start to run more and more true. Finally, as the edge is 'found', the edge finder will crawl up the side of the workpiece. In this precise

Fig. 1.5   As the edge finder approaches the target surface, the amount of runout will reduce until it is running exactly true.

Fig. 1.6   Finally, when the edge is located, the tool will be seen to step out as the ball end walks along the edge of the workpiece. At this point the edge of the work is off from the machine axis by the radius of the ball.

position, the edge of the work is a distance from the quill axis, equal to the tip radius. For example, the wobbler shown has a ball diameter of 5mm. When the edge is detected, the centreline of the quill is therefore 2.5mm from the edge. The mill or lathe dials can be zeroed and then advanced 2.5mm where they are zeroed again, to pick up the edge of the workpiece as a datum.

DRILLING AND REAMING

For simple plate parts, drilled holes should be centre-punched before they are drilled. If a hole is being drilled in the lathe, no punch mark is needed, but the hole should be centre-drilled first. A centre drill is just a short rigid drill that will pick up on the centre of the workpiece without wandering off course. Once the hole has been centre-drilled, progressively larger drills can be used in the normal way to get the hole to the final size.

For holes where an accurate diameter is needed, a reamer is the best tool for the job. This is effectively an accurately ground drill, but it should only be used to remove the minimum amount of material from the work. For a 6mm hole for example, you should drill to 5.8mm or 5.9mm before using the 6mm reamer to finish. Use a slow chuck speed for reaming, and feed it in with some sensitivity.

Reamers can be hand reamers or machine reamers. Hand reamers have a longer tapered section to help the operator align the reamer in the drilled hole, but for this reason they are only suitable for through holes. Machine reamers are parallel right up to the leading edge, aside from a small chamfer. These have more uses in model engineering, and can be used to make accurately sized holes using a range of machine tools.

D-BITS

D-bits are homemade reamers. They are simple to produce, work well, and allow the builder to ream holes in non-standard sizes. The material to use is a tool-steel or silver-steel rod. This can be turned to the final required diameter of the hole. Then it can be heated to red hot and quenched in water to give it a hardened working surface. Check with a small file, and if it skims over the surface without cutting, the steel is nice and hard.

Next, a bench grinder is used to create the shape shown in Fig. 1.7. The important things to note are that the remaining 'D'-shaped part of the tool should be ground to just less than half the bar diameter – never more than half, or the tool will rub. The end can be left square to create a flat-bottomed hole, but relief is required on the non-cutting corner and under the cutting edge. A small flat is ground on to the leading edge of the tool to help it bite.

D-bits work well, but the less material they have

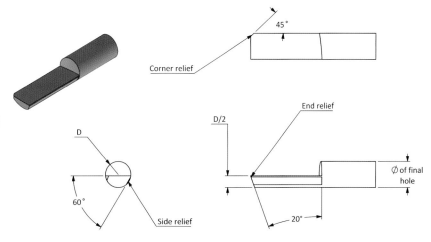

Fig. 1.7 Suggested D-bit geometry. D-bits can be thought of as custom reamers, and as such should only be used to remove the smallest amount of material possible. When grinding the D-bit the remaining 'D' should be half the bar diameter or less to avoid rubbing.

to remove, the better. Aim to drill the hole to about 0.1mm undersize, and then finish with the D-bit.

LATHE TOOL CENTRE HEIGHT

To cut at its best, a lathe tool should be set at the centreline of the workpiece. A simple way to check and adjust this is to trap a short steel rule between the tool tip and a piece of rod held in the chuck. When the tool centre height is correct, the rule will sit vertical.

THREE-JAW CHUCKS

Three-jaw chucks are a great time saver, clamping round or hex bar along the lathe centreline without the need to check alignment. However, they should be thought of as approximate devices. Modern chucks are actually very precise, but they are not exact. The only way to ensure two features machined on a bar are concentric is to do them in one setting. Once the part is repositioned or reversed in the chuck then the datum is lost and so features will not be exactly in line. For ornamental parts this doesn't matter, nor for turning a bolt from hex bar, but it should be kept in mind when thinking through machining steps to ensure that accuracy is not lost where it is needed.

CROSS-DRILLING A WORKPIECE

Being able to accurately cross-drill a shaft or circular workpiece on the centreline can be useful. One of the simplest ways to do this is to create a drilling guide. This is turned to the same diameter

as the workpiece and centre-drilled, then drilled to the final drill size on the lathe. On the drill press the workpiece and the drill guide can then be clamped in the vice, and by feeding the drill gently through the guide you should get an accurately placed hole in the part.

HONING SMALL CYLINDER BORES

For a small engine to run at its best the cylinder walls should be polished to remove any machining marks. In full sized engines there are hones to do this, but in a small engine we need a different solution.

A small bore can be polished using metal polish or toothpaste in combination with a wooden dowel turned to be a tight 'wringing fit' in the bore. The wooden dowel can then be turned at a slow speed in the lathe whilst the cylinder is moved up and down the dowel by hand. After a short while the bore should appear polished, without any tool marks. Protect the lathe bed from any polish or toothpaste during this process.

MACHINING A BAR TO LENGTH

Machining a piece of bar to length is a three-step process. First, both ends of the bar need to be faced off square in the lathe for a datum measurement. For this reason, the starting blank needs to be slightly over-long. With the bar ends square, the part can be removed from the chuck and the length measured with a vernier, caliper or micrometer. From this length an amount to be removed can be calculated from the specification.

To remove exactly this amount, set the top slide on the lathe to zero, taking out any backlash in the screw. Advance the lathe saddle until the tool just touches the workpiece, and lock the saddle firm. Then take progressive facing cuts, advanc-

Fig. 1.8 Cross-drilling a round component using a guide. The guide piece is the same diameter as the workpiece so that both components can be clamped in the vice jaws simultaneously.

ing the top slide the right number of graduations. If more than 3mm or 4mm needs to be removed, then it is worth getting close and then recalculating the final cuts to take out any error.

TURNING A SHOULDERED PART

The technique for this process is similar to turning a part to length, but the length and diameter have to be watched at the same time to get the part correct. The easiest method is to concentrate on the diameter and make the reduced shoulder over-long, and then turn the shoulder to final length using the process described to machine a part to length.

Measure the diameter regularly and calculate the number of graduations needed on the cross-slide to get to final size. On the last cut up to the shoulder, stop the tool at the end and then extract it using the cross-slide to create a 90-degree shoulder. Now measure the length of the smaller diameter part and reduce as needed using the top slide.

CREATING A RADIUS ON A PART

When adding a radius around a hole, it is important to get it concentric; it is very easy to see when

Fig. 1.9 Filing buttons are a useful tool to radius a component. Made from tool steel, they can be heated to red hot and quenched so that they become hard. Then the file will be found to skip over the work when the button is reached.

the two features are not co-axial. Filing the radius is fine, but a guide is needed to get it right, and filing buttons are commonly used to make this operation easier. A filing button is just a piece of tool steel turned with a shoulder, the small diameter being a close fit in the hole of the part and the larger diameter being the curve needed on the outside.

Ideally, the button is heated to red hot in the hearth and then quenched in water to make it hard. The button can now be held in the hole with a clamp or bolt, and a file used to file the corner flush to the button. If the button has been hardened the file should skim across the part once it is down to size. For wider parts a filing button each side is a good idea so that the radius doesn't taper across the width.

MACHINING A FLYWHEEL

To look correct, the flywheel needs to run true when it is spinning on the crankshaft. Lathe chucks are very good at holding the workpiece central, but they are not perfect. If a flywheel is machined whilst held in the three-jaw chuck it is likely that it will wobble when fitted to the axle. The only way to get the flywheel to run perfectly true is to use an arbor to mount the flywheel for a finishing cut to remove any machining error.

The first step is to roughly machine the flywheel to size. In the case of a simple marine-style flywheel, the three-jaw chuck can be used to hold the flywheel blank and the axle hole can be centre-drilled, drilled and reamed to final size. Also in this setting, any mounting bosses or shoulders can be added. At this stage all the machined features will be perfectly concentric, but the outside edge may not be, depending on the condition of the chuck. To true up the outside face we need an arbor.

To create an arbor, a piece of scrap bar can be placed in the three-jaw chuck and turned to have an axle to fit the flywheel. Machining the arbor on the lathe in this way will give a reference that is exactly on the lathe centreline, removing any errors in the chuck. A thread may be added to the end of the axle to clamp the flywheel, or a flat can be filed on the axle if the flywheel has a grub screw.

With the flywheel on the arbor the runout from the chuck will be obvious and you can take light cuts until they go from intermittent to continuous. Now you have a perfectly true flywheel.

TRANSFER DRILLING

A useful process where aligned holes are needed is transfer drilling. This removes the risks of measurement error creating misalignment. The process is to mark out and drill one part and then use this as a template to make the holes in the second part. An engineer's clamp is all that is needed to hold the parts together for drilling. Where one hole is tapped for a thread and the other is a clearance for the screw, concentration is needed to ensure that you drill the correct diameters in both parts.

ECCENTRIC OR OFF-SET MACHINING

The crank discs on these engines are examples of off-set or eccentric machining. Not only must the crank pin be the correct distance from the axle, it must also be parallel to it. Therefore, the hole for the crank pin is best drilled in the lathe. One process to achieve the required off-set is to pack out one jaw of the three-jaw chuck to put the workpiece off centre. So to start, the outside of the crank disc can be machined along with the centre hole and any shoulders. Now a packing piece must be calculated to give the correct throw on the crank pin. An approximate formula for this is:

$$Packing\ piece = 1.5 \times offset \times \left(1 - \left(\frac{1}{8} \times \left(\frac{offset}{diameter}\right)\right)\right)$$

This is all right for non-critical (cosmetic) eccentrics but unfortunately the formula gets less exact as the main bar diameter decreases and the throw increases.

If more accuracy is needed then it may be necessary to use this next formula, kindly shared by Marvin Klotz, which compensates for the width of the contact area of the jaws of the chuck. Marvin is a retired aerospace physicist and now spends his hobby time making engineering models and deriving formulae for model engineering activities. His more detailed formula is as follows:

$$Packing\ piece = 1.5 \times e - r + \left(0.5 \times \sqrt{(4r^2) - (3e^2) + (2ew \times \sqrt{3}) - w^2}\right)$$

where:
e = eccentric off-set
r = radius of the workpiece
w = width of the jaws

It's quite a task keying this into your calculator.

Work out the brackets first, then do the multiplication steps, then the additions, and finally the subtractions. As an example, if the specification of an engine is for a crank throw of 6mm and the overall disc diameter is 19mm. Using the formula, that gives us:

$$Packing\ piece = 1.5 \times 6 - 9.5 + \left(0.5 \times \sqrt{(4 \times 9.5^2) - (3 \times 6^2) + (2 \times 6 \times 2 \times \sqrt{3}) - 2^2}\right) = 8.02mm$$

Packing piece = 8.02mm

So a packing piece of 8mm against one jaw of the chuck would give the required off-set with enough accuracy to create the eccentric.

The lathe can be used to create a small nugget of bar the correct length, which can then be used to space the workpiece from one of the jaws. In this setting the crank-pin hole can be drilled and tapped for the crank pin.

A word of caution should be given regarding safety with this set-up. It is clearly not how the three-jaw chuck was designed to be used. If in doubt, you can just use this method to mark a part by turning the lathe by hand and then drill it on the drill press; but with a slow spindle speed and light drill pressure, there should be little problem. The four-jaw chuck is another option, but the three-jaw method is a useful technique to be aware of even if it is seldom used.

CENTRING IN THE FOUR-JAW CHUCK

If the centre of the workpiece has been marked and centre-punched, then the easiest set-up on the four-jaw chuck can be done with a floating centre. Fig. 1.10 shows a piece of square bar being centred for drilling. The floating centre will waggle around as the chuck is turned by hand, and a DTI (dial test indicator) will show the runout. If the DTI is placed over the work, then when the dial runs fully clockwise the work is highest and the top chuck jaw should be tightened to push it down. When the DTI runs fully anti-clockwise the workpiece is low and the top jaw should be loosened. Working progressively round the chuck should soon centre the workpiece.

If you are trying to tighten a jaw to move the workpiece down but it is too tight, then try backing off the opposite jaw first. Also be aware that the jaws on either side may be gripping the work and may be working against you, so some sympathy for how the jaws work together is needed. Packing pieces of scrap metal can be used to allow the workpiece to be moved about between the jaws without scratching it.

If a part already has a hole or lug that you need to centre, then the same adjustment process can be used but without the need for the floating centre. Instead, rest the DTI tip on the body or bore of the feature to be centred.

In the case of a part that is a regular shape,

Fig. 1.10   Centring a workpiece in the four-jaw chuck. In this set-up the required centreline of the workpiece has been centre-punched. The floating centre can then pick up this centre mark, and the runout of the component is shown by the DTI (dial test indicator).

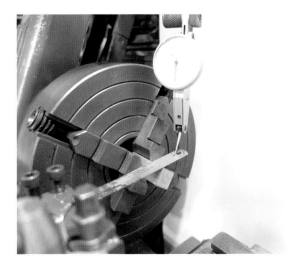

Fig. 1.11   If the bar stock is a regular shape, then the high points can deflect a spring contact arm, which can be used to move the DTI. The contact arm might be a steel strip, or an old rule, or a hacksaw blade with the teeth ground off.

another process using a spring contact bridge can be employed. The advantage is that there is no need to find the centre first. A steel rule or old hacksaw blade can be clamped in the tool post and set to run over the high points of the bar. The DTI can then be used to read the high points, and the same adjustment process followed to centre the part. This is a quick and useful technique for drilling the centre of a square bar, for example, as shown in Fig. 1.11.

LATHE TOOLS

Lathe-cutting tools come in all sorts of types. There are left-handed and right-handed tools, thread-cutting tools, parting-off and profiling tools. The most useful tool is a right-handed tool with a 60-degree point. This will be able to cut both the face of the work and the outside diameter, and will be capable of creating 90-degree shoulders. Convention states that a right-handed tool cuts from the right, in other words towards the lathe chuck, which is the most common direction to machine.

Tools can be purchased with replaceable inserts; these are nice because the angles of the cutting faces are already set for you, and when the tool is blunt you just replace (or rotate) the insert.

Inserts are available in a huge range of shapes, but sometimes it is necessary, or preferable, to grind your own tool. This takes practice, but is simple enough using a bench grinder. In the simplest terms, there are three faces that need to be ground, and each one of these faces needs to be angled in two planes. Fig. 1.12 shows a lathe tool with some ground faces. The *rake* of a cutting face is the angle at which it cuts into the workpiece; the *relief* is the clearance behind the cutting edge and is necessary to stop the tool rubbing. Most tools also have a small radius on the tip, which improves tool life and gives a better surface finish.

Looking at Fig. 1.12, you can see that the end and side faces both have a relief angle and a cutting angle. A tool with a greater relief angle usually has a lower rate of wear, but because there is less material to support the cutting edge the tool can break more easily; also it cannot conduct heat away so efficiently. The top face has two rake angles because it can cut both 'into' and 'along' the workpiece. These angles are identified as a 'side rake' angle and a 'back rake' angle. The rake angle sets the angle of shear for the cut. A greater rake angle reduces cutting forces and gives a better tool life, but too much rake can make the tool fragile.

Fig. 1.13 shows the various facets of a tool, and which faces need to be cut. Different materials are best cut using slightly different angles, and the table gives some suggested angles for the critical faces; but in summary, harder materials have smaller rake angles, and softer ones have greater rake angles. The exceptions are brass and bronze, which are usually cut with a zero or negative rake, to prevent the tool digging in.

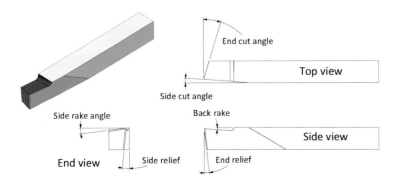

Fig. 1.12 *Diagram of lathe-tool notation. The tool shown is a typical right-handed tool for a lathe, which cuts from right to left and can also cut across the face of the work.*

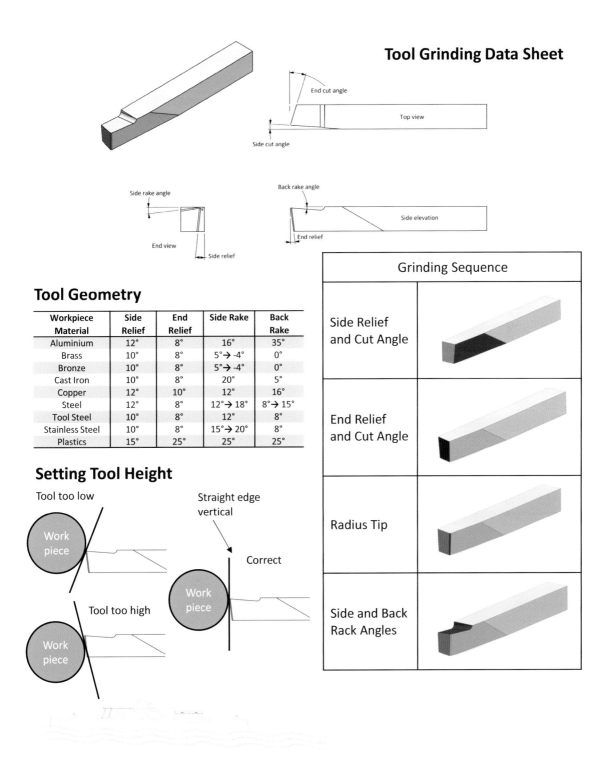

Tool Grinding Data Sheet

Tool Geometry

Workpiece Material	Side Relief	End Relief	Side Rake	Back Rake
Aluminium	12°	8°	16°	35°
Brass	10°	8°	5° → -4°	0°
Bronze	10°	8°	5° → -4°	0°
Cast Iron	10°	8°	20°	5°
Copper	12°	10°	12°	16°
Steel	12°	8°	12° → 18°	8° → 15°
Tool Steel	10°	8°	12°	8°
Stainless Steel	10°	8°	15° → 20°	8°
Plastics	15°	25°	25°	25°

Setting Tool Height

Grinding Sequence

Side Relief and Cut Angle	
End Relief and Cut Angle	
Radius Tip	
Side and Back Rack Angles	

Fig. 1.13   A lathe-tool reference guide presented in the style of a poster for the workshop wall.

The data is presented in the form of a poster, which you can copy and print out for your workshop wall.

SILVER SOLDERING

To be able to do a good silver-soldered joint, it is not necessary to have a deep understanding of the metallurgy of the process. Instead, a three-step approach can be used: clean, flux, heat.

Clean metal is important to form a strong joint, and mechanical abrasion is all that is needed. Coarse and fine abrasive pads are useful for bringing the metal up to a bright finish. Wipe the dust off with a soft rag or compressed air.

The best flux is a powdered form. This can be mixed with water to create a flux paste and also used as a dip for a warmed silver-soldering rod, creating a flux-coated rod for your joint. Out of the fluxes available Tenacity 5 is less easily exhausted than some, and can be used with stainless steel as well as other metals, so is a good choice for all round silver-soldering.

Heating the work requires two things: a brazing hearth and a gas torch.

A brazing hearth: The brazing hearth needs to reflect the heat from the torch to avoid wasting energy. Normal bricks and firebricks won't work well here, as they will absorb a lot of heat. Ideally you will have some vermiculite bricks – these are not a large investment, and they will enhance the capability of your silver-soldering equipment.

A gas torch: A plumber's torch will just about do a boiler of this size. Propane or Mapp gas will work. You don't need a super-hot, intense flame, but rather a high quantity of heat from a broader flame to get the whole workpiece hot.

Only when the work is glowing red hot should you add the silver-solder rod. At this point you should also see the flux turn from a dark paste into a clear liquid. Warm the rod in the flame

and dip it in the flux powder and then apply to the join and allow it to melt and flow. Aim to have the heat of the work melt the rod and not the flame. Keep heating the work as you move along the joint, but place the flame nearby, rather than directly on the rod.

PICKLING

Pickling is a dilute acid bath used for cleaning up parts after silver soldering. These days the best option for the environment and for safety is citric acid. This can be purchased from brewer's shops. Two teaspoons in a litre of hot water will be strong enough to pickle any soldered parts.

SOFT SOLDERING

Soft soldering can be used on model steam engines anywhere except for the pressure vessel. As with silver soldering, cleaning the joint is the vital first step. A liquid flux can be used to create a fillet on the joint, and the solder wrapped into position. This works well, and is easier than trying to feed in the solder later on. Heat has to be applied to the parts being joined, rather than to the solder itself – this way the solder will only melt when the neighbouring parts are hot enough. The melted solder should flow into the joint with capillary action.

Pickling is not used for soft solder joints; instead, clean up afterwards with hot soapy water. The soap helps to neutralize any acids in the flux.

INTERNAL AND EXTERNAL THREADING

Internal threads are cut with a tapping tool. External threads are cut with dies. In both cases some light oil or cutting fluid should be used, the exception being brass, which can cut quite nicely dry, particularly in the larger sizes.

With round or hex parts, the lathe can be used to get threaded holes nice and square to the workpiece. For tapping, the tap can be held in the tailstock chuck with the chuck tightened just hand tight. The workpiece can be rotated by hand whilst the tailstock is pushed to create a

BUILDING A BOILER TEST PUMP

All pressure vessels should be tested hydraulically, and not with compressed air, as testing with a non-compressible fluid is the only way to avoid a sudden release of energy in the event of failure.

A capable test system can be made from a cheap plant sprayer. Tests have shown that these can produce pressures of up to 200psi, at which point the most likely thing to fail is the pump trigger. When selecting a sprayer, look for one with a screw-on nozzle as this can be used to attach a connection hose.

To make a pressure-tight connection to the boiler, avoid silicone tubing as this is too soft and go for something such as PTFE, or flexible PVC hose or polyethylene. A union can be made as follows:

Measure the inside of the tube you are using. Then make a tube insert that is 0.2mm larger in diameter than this measurement, and add some grooves to help it grip the tube. This part will also need a flange to fit inside the sprayer nozzle. Push this insert into the tube and measure the outside diameter over the tube and insert area.

Now make a plain collar with an inside diameter 0.2mm smaller than this external measurement. Push this support collar over the insert, and you have a very capable joint.

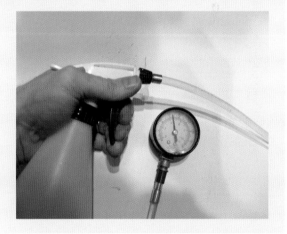

Fig. 1.14   A simple pump from a plant sprayer can produce reasonable pressures, here shown at 65psi. Some ingenuity is required to attach the hose to the nozzle, but most plant sprayers have a screw-on nozzle that lends itself to holding a barbed hose insert. The insert should be 0.2mm larger than the hose inside diameter, and the securing collar should have an inside diameter 0.2mm smaller than the diameter of the hose over the insert.

Fig. 1.15   Bespoke die holders are available for tailstocks, but a standard die holder can be held square to the workpiece just using the face of the tailstock chuck against the die. The tailstock can be used to apply light pressure to start the cut, and the tool post can stop the holder turning.

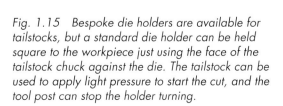

Threading Reference Tables

B.A. Threads

Thread	Tapping drill (mm)	Clearance drill (mm)
0BA	5.10	6.00
1BA	4.50	5.40
2BA	4.00	4.80
3BA	3.45	4.20
4BA	3.00	3.70
5BA	2.65	3.30
6BA	2.30	2.85
7BA	2.05	2.55
8BA	**1.80**	**2.25**
9BA	1.55	1.95
10BA	1.40	1.80
11BA	1.20	1.60
12BA	1.05	1.30

B.S.F. Threads

Diameter	TPI	Tapping drill (mm)	Clearance drill (mm)
3/16"	32	3.95	4.90
7/32"	28	4.63	5.70
1/4"	26	5.35	6.50
5/16"	22	6.75	8.10
3/8"	20	8.22	9.70
7/16"	18	9.67	11.30
1/2"	16	11.1	13.00

Threads in **bold** used in Making Model Steam Boats

Mechanical Engineering Threads

M.E. Threads 32 tpi	Tapping drill (mm)	Clearance drill (mm)	M.E. threads 40 tpi	Tapping drill (mm)	Clearance drill (mm)
1/8"	2.36	3.50	1/8"	2.40	3.50
5/23"	3.00	4.20	5/32"	3.20	4.20
3/16"	**3.90**	**5.00**	3/16"	4.00	5.00
7/32"	**4.60**	**5.80**	7/23"	4.80	5.80
1/4"	**5.50**	**6.60**	1/4"	5.60	6.60
9/32"	6.30	7.50	9/32"	6.40	7.50
5/16"	**7.00**	**8.20**	5/16"	7.20	8.20
3/8"	8.70	9.80	3/8"	8.80	9.80
7/16"	10.10	11.50	7/16"	10.40	11.50
1/2"	11.90	13.10	1/2"	11.90	13.10

Metric Coarse Threads

Diameter	Pitch	Tapping drill
M2.0	0.40	1.6mm
M2.5	0.45	2.05mm
M3.0	0.50	2.5mm
M3.5	0.60	2.9mm
M4.0	**0.70**	**3.3mm**
M5.0	0.80	4.2mm
M6.0	1.00	5.0mm
M8.0	1.25	6.8mm
M10.0	1.50	8.5mm
M12.0	1.75	10.3mm

Metric tapping drills = diameter - pitch

Whitworth Threads

Diameter	TPI	Tapping drill (mm)	Clearance drill (mm)
1/16"	60	1.20	1.70
3/32"	48	1.90	2.44
1/8"	40	2.55	3.57
5/32"	32	3.20	4.00
3/16"	24	3.70	5.16
7/32"	24	4.50	5.60
1/4"	20	5.10	6.75
5/16"	18	6.50	8.30
3/8"	16	7.80	9.90
7/16"	14	9.30	11.50
1/2"	12	10.50	13.10

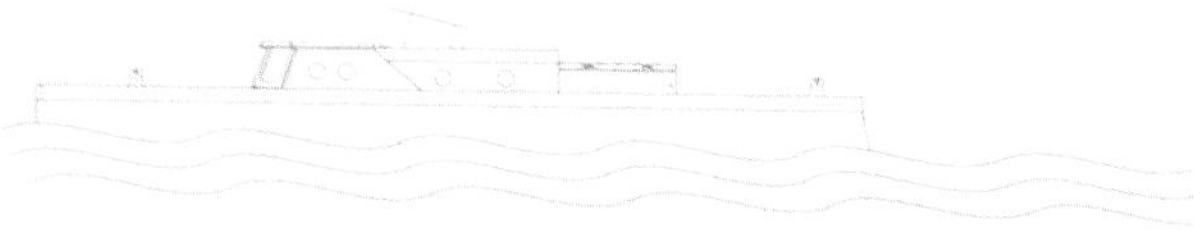

Fig. 1.16   *Threading tables for the workshop presented in the style of a poster for the workshop wall.*

READING DRAWINGS

The plans in this book are drawn using third angle projection. This refers to the layout of the views on the page.

Fig. 1.17 shows a house drawn in both first angle and third angle layouts. The information is the same in both cases, just the layout is different. Also given are the standard projection symbols, which show two views of a cone. This symbol tells the reader which projection system is used in the drawing.

In the third angle projection, the side view is drawn on the same side of the part as the observer. In first angle projection, the same view is drawn on the opposite side of the part.

A cross-section view is also shown. The viewing direction is given by the arrows on the parent view, and hatching shows solid areas of the part. Cross-section views are used to show hidden details.

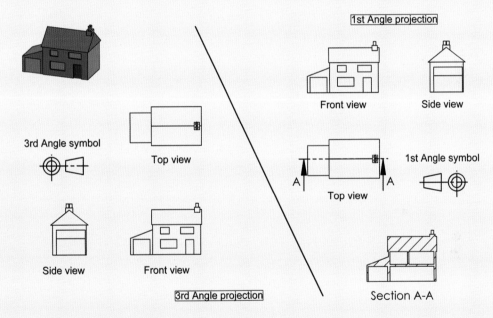

Fig. 1.17 Drawing projections can be first angle or third angle. Third angle is perhaps more common and is used for the drawings in this book.

To ensure drawings are clear to read, the minimum information is always used to detail how a part should be made. This includes the number of views and the number of dimensions used. When reading drawings, the builder should always look for lines of symmetry and dimensioned holes or radii that are carried throughout the part. These are used to save cluttering up the drawing with repeated measurements.

You will see 'PCD' marked on some drawings. This stands for 'pitch circle diameter', and it is used to show where a ring of features should be located by giving a centre point and a diameter to work from. An example is the wheel nuts on a car. These are in a circular pattern, and if you want to find a new wheel to fit, then the PCD of the hole patterns must be the same.

controlled pressure to help the tap cut. There is a lack of sensitivity cutting a thread like this, so for small sizes (smaller than about 6BA) it is better to start the thread in the lathe and then move the work to the bench vice to finish by hand. This will get you a thread perpendicular to the axis of the part without the risk of snapping the tap.

The lathe can also be used to cut external threads using the same process, but this time the die is not held in the tailstock chuck, but rests on the face of the chuck to help set it square to the workpiece. Once again, the tailstock can apply pressure, and the tool post can be set to stop the die holder rotating, whilst the chuck is rotated by hand.

In both cases the tap or die should be 'backed out' every few turns to break the swarf and stop it binding up.

Fig. 1.16 lists the suitable drill sizes for common model engineering threads. The bold line items are the threads used in this book. The initials 'tpi'

refer to 'threads per inch', and describe how fine or coarse a thread is.

BA threads are metric threads, and notable for the rounded tip and root of the thread form, which makes them stronger.

ME threads are mechanical engineering threads. 32tpi is useful for parts that are frequently removed, such as boiler filling plugs and lubricator lids; 40tpi is useful for permanent fixtures such as boiler sight-glasses and pipe unions.

Finally, if you purchase a Mamod-style safety valve for the Pond Runner model, you will need a tap that is ¼in × 26tpi, sometimes called ¼in BSF (British Standard Fine). The tapping drill for this thread is 5.3mm.

Metric threads are common in Europe, but the large sizes have a very coarse pitch. In the model boat world, the M4 thread is commonly used for small propeller fittings. Fig. 1.16 is presented in a full-page format to be copied and kept for reference on your workshop wall.

CHAPTER TWO

THE POND RUNNER: A MODEL OF THE SIMPLEST DESIGN

If you are looking to get out on the water as soon as possible and to build a live steamboat without the concern of boiler theory or hull design, then this is the chapter for you. The Pond Runner is a single-cylinder, screw-driven launch, 500mm in length and with a beam of 100mm. The hull is open top, and a number of purchased parts are used in the model to facilitate the build. Specifically these are:

solid fuel tablets
safety valve (Mamod style)
propeller
propeller shaft
stainless-steel spring

Some small 8BA screws will also be needed: at least three 8BA 6mm long hex-head screws, two 8BA 6mm long countersunk screws, and two more 12mm long. Whilst you are ordering from a model engineering supplier, consider a box

wrench for the hex screws: it is not expensive and is well worth having in your toolbox. An M4 grub screw will also be needed.

Some Loctite retaining compound is required for the crankshaft assembly. A medium to high strength is best – 603 compound would be a good choice, or Truloc 268, which is the equivalent.

The main tube for the boiler is a piece of 20-gauge copper pipe, 1¾in in diameter, and you will need some 18-gauge copper sheet for the end plates. If you order a 12in (30cm) length of the copper tube, this will be enough for both boilers described in this book. The safety-valve bush is made from bronze and is designed to work with a standard Mamod safety valve, which uses a ¼in BSF thread of 26tpi (threads per inch).

The hull is a small plywood construction and features a flat bottom for an easy build and a stable vessel.

Fig. 2.1   The Pond Runner's maiden voyage on Eastville Lake. Its performance was modest but reliable.

THE ENGINE

This engine uses the common oscillating cylinder design, which is simpler and has fewer parts than an engine with slide valves. The cylinder has the pivot above the steam ports, which makes drilling the pivot hole less critical as there is no danger of it breaking through to the cylinder bore. The off-set parts of the build, including the cylinder and the crank disc, are made without the need for a four-jaw chuck, and the piston, piston rod and big end are machined from one piece of material for a simpler assembly.

Looking at the drawings, it is worth noting a couple of things. First, the two steam ports are different. Only the exhaust port goes right though the frame: the inlet port is drilled just halfway through and then meets another drilled hole coming in from the side of the frame. Getting these ports the right way round affects the direction of rotation of the engine, so it needs to be right, otherwise your boat will go backwards.

Second, the crank and main bearing both share some of the space within the thickness of the frame. The crank disc is thin, but has a boss to help it join securely to the axle. This boss protrudes into the frame and so the main bearing has to accommodate this, so take note of how both the bearing and the crank disc fit into the

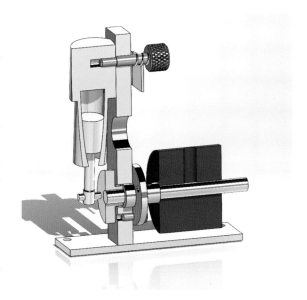

Fig. 2.3   Cross-section of an engine bearing. Note how the bearing and the crank disc both use up some of the frame thickness. The bearing sets the crank-disc position to hold it off the frame face. The crank disc has a boss to help it sit perpendicularly to the main axle, but this boss is a clearance fit in the frame.

frame. The bearing boss is snug to the frame, but the crank-disc boss has some clearance to allow it to rotate.

Finally, note that the frame ports are not dimensioned; instead, they are drilled using a jig. This method ensures that the ports are correctly positioned regardless of any accumulated inaccuracies that may have built up. Following the drilling of the ports in the frame, the exhaust port is then used to locate the steam port in the cylinder, again ensuring its position is correct.

THE FLYWHEEL

A nice place to start is the flywheel, which is a job for the lathe and starts with a piece of iron, steel or brass if you like. As a rule, it is best to turn the flywheel to size and then 'true' it up on a mandrel/arbor to get it running exactly.

To start, face one end of the bar and centre-drill, drill and ream it to a final size of 4mm. Add

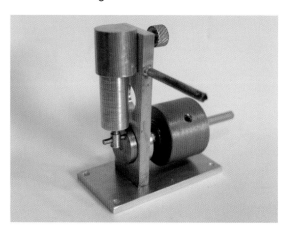

Fig 2.2   The Pond Runner engine featuring a single oscillating cylinder and a one-piece piston and connecting-rod assembly.

the small shoulder on the end, and then either part it off or remove it from the chuck and saw it off in the vice. Either way, place the flywheel back in the chuck with the 'sawn' face outermost, and machine it square.

Over on the drill press the flywheel can be drilled and threaded to take an M4 grub screw. If your chosen tap for the grub screw is not long enough to reach the axle hole, simply counter-bore the hole a little, to create a shorter threaded section. To locate this hole accurately, make a drilling gauge from a small piece of bar. This should be the same diameter as the flywheel and with a 3.3mm hole in the centre. Then hold both the flywheel and the gauge in the drilling vice, and drill through to the axle hole. Thread the cross-drilled hole M4, and then just push the 4mm reamer through the axle hole to tidy any burrs.

The next job is to machine an arbor to hold the flywheel. The arbor will be the same size as the axle, but the important thing is not to remove the arbor from the chuck until the job is finished, otherwise you will lose accuracy. Take a piece of scrap bar and place it in the three-jaw chuck with enough protruding to take the flywheel. Because 4mm is quite thin and the arbor needs to be quite

Fig. 2.5   Final truing of the flywheel rim should be on an arbor. This is the only way to get a flywheel to run exactly true. The arbor needs to be a good fit in the flywheel hole, and must not be removed from the chuck at any point, or an error may be introduced.

long, the free end should be supported with the tailstock. So centre-drill the end and bring up the tailstock with a fixed centre to hold the workpiece.

Now turn a 4mm spigot, long enough for the flywheel. Fit the flywheel and wind in the grub screw to mark the arbor. Then file a flat where the grub screw touches the arbor. Now refit the flywheel, secured with the grub screw against the flat.

With the fixed centre back in place, light machining cuts can be taken to get the edge of the flywheel running true. The flywheel is only driven by the grip of the grub screw, so cuts must be light and some oil may help. You can use the fine feed if your lathe has one, to get a nice finish on the rim. The result should be a flywheel with very little runout.

THE CYLINDER

The cylinder is made before the piston so the piston can be made to fit. The actual diameter of the cylinder bore is unimportant: more significant is that the bore should be parallel and smooth, and perpendicular to the port face.

To start, cut and turn a piece of 16mm brass

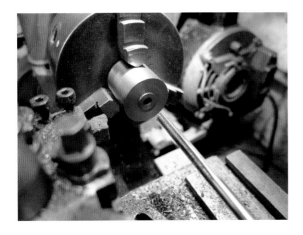

Fig. 2.4   Machining a flywheel bore. Always centre-drill and then drill in increasing sizes, finishing with a reamer, to get a good fit on the axle. Reamers work best when they are removing the smallest amount of material.

Fig. 2.6 *The cylinder port face can be machined in the lathe using a vertical slide (as shown here) or in the milling machine. It should not be released until the pivot hole has been drilled and tapped, to ensure the thread for the pivot pin is perpendicular to the face just machined.*

Fig. 2.7 *Finding the edge of the cylinder using an edge finder will allow accurate positioning of the pivot hole. The edge finder can also find the centreline by finding the mid-point between the vice jaws.*

bar to length. Then using the milling machine or vertical slide in the lathe, machine a flat on one side, 2mm deep. Also in this set-up, find the centreline of the part using an edge finder against the vice jaws, and measure from one end to drill and tap the cylinder pivot hole. Doing this in the same setting will ensure the hole is perpendicular to the flat previously machined.

An optional but worthwhile enhancement is also to remove the material around this pivot hole; this modification reduces the amount of cylinder area in contact with the frame, and therefore increases the chance of the bit over the steam ports making good contact. It also means that any deformation around the pivot pin hole doesn't affect how well the cylinder sits on the frame.

Now place the part in the three-jaw chuck with the flat against one of the jaws, ensuring that at least 20mm of the part is sticking out. In this setting the cylinder bore can be centre-drilled, drilled 23mm deep, and reamed to an 8mm bore. If a reamer is not available a D-bit can be made to finish the bore parallel and create a flat bottom to the hole. To finish, the outside of the cylinder can be reduced to 10mm diameter, along the 20mm length.

To remove any machining marks in the bore, a hardwood lap can be turned in the lathe to be a wringing fit in the cylinder. Then running the lathe slowly and with some metal polish, the bore can be polished to a smooth, bright finish.

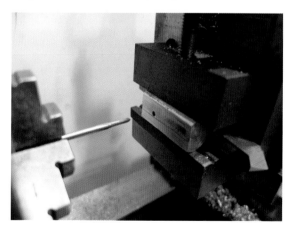

Fig. 2.8 *Drilling and tapping for the cylinder pivot pin should be done before the part is released from the vice. The design of the cylinder is such that the depth of this hole is unimportant – it can even go right through. The chuck can be used to hold the tap, but it must only be turned by hand.*

Similarly it is necessary to remove any machining marks from the port face of the cylinder. This can be done using the finest grade of wet'n'dry paper (1200 grit or greater) and taping it to a flat surface, such as a piece of tempered glass. Add some oil or water, and then use light pressure

Fig. 2.11   Lapping the cylinder port face is important to provide a steam-tight valve system. Wet'n'dry paper of 1200 grit or more is ideal for this.

Fig. 2.9   The piston bore and outside of the cylinder are machined in one setting. Ensure that there is enough material sticking out of the chuck for the outside machining. The location of the piston bore is set by the previously machined flat on the cylinder resting on one of the chuck jaws.

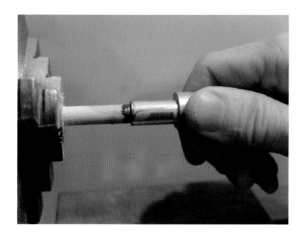

Fig. 2.10   The cylinder bore can be polished using a wooden dowel turned to be a wringing fit in the cylinder. Metal polish is then used with the dowel, with the lathe running and the part being worked by hand.

and a circular motion to polish the face smooth. It is vital that the paper is flat: if it is allowed to 'pucker up' then the edges of the port face will become rounded, which will not help the cylinder seal against the frame.

THE PISTON

The piston, piston rod and big end are machined from a single piece. The only critical things are the piston diameter and the hole in the big end, which needs to be perpendicular to the piston axis. Start by placing a piece of brass in the three-jaw chuck, with enough protruding for the whole assembly. The piston will be on the outer end of the part and will be the main part to get right. So undercut an area beyond the piston to a diameter of less than 8mm so we can work on the piston and trial fit the cylinder without anything getting in the way.

Reduce the piston diameter close to 8mm and then start trial fitting the cylinder until it is a tight fit. To reduce the piston from a tight fit to a sliding fit, a piece of fine wet'n'dry paper wrapped on a file can be used to polish the diameter. This will remove any machining marks and fractionally reduce the size. Proceed carefully and keep checking with the cylinder until you can slide the piston all the way down the cylinder. When the fit is fractionally too tight, stop using the paper and try some metal polish between the piston and cylinder, and work by hand to get a nice fit. When the cylinder is pulled from the piston it should make nice 'pop' sound, indicating a gas-tight fit.

Now that the working surface of the piston is complete, the remainder of the part can be reduced to create a connecting rod and big end.

Before parting off the work, transfer over to the drill press and cross-drill the big end for the crank pin. A V block is useful to ensure the workpiece is horizontal and secure, or a vice with a parallel can be used. Take some time to ensure the part is drilled centrally.

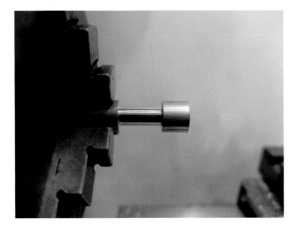

Fig. 2.12   Before machining the piston itself, some material should be relieved beyond the piston, enough to allow a trial fit of the cylinder. For this reason, the material must stick out from the chuck equivalent to the cylinder-bore length.

Fig. 2.13   The working part of the piston should be machined to be a sliding fit in the cylinder bore.

Fig. 2.14   Trial fit of the piston in the cylinder bore. Once the piston can just fit into the cylinder, some wet'n'dry paper on a file can be used to polish the piston surface down to a sliding fit.

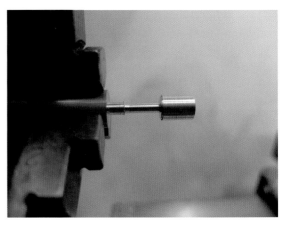

Fig. 2.15   Machining the piston rod and big end. Light cuts should be used to avoid breaking the part. Exact dimensions are not critical here, just enough to clear the crank disc.

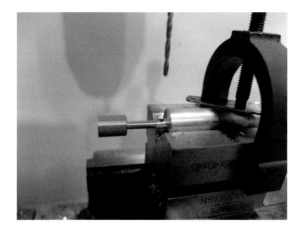

Fig. 2.16   Cross-drilling the big end for the crank pin can be done on the drill press with the part held in a V block or vice. Note the scrap brass used under the V-block clamp to prevent it marking the bar stock.

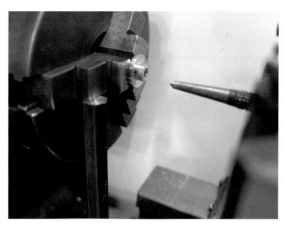

Fig. 2.18   An alternative method for marking the three mounting holes, using a hard stop for the chuck jaws rather than the level.

To finish, return the bar to the lathe and part the component from the stock. The piston is now finished, and should make a healthy 'pop' noise when you pull it from the cylinder.

THE MAIN BEARING

The main bearing is a simple turning job, the only critical dimensions being the centre bore and the length of the shorter shoulder, which gives the crank disc its position. The three mounting holes can be located with adequate accuracy using a small level on the chuck jaws, as shown in Fig. 2.17, or just a piece of bar the right length (Fig. 2.18), and marking with the lathe tool or a punch held in the tool post.

An oil hole is added between two of the mounting screws.

Fig. 2.17   Three evenly spaced mounting holes for the bearing can be marked with a small level on the chuck jaws. This is not suitable for very accurate work, but perfectly acceptable here where the frame can be drilled to match.

Fig. 2.19   The oil hole in the main bearing should be drilled mid-way between two of the mounting holes to ensure the correct orientation on the final assembly. A centre drill can produce an accurate hole with a small countersink to hold a drop of oil.

THE CRANK DISC

The crank disc starts life as a piece of 16mm steel bar cut to 10mm long with the end faces machined true. In the three-jaw chuck the part is then drilled through and reamed to 4mm diameter. Before reducing the crank-disc thickness, it is better to drill the off-set hole for the crank pin so that the part can be held more securely in the chuck. The off-set hole can be made using the three-jaw chuck with a piece of packing against one of the jaws. As mentioned previously, this has to be done using some care and a slow speed to stay safe. The height of the packing piece should be approximately 6.8mm, but it is worth checking this number against the lathe being used, which could have wider or narrower jaws.

The formula is:

$$Packing\ piece = 1.5 \times e - r + \left(0.5 \times \sqrt{(4r^2) - (3e^2) + (2ew \times \sqrt{3}) = w^2}\right)$$

where:
e = eccentric off-set
r = radius of workpiece
w = width of jaws

Fig. 2.20 shows the packing piece set up for drilling the off-set hole. The hole diameter needs to be an interference fit with a 2mm pin. If you have a No. 47 drill in your drill box this would be perfect, as it is 1.9939mm, giving a 6μm (micron) interference; if not, a $^5/_{16}$in drill might be all right – at 1.9844mm it gives a 15μm interference with the crank pin.

Fig. 2.21 *Creating a shoulder on the crank disc. Leaving the crank disc over-long helps the chuck to hold the part square.*

Next the part can be held in the three-jaw chuck and the shoulder turned to length and diameter. The length is more important here; the diameter needs to be just less than the hole in the frame. Finally, the part can be held in the three-jaw chuck by the boss, and then the crank disc reduced in thickness to 3mm.

THE CRANK PIN

The crank pin is a piece of 2mm silver steel cut to 12mm long and trimmed on the lathe. On one edge a chamfer is added to assist its assembly into the crank disc.

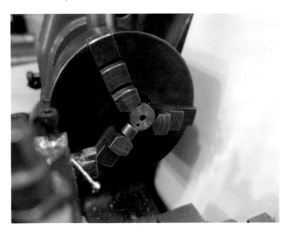

Fig. 2.20 *Off-set drilling can be achieved in the three-jaw chuck with the correct amount of packing. Use a slow speed and light cutting pressure.*

Fig. 2.22   The crank disc can be turned to final thickness by holding the part by the previously machined shoulder, and taking light cuts.

Fig. 2.23   The pivot pin should be made from steel to be strong enough. Take care to create a square shoulder where the thread meets the boss of the screw. This will help it to pull up perpendicular to the cylinder port face.

THE AXLE

The axle is a piece of 4mm silver steel bar cut to a length of 60mm with the ends trimmed on the lathe.

THE CRANK ASSEMBLY

The crank pin should be pushed into the crank disc using a vice or press. Take some time to ensure it is square before pushing it home. If there is a problem with the pin being loose in the crank disc, then Loctite retaining compound can be used to glue it in place.

Once the pin is set, the axle should be assembled to the crank disc, again using Loctite.

THE DRILLING JIG

This simple but important part gives the best chance of having a working engine without any adjustment. Critical features are that the part must be 5mm wide, and the two holes drilled where shown and on the centreline. The top hole is tapped 8BA to match the pivot screw.

THE PIVOT SCREW

This is a simple turning job but is quite tiny. It needs to be made from steel to be strong enough. Turn the small end first and add the 8BA thread.

Next machine the long shoulder to 3mm diameter.

Finally, either knurl the top and then part it off from the bar stock, or, if a knurler is not available, just part it off and add either two spanner flats using the mill, or just cut a slot using the hacksaw, for a flat-blade screwdriver.

THE FRAME

The frame is a piece of 4.75mm ($^3/_{16}$in) brass flat, 18mm wide and 60mm tall. Only some holes are dimensioned in the drawing, and these should be marked and drilled first. The holes for the bearing screws can be transfer-drilled by fitting the bearing and drilling through and then tapping 8BA.

The port holes are drilled using the drilling jig. The bearing must be installed at this point as the axle is used as a reference for the jig. Secure the jig at the pivot hole using the pivot screw and some washers. Then rotate the bar until it hits the axle, which should be in the bearing. The first small hole can now be drilled, but make sure you know if it needs to go right through or not. *Only one of the port holes goes right through, and it matters which one* in order to get the engine

Fig. 2.24   *The engine frame holes marked and drilled.*

Fig. 2.25   *Transfer-drilling of the bearing mounting holes can be done in the drill press, ensuring that the oil hole is positioned correctly. Remember that the mounting holes are larger than the hole needed for the thread, so use a drill the same size as the bearing holes to mark the frame, and then switch to a smaller drill to drill for the thread.*

running in the correct direction. Once one hole is drilled, then rotate the jig all the way over until it rests on the other side of the axle and drill the second hole.

There are two holes in the lower edge of the frame to mount it on a base, and a hole in the side to connect a steam pipe. This side hole links up with the steam inlet port, and is the hole that has not been drilled through. To ensure that the face of the frame is flat, it should be lapped in the same way as the port face on the cylinder. Find a flat surface, such as a piece of glass, and tape some of the finest wet'n'dry paper to it. Add

some oil or water, and then use light pressure and a circular motion to polish the face smooth.

To get the frame to fit the base exactly, mark, drill and tap just one of the holes in the bottom of the frame. Then use an 8BA screw to secure the frame to the base. Set the parts square, and

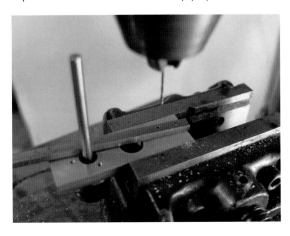

Fig. 2.26   *The drilling gauge specified in the plans can be used against both sides of the axle to position the port holes exactly. Note that only one hole goes right through.*

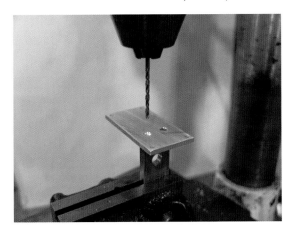

Fig. 2.27   *One of the frame mounting holes can be marked, drilled and tapped to the plans; the second one should be transfer-drilled from the base to create an exact fit.*

transfer-drill the second hole from the base to the frame.

THE SPLASH GUARD

A small but important part is the splash guard. This is optional, but it does prevent hot steam and oil hitting your hand when you are trying to start the engine. It is just a small piece of metal drilled and bent to deflect any exhaust emissions. The part can be used to transfer holes to the side of the engine frame for mounting with 8BA screws.

THE BASE

The base is a simple marking out and drilling job. The two holes in the centre of the plate are also countersunk for the frame mounting screws. Refer back to the frame description to understand how to get these holes to align perfectly with the frame screw holes.

FINAL ASSEMBLY AND FINISHING

The final machining step needs the engine to be fully assembled so the steam port in the cylinder can be transfer-drilled through the exhaust port. However, before drilling this hole, the cylinder must be at its full oscillation on its exhaust stroke. Take a moment to study Fig. 2.28, which shows the correct position. Then using a 1mm drill bit, transfer-drill the position of the exhaust port into the cylinder.

Remove all the parts and clean away any swarf with compressed air or by blowing.

Put the engine back together with some light oil, and turn it by hand to check for tight spots. If you think the engine is running smoothly, try taking the flywheel off and turning it by the axle. This removes the mechanical advantage of the flywheel and will make you more sensitive to tight spots in the motion.

If you can feel some friction, try just the axle in the bearing and the piston in the bore to work out the problem. If it is only tight when the whole engine is assembled, it is most likely that the crank pin is not exactly square. Try turning the engine over and looking for a gap between the cylinder

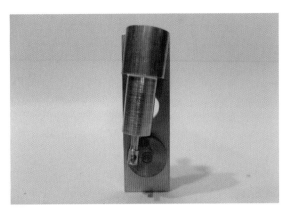

Fig. 2.28   The correct position of the cylinder to have the cylinder port hole drilled through the exhaust port. The engine needs to be assembled and oscillated to this position, then the cylinder port can be drilled through the exhaust port. This approach should take out any built-up errors in the assembly.

and frame. If the crank pin is not square it may lift the cylinder during part of the cycle, which can cause stiffness. If necessary, open out the hole for the crank pin a fraction and see if this eases it.

It is also important that the pivot pin is square to the cylinder face, and that the spring is able to pull the flat face of the cylinder and the frame together. Try just the cylinder, pivot assembly and frame together and look for any daylight between the port faces. If there is any gap, then steam will leak, and with the simple boiler on this project, we don't have much steam to spare.

If you suspect the pivot pin is not square to the cylinder face, then opening out the pivot hole in the frame may allow the spring to pull the faces square – but opening out the hole too much will make for a rattly engine, so some judgement is needed. Also check that there are no burrs around the pivot holes, which could stop the faces pulling together. Any burrs here can be removed by twisting the point of a larger drill by hand against the hole edge.

If you suspect the face really isn't flat enough – and if you didn't include this in the original cylinder machining – a more drastic option is to

Fig. 2.29   If steam leaks from between the cylinder and the port face, adding a recess around the pivot pin may resolve the issue, but ensure that it is perpendicular to the pivot-pin hole.

machine out the area around the pivot pin, but leaving some material to support the cylinder edge beyond the pivot, and of course enough at the other end to seal the steam ports. This modification reduces the amount of cylinder area in contact with the frame, and therefore increases the chance of the bit over the steam ports making good contact.

If compressed air is available, then this is ideal for running in an engine, and adding oil will help highlight any leaks. Experiment with the spring tension on the pivot screw by either loosening the screw or adding washers under the spring to reduce and increase spring tension. You want to achieve the lowest tension whilst still retaining a steam-tight fit of the cylinder on the frame at maximum working pressure.

Once the engine is turning over smoothly, it should run on compressed air happily.

COMPRESSED AIR

Compressed air for a short running test does not necessitate a workshop compressor. The gardening department at the hardware store will have an appliance we can use. In the plant sprayer section, there are not only trigger spray guns, but also pressure-based plant waterers. These systems contain a pump and release system that can be used to build up a small container of compressed air, enough to power a small steam engine for a few minutes. Some such systems are shown in Fig. 2.30. Depending on the design, some ingenuity might be needed to attach a hose from the pressure tank to the engine, but it is worth bearing in mind if you are working on a budget.

Fig. 2.30   In the absence of a compressor, pressure-based plant sprayers are a possible source of stored air pressure.

OSCILLATING ENGINE DESIGN

Simple oscillating engines have been around for many years, but they still offer plenty of variables for experimentation, and they are a favourite machining project for beginners. Dimensions can be varied to create a larger engine or one with a longer stroke, although there are limits to this, governed by the geometry.

Designing Your Own Engine

Let's set the crank throw to be 10mm. This means the piston stroke will be 20mm, and let's suggest a piston height of 10mm. In an oscillating design there is a side load on the piston each time it oscillates the cylinder and so the piston will typically be equal to, or taller than, its diameter to avoid it jamming in the bore.

We need to ensure that when the crank is at the bottom of its rotation, the piston doesn't hit the crank disc, and so now we can sketch in a suitable connecting rod length.

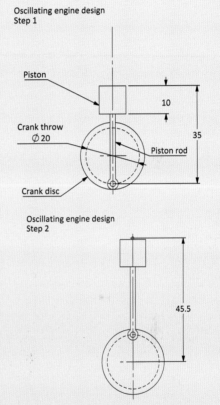

Fig. 2.31   Oscillating engine design – step 1: define the crank throw.

Next you can take the piston and connecting rod parts and draw them at the top of the crank rotation, known as 'top dead centre' (TDC). Now you have the position of the top of the cylinder defined, and also the cylinder steam port position, which will need to be just above the piston at TDC. Finally, you need to add the two steam ports in the frame. At their closest these can touch the central cylinder port just drawn. In reality these will need to be placed on an arc, but while we are defining the pivot position just putting them

Fig. 2.32   Oscillating engine design – step 2: determine the port height.

on each side will suffice. Drawing a construction line from the outside ports to a tangent on the crank-pin path will show where the pivot needs to be for these port positions.

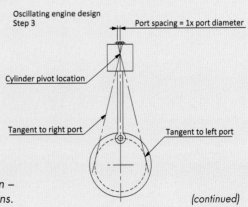

Fig. 2.33   Oscillating engine design – step 3: locate the port positions.

(continued)

(continued)

When designing your own engine the basic requirement is that there is enough oscillation on the cylinder to allow it to switch between the inlet and exhaust ports. The amount of oscillation is a combination of the crank throw and the distance the cylinder pivot is from the crank. Out of these it is best to decide on the crank throw at the beginning, based on the model you are making.

Once you have a crank throw defined, you have automatically defined the piston stroke, which will be twice the crank throw. If you add to this your proposed piston height you will start to see where the cylinder will need to be. *See* the worked example on the previous page.

Of course, you don't have to have the ports touching like this. If you place them further apart, the pivot will move accordingly. Having them further apart will make the steam admission later in the engine cylinder, and the steam cut-off earlier too. This would be a more economical set-up, but there needs to be enough steam admitted to get enough of a power stroke, to sustain the engine for a whole revolution.

Port spacing and size are key areas for experimentation. Some engineers have found that having a larger hole in the cylinder so that there is some overlap between the ports makes a better performing engine. Other people have had improved results by enlarging the exhaust hole a little.

It is also true that minimizing the distance between the cylinder pivot and the crank will help the cylinder oscillate more, and potentially allow larger steam ports to be used. However, higher oscillations can be expected to create more wear, and if you look at commercial engines, maximum oscillations are about 25 degrees, which is a good compromise between wear rate and port spacing.

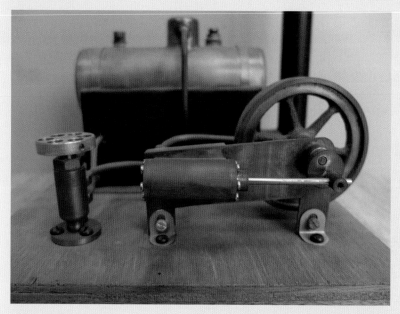

Finally, we should mention double-acting oscillators. This is possible by using upper and lower ports in the frame and cylinder, and the pivot is usually mid-distance between the ports. For the return power stroke to work, the cylinder has to be sealed at both ends, which means using a steam-tight guide for the piston rod. One of the consequences of this is that the piston can afford to be thinner, as the oscillating forces will be partly supported by the cylinder guide.

Fig. 2.34   An old steam engine with a double-acting oscillating cylinder. The cylinder must be sealed at both ends for this to work.

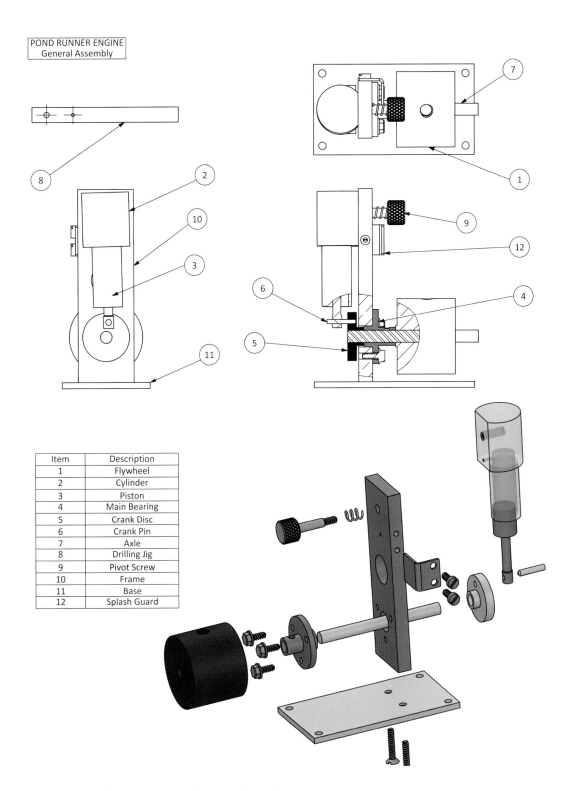

Item	Description
1	Flywheel
2	Cylinder
3	Piston
4	Main Bearing
5	Crank Disc
6	Crank Pin
7	Axle
8	Drilling Jig
9	Pivot Screw
10	Frame
11	Base
12	Splash Guard

POND RUNNER ENGINE
General Assembly

Fig. 2.35   Pond Runner engine drawings sheet 1.

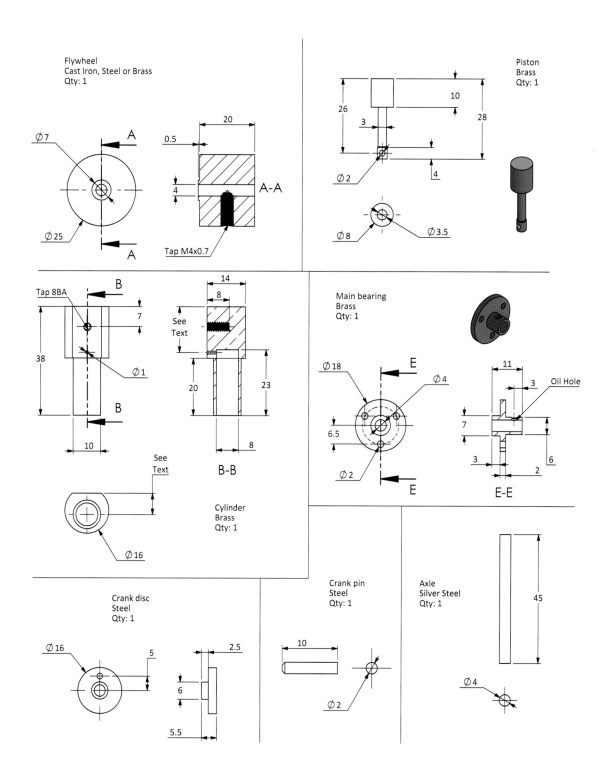

Fig. 2.36   Pond Runner engine drawings sheet 2.

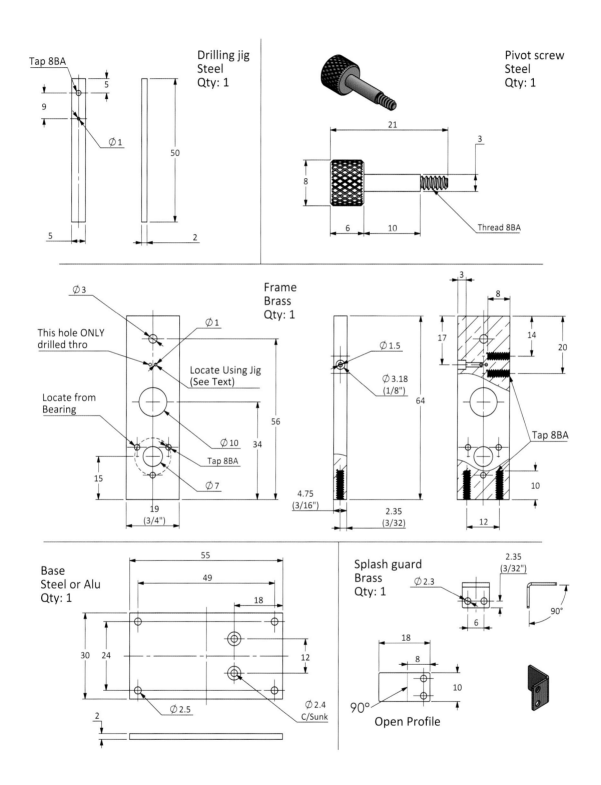

Fig. 2.37   Pond Runner engine drawings sheet 3.

THE BOILER

The boiler for the Pond Runner is only small, and in years gone by would have been made from thin brass tube. You can do this if you like, but it can't be recommended in this text, because some cheaper brass can (over many years) become porous through a process called dezincification.

Fig. 2.38 The simple pot boiler for the Pond Runner.

So for a safe boiler in the long term, copper is preferred. Working with copper will also develop skills for larger boiler work if this should come up in future projects.

The design has a short smokestack, which acts as a fire tube to increase the heating area; there is a bronze bush for a safety valve, and the steam supply pipe goes through the firebox to try to reduce condensation. The flat end plates have no support stay. This is unusual and only possible with very low pressure 'toy' boilers. The standard Mamod safety valve specified is set to release between 18 and 22psi.

It should be said that this style of boiler is particularly inefficient. The exposed top surface and end plates combined with the thickness of the copper means a fair amount of the heat produced will be wasted. In particular, it was noted that the model ran more slowly in wet weather with raindrops removing heat from the boiler shell through evaporation; however, it has proved to be capable enough for this model, and its simplicity is valuable as a beginner project boiler.

The end plates for the boiler are made from

LIGNUM VITAE

Any hardwood should work for the formers, but there is an African timber called Lignum Vitae, which is part of a small family of timbers that are so dense, they don't float. In addition to its density, Lignum Vitae is very 'waxy', a property that means it has been used for pulleys and stern tube bearings on full-sized ships in the past. John Harrison famously used Lignum Vitae for some bearings on his early maritime sea clocks.

Lignum Vitae machines easily on the lathe, very much like machining plastic, and a good finish is easy to obtain. It is a very tough wood, and mallets, skittles and bowling balls can be found made from Lignum Vitae, all of which makes it a good choice for our boiler formers.

Fig. 2.39 Hardwood former for the boiler end plates.

18-gauge copper discs. To flange the edges, a former is needed, which should be turned from aluminium, steel or hardwood to a diameter of the boiler shell outside dimension of 44.45mm (1.75in). A generous radius should be added to the help the copper flange form without cracking. To hold the blank copper discs to the former, a clamping plate is used. This can also be steel, aluminium or hardwood and turned to a smaller diameter of 40mm to allow for the forming process. A particularly suitable hardwood is called 'Lignum Vitae'.

BOILER BUILD

Mark two 60mm diameter discs on some 18-gauge copper sheet using the dividers. Also mark a 45mm-diameter circle on the same centres, just to help align the blanks on the former. The blanks will need annealing in the brazing hearth. To anneal, heat to glowing red and leave to cool or quench in water to speed things along. Then load each blank on to the former, align centrally, secure with the clamping plate, and progressively form the edge flange with a plastic-faced hammer.

The annealing and forming steps will need repeating to get the final shape without the copper cracking or rippling – typically five or six times. Finally, the finished end plate can be trimmed on the lathe, holding it in the reverse

jaws and using a boring tool to take light cuts and trim any unevenness off the edge of the part. Copper is quite 'chewy' to machine but a sharp tool, light cuts and some oil should help.

The main body of the boiler is a length of 1¾in copper tube in 20 gauge. Thicker metal will affect the performance of the boiler, and thinner will impact safety, so aim to get 20-gauge copper.

With the end plates complete, trial fit them to the copper tube and measure the overall length. This length will vary from build to build because

Fig. 2.41   The flanged plates can be trimmed to neaten the edges. A sharp tool and cutting oil will help when machining copper, which is quite 'chewy'.

Fig. 2.40   Using the hardwood formers to create a flanged end plate.

Fig. 2.42   To cut a tube square, a wrap of paper can be used to mark a straight edge to file to.

it depends on the radius of the flanged end plate. Trim the boiler tube to get the total length with the end caps to be 120mm. The boiler shell can be trimmed by cutting and filing, as the edge will be covered by the flange and not visible; or it can be trimmed on the lathe using the fixed steady to support the workpiece. If you are cutting and filing the tube, wrapping a piece of paper round will provide a 'square' edge to work to.

Fig. 2.43 *Marking the boiler barrel 180 degrees apart – step 1. Measure the boiler circumference with a piece of paper cut to size.*

To mark out the boiler tube for drilling, we need two marks 180 degrees apart on the shell. Wrap a piece of paper round the tube, and fold, mark or cut it so you have a piece of paper equal to the tube circumference. Fold the paper in half and make a small cut on each corner. Now wrap the paper back round the tube and you have two marks to indicate 180 degrees apart.

Jenny calipers can now be used to mark off the location of the holes along the length of the barrel.

Centre-punch and drill out the holes to final size, starting with a 3mm drill and working progressively upwards to create circular holes without deforming the copper.

SAFETY-VALVE BUSH

The safety-valve bush is a small piece of 10mm ($^3/_8$in) bronze. Turn an 8mm-diameter shoulder on the bar and part off the component to length. Hold it in the three-jaw chuck by the new shoulder and centre-drill, drill and tap with a ¼in BSF thread of 26tpi. The tapping drill for this thread is 5.3mm. Skim the top of the bush in the same setting to ensure it is perpendicular to the thread just cut.

Fig. 2.44 *Marking the boiler barrel 180 degrees apart – step 2. Fold the piece of paper in half and cut the corners to find the mid-point.*

Fig. 2.45 *Marking the boiler barrel 180 degrees apart – step 3. Wrap the paper back round the boiler to locate two points, 180 degrees from each other.*

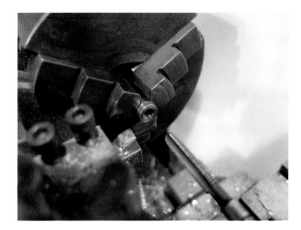

Fig. 2.46   Machining the safety-valve bush is a straightforward job. The lathe chuck should be turned by hand with the tap held in the tailstock chuck, to create a thread perpendicular to the top face.

SMOKESTACK

The smokestack is a piece of 15mm copper pipe cut to length with the edges tidied up on the lathe.

STEAM-FEED PIPE

The steam-feed pipe is a piece of $1/8$in copper tube – something 150mm long will be more than enough. Anneal the tube and then carefully bend it at 90 degrees, leaving a length on one end equal to the boiler diameter. You can just bend

it with fingers, but don't go too tight so that it buckles. The tube needs to be positioned in the boiler as shown in Fig. 2.47. The steam feed needs to be high up in the boiler to avoid sucking in water, but not so high that it is touching the boiler shell. A 2mm gap here will be fine.

SOLDERING THE BOILER

Clean all the parts to be joined with abrasive and then dust off or wash off any debris. Mix some of the tenacity flux with clean water into a thick paste and apply it to each part as you slide it into position. Put in the smokestack and steam feed before the end plates so you can see where they are positioned. Then add the end plates and safety-valve bush and place in the brazing hearth.

Brazing is a simple operation – the biggest mistake for the novice is adding the silver-solder rod before the work is hot enough, so spend some time working the flame all around the job before focusing on the first area to be joined. Dip the rod in the flame and in the flux to create a flux-coated rod, and then work from one end of the boiler to the other, soldering as much of the end plate as you can access. Use some barbecue tongs to rotate the workpiece so you can access any unsoldered areas on the other side.

Fig. 2.47   The steam take-off pipe should be towards the top of the boiler shell to prevent water being drawn into the engine.

Fig. 2.48   Pressure vessel after silver soldering.

While the work is cooling the pickling bath can be prepared. Citric acid is a much safer alternative to the traditional stronger acids, and is a very effective pickle given a little more time. It can be purchased from a brewery supplier in crystal form. It works best if mixed in hot water: two teaspoons per litre, in a Tupperware container large enough for the boiler. After a soak and given time to cool down, scrub the boiler with abrasive cloth and then return it to the pickling bath until it is clean.

TESTING THE BOILER

It is important to test the boiler for leaks and to ensure that all joints are safe. The first check is a visual inspection of the solder joints, where you should see neat fillets of silver. The fillets should flow down to a smooth blend with the copper parts.

To pressure test, water should be used, because it will not compress and store energy as air can. The best equipment is a simple pump and pressure gauge as shown in Fig. 2.51.

If you need to buy a pump, then one of the best and most economical options is a plant spray bottle. These simple devices can easily pump 200psi, and so all that is needed to test the boiler is a suitable piece of hose attached to the nozzle.

The usual test procedure is to pump up to twice the working pressure (40psi for this build) and leave the vessel to hold that pressure for ten minutes. If all is well the gauge will not have changed. If the pressure has dropped, do the test again with the vessel on a paper towel to try to detect where the leak is.

If remedial work is needed, then the water must be emptied from the boiler and all the joints refluxed before reheating and attending to the leaking joint.

If a gauge is available but not a pump, then the boiler can be tested by filling it with water and heating it. Heat should be applied gradually

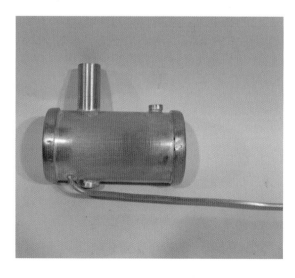

Fig. 2.49   Pressure vessel after cleaning in a citric acid pickling solution.

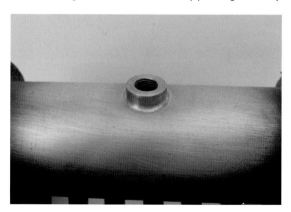

Fig. 2.50   Close-up of a good, filleted silver-solder joint.

Fig. 2.51 A typical hydraulic boiler-test pump and gauge.

Fig. 2.52 An alternative method for pressure testing, by filling the vessel full of water and heating it. A repurposed bicycle-pump gauge is shown here, being used to monitor the pressure.

because the pressure can climb quite suddenly, but it is a work-around for anyone without a pump. You will, of course, need a gauge, but something taken from an old bicycle pump, connected with a threaded boss or just with some hose and a few hose clips, will work.

THE FIREBOX

The firebox is made from two folded parts. Brass, copper or steel will work here, but not aluminium as we need to solder it. Something about 0.5mm thick is ideal, as this will be strong enough whilst it will still fold easily. Note in the drawing that both parts are similar in terms of their external dimensions, but one has the firebox door cut in it and the other has a hole for the steam pipe.

Cut the material to size, and mark the edge flange to be folded and the semi-circular cut-out for the pressure vessel; also the firebox door on one of the parts. The vent holes are most easily cut using a pilot drill followed by a step drill. A step drill is less likely to snag the thin sheet, and if you

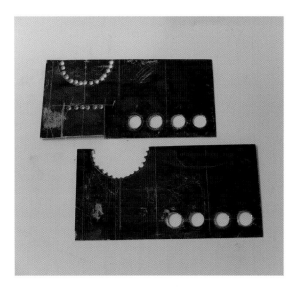

Fig. 2.53   The brass sheet for the firebox housing can be marked out and cut by hand, using shears for straight cuts and chain drilling for curves.

Fig. 2.55   The finished firebox with the pressure vessel in place.

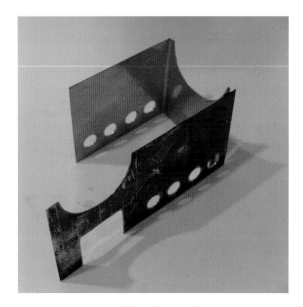

Fig. 2.54   One half of the firebox folded.

drill the hole to size and then just touch the edge with the next step up, it will remove any burr. Turn the part over and you can then use the step drill to de-burr the reverse side too.

Make the other cut-outs by chain-drilling close to the marked line with a 3mm drill, and then cutting with the tin snips. A small file can then be used to shape up to the marked line. If the semi-circular cuts are not perfect, don't worry, because small variations will be covered by the flanged end plate of the boiler barrel.

Mark and drill the hole for the steam pipe by offering up the pressure vessel to the panel to find an approximate location. The hole can be drilled oversize to cover any small error.

Folding can be done by hand in the vice. Just ensure the part is perpendicular to the vice jaws by checking with an engineering square each time. If the part needs to be hammered to get the fold sharp enough, place some wood on the fold and hit that, to avoid marking the work.

To finish, both parts need to be soldered together. Soft soldering will be good enough for the expected temperatures, but you can silver solder if you like. Fig. 2.55 shows the finished assembly.

THE BASE

The base is a 2mm thick piece of metal cut to the shape shown in the drawing, and drilled with the hole pattern given. The corner holes are just for holding the boiler to the boat hull, and the two counter-sunk holes will secure the boiler to the base.

THE BOILER BAND

The boiler band is made from a 0.5mm-thick strip of brass, 10mm wide by 190mm long. Make two 8BA nuts out of hex or square bar, and then silver solder one to each end of the strip. The band is tensioned with some 8BA countersunk screws through the base, and the tension holds both the pressure vessel to the firebox and the firebox to the base. Two 8BA countersunk screws will be needed, about 12mm long.

Fig. 2.56   Silver soldering the burner tray.

THE BURNER

The burner tray is made from three pieces of thin brass, with a fourth piece being used as a handle. The tray dimensions are such that the Mamod round tablets or the rectangular MSS tablets should fit.

The whole assembly should be silver soldered. Silver soldering is most easily done with the tray upside-down in the hearth with the handle bent flat. The handle can be lifted to the desired shape later on.

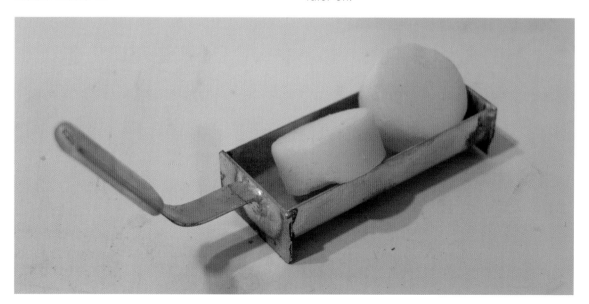

Fig. 2.57   Burner tray with the handle formed.

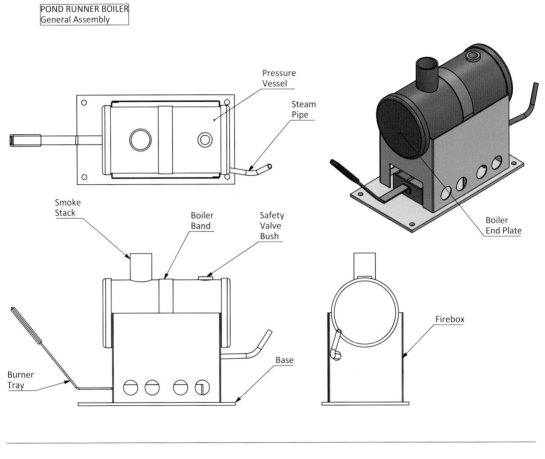

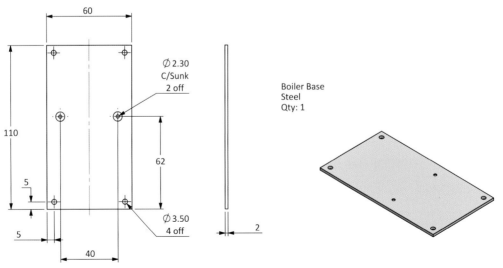

Fig. 2.58   *Pond Runner boiler drawings, sheet 1.*

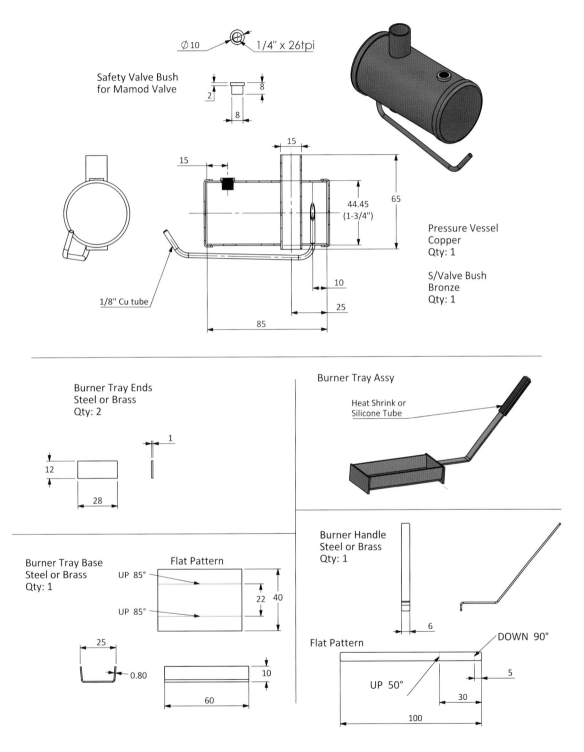

Fig. 2.59   Pond Runner boiler drawings, sheet 2.

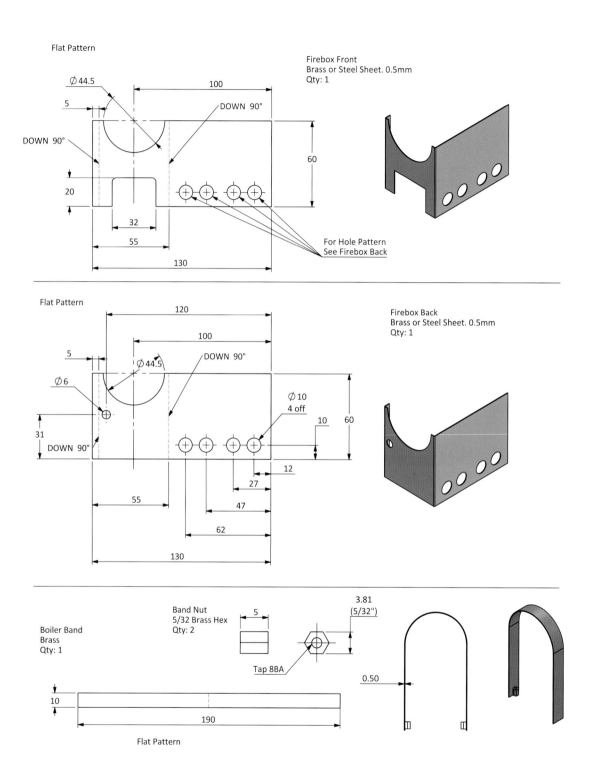

Flat Pattern

Ø44.5

100

DOWN 90°

Firebox Front
Brass or Steel Sheet. 0.5mm
Qty: 1

5

DOWN 90°

60

20

32

55

For Hole Pattern
See Firebox Back

130

Flat Pattern

120

100

Firebox Back
Brass or Steel Sheet. 0.5mm
Qty: 1

5

Ø44.5

DOWN 90°

Ø6

Ø10
4 off

10

60

31

DOWN 90°

12

27

55

47

62

130

Boiler Band
Brass
Qty: 1

Band Nut
5/32 Brass Hex
Qty: 2

5

3.81
(5/32")

Tap 8BA

0.50

10

190

Flat Pattern

Fig. 2.60   Pond Runner boiler drawings, sheet 3.

HULL BUILD

Inside the hull, bulkheads are kept to a minimum to allow for a large engine room with plenty of access to stoke the fire.

The first step is to mark out and cut the bottom of the boat. The grid of dimensions shown in the drawing should achieve a curve that is close enough. The best wood for this job is plywood, but ensure that it is at least 9mm thick as the sides will need to glue to the edge.

The block of wood given in the plans can be glued to the base at the bow. This will be shaped to match the base profile and is known as a breasthook. The bulkhead at the stern, known as a transom, should be made from a rectangle of 9mm plywood, and a similar rectangle can be glued into place to form the back of the engine room. Both should be set perpendicular to the base.

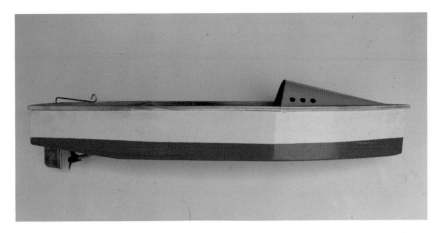

Fig. 2.61 The simple hull for the Pond Runner boat.

Fig. 2.62 The flat hull bottom with the breasthook, bulkhead and transom glued in place.

Once the glue is dry, a sander or sanding disc can be used to blend the block at the bow to match the base profile, and sand the bulkhead and transom to be flush with the base.

To create the raised rear section, a kerfing cut is made just behind the rear bulkhead. This is a cut part way through the wood to allow it to bend. The plans indicate a support block of the correct size to establish the required 8-degree angle. So cut the support block and sand it square. If you are a smartphone user there are free applications that are good for approximating angles such as this.

Make one or two kerfing cuts (depending on your saw-blade thickness) with a tenon saw, as shown in Fig. 2.64. A bandsaw is also an option to create the kerfing cuts, depending on your experience.

The sides start life as long rectangles of 6mm

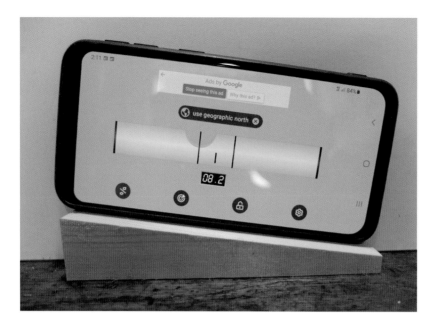

Fig. 2.63 Using a smart-phone app to check the angle of the support block.

plywood. A series of kerfing cuts 15mm apart are used around the tightest curves of the boat at the bow. The design is such that one side should be added to the base section first and left over-long at the front for final finishing.

To assemble the first side, start with the base clamped to the bench, but put some newspaper underneath so that it doesn't get stuck there. Add glue to the kerf, and push the support block into place to lift the stern section to the required 8 degrees (see Fig. 2.65). Next, glue one side. Clamps can be used to hold the side in place, or, if necessary, some nails driven into a baseboard can help form the sides around the base profile.

Fig. 2.64 Kerfing cuts, which are cuts partway through the timber, can be made to allow the wood to curve without splitting.

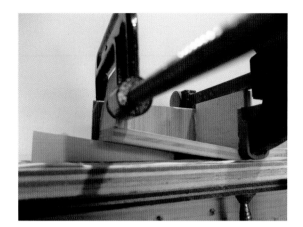

Fig. 2.65   Using the support block to set the angle of the raised stern section whilst the first side is glued.

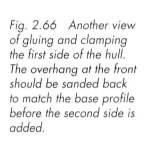

Fig. 2.66   Another view of gluing and clamping the first side of the hull. The overhang at the front should be sanded back to match the base profile before the second side is added.

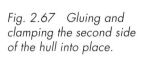

Fig. 2.67   Gluing and clamping the second side of the hull into place.

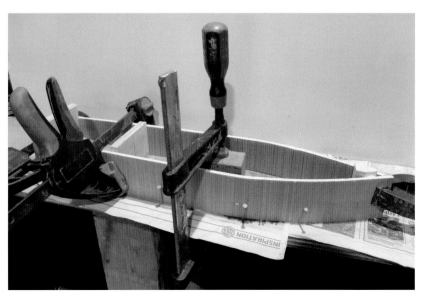

Once dry, the overlong planking at the bow will need sanding back to match the angle of the block. Then the second side can be added using the same process. Like the first side, the overlong front edge will need sanding back to create the final point at the bow.

The basic hull structure is now complete. It should be possible to place the steam plant in the hull to find a good position where burner access is assured but the engine is not too far back, as we need to access the flywheel for starting.

FITTING OUT THE HULL

The propeller shaft can be bought from a model shop. It should be 5in (125mm) long. The suggested propeller is three-bladed and 30mm in diameter. However, before ordering the propeller, it is worth checking the direction in which the engine rotates. As drawn, the engine is designed to use a left-handed propeller. This was chosen because the right-handed thread that secures the propeller to the shaft will not be exposed to an 'undoing' force when the boat is running. Typically, the 'hand' of a propeller is the direction it turns as viewed from the back of the boat. If the propeller turns clockwise from this view, it is right-handed, if anticlockwise, it is left-handed.

The most difficult part of the build is align-ing the propeller shaft and engine both radially and axially. To assist in this, the engine plinth is made first and is then used to create a drilling guide *and* to support the finished engine, thus helping both to be set with the same angle. The engine support block is just a piece of wood sanded to 12 degrees. At this stage it can be as long as you like, and needs to be wider than the engine base.

The drilling guide for the propeller is just a block drilled with a 6mm drill bit at a position as shown on the plans. To drill the angled hole, the gauge block can be set on the engine support block, so the drill starts at the marked location and then goes through at 12 degrees.

Now it should be possible to clamp the drilling gauge in the boat hull, up against the rear bulkhead. Make sure it is central, and then drill the angled hole for the propeller shaft. A 'long series' drill or 6mm flat bit may be needed to reach all the way through the hull. Drill through the bulkhead and then let the tip of the drill mark the raised floor section at the back of the boat. Then take a normal drill and drill a divot at this point. Then return to the long series drill and drill the angled hole right through. The purpose of the divot is just to stop the long drill wandering up the sloped floor section, which is quite likely to

Fig. 2.68   The guide block for the propeller shaft can be drilled at an angle to match the engine angle, by resting the block on the engine plinth itself.

happen given the shallow angle at which they meet.

If all has gone well, you should be able to push the propeller shaft through and find a position so the propeller sits clear of the hull but in front of the rudder position. In full size boats, the recommended propeller tip clearance is 12 per cent of the diameter. So for the 30mm propeller, aim for a hull clearance of 3mm to 4mm. If something is wrong, don't worry. Enlarge the hole in the bulkhead, or file the hole in the hull to find a good position. Before gluing the propshaft tube in place, put the engine plinth in the hull and place the engine on it to check that you can get the engine shaft and prop-shaft aligned.

The best approach is to first remove the flywheel and crank from the engine. Take a 4mm piece of silver steel and slide it through the prop tube and into the main bearing of the engine. The rod will ensure the engine and propshaft are perfectly aligned. Now it is a case of sliding the engine plinth and tilting the prop tube to find a position where everything lines up. When you are happy, both the engine plinth and prop tube should be glued in with the silver-steel rod holding the alignment. Use

Fig. 2.69   Drilling the propeller-shaft hole in the hull using a long-reach flat bit.

Fig. 2.70   A 4mm steel rod should be used to position the propeller tube and engine in alignment. With the rod in place, both the tube and engine plinth can be glued. If further adjustment is needed, then shims can be placed under the engine to find the easiest running position.

wood glue for the engine plinth and epoxy resin for the prop tube.

Once the glue is dry and before removing the steel rod, try screwing the engine down to the plinth – keep checking that the alignment rod slides smoothly. If it gets tight then you'll need to try some washers or off-cuts of brass under the engine base to try to find a setting where the engine is secure but the alignment good. It is worth spending some time getting this as good as you can, as it will minimize friction in the drive train and put more of our modest power into the water.

The propeller shaft should be installed next with a generous amount of light grease. The coupling to the engine output shaft is a short length of silicone tube. This should have enough strength to transmit the power without causing a lot of friction in the system. The gauge block used to set the angled stern section should now be glued inside centrally at the stern. This will create a support for the rudder.

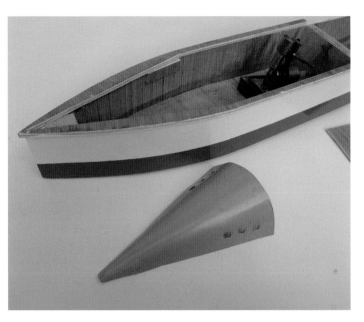

Fig. 2.72   Capping at the bow is made from some offcuts glued to the edge of the sides and sanded to match the curve. The aluminium splash hood is also shown in this image.

Fig. 2.71   The support block can be glued into the rear of the hull to create a level area for the rudder tube.

Before going any further, a float test with the engine and boiler fully fuelled is a good idea, to check the trim of the hull. In this case, 50g of lead was added to the stern to set it level. This lead was stuck in with epoxy resin.

Once the boat is trimmed, the rear deck panel can be tacked into place. You can glue it if you like, but a couple of tacks allows for maintenance access later on.

The sides and curved bow section of the hull have capping pieces to give a neat finish. The straight sections are just 8mm-wide off-cuts of 6mm plywood glued into place. For the curved section the strips are cut wider to allow for the curve. Once all the edge pieces are in place, they can be sanded to match the profile of the hull with a slight overhang on the outside. The result should be that the front capping pieces are curved on the outside but straight on the inside, which will make fitting the splash hood much easier.

At the very back, drill a vertical hole for the rudder, ensuring that it places the rudder clear of

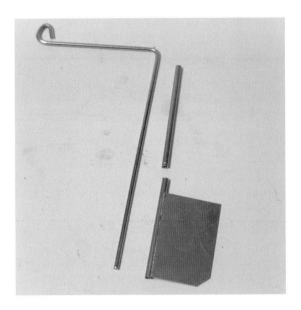

Fig. 2.74   The rudder can be crimped to the rudder shaft, so that removal is possible later on.

Fig. 2.73   Rudder parts made from brass and soft soldered.

Fig. 2.75   The steam connection from the boiler to the engine can be just silicone tubing, given the pressures expected from the boiler, secured with zip ties if needed.

the propeller. It should be a 3mm hole into which a 3mm brass tube can be glued. The rudder parts are shown in Fig. 2.73. The rudder itself is a piece of brass plate cut to the size shown in the plans and soft-soldered to another piece of 3mm brass tube. To assemble the rudder, take a 2mm piece of brass rod and bend it to create the tiller. Push the straight part of the tiller down through the 3mm brass tube, and slide the rudder on the bottom. To make the rudder, grip the shaft, and the 3mm piece of brass tube can be crimped very slightly with some wire cutters (Fig. 2.74): this will create a friction fit to the rudder shaft.

The boiler can be installed next. Ensure it is central left/right, so that the boat sits level. Make sure there is room at the bow for the burner to be removed. The closer you can make the boiler to the engine the better, as long steam-feed pipes lose heat. Then mark the base and drill for short wood screws.

The simplest connection between the boiler and engine is a piece of silicone tube. If it is a tight fit, then it can just be pushed into place, or if necessary cable ties (zip ties) can be used to help it grip the copper tubes.

THE SPLASH HOOD

The splash hood can be a piece of any metal 0.5–0.7mm thick, cut to the template. Aluminium works best if you have some, because it doesn't

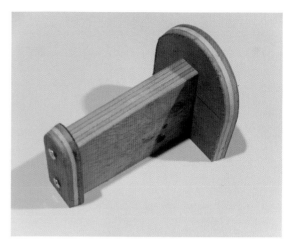

Fig. 2.76   A possible former for curving the splash hood. It consists of two wooden end plates sanded to match the hull, with a spacing block between them.

spring back as much as some materials. The challenge with this part is that the bend is not a constant radius, but gets tighter towards the bow. The best thing is to create the large radius first and then use progressively smaller radius formers to get the final shape. It is not an exact science, so use whatever you have to form the part, but try to avoid hitting it, which will mark it. A wooden former as shown in Fig. 2.76 is also an option.

To make the hood fit the hull, add some blocks of scrap wood, as shown in Fig. 2.77, to support the back edge. The front edge should rest on the breasthook at the bow.

Fig. 2.77   Two offcuts of wood can be used to create support blocks for the splash hood.

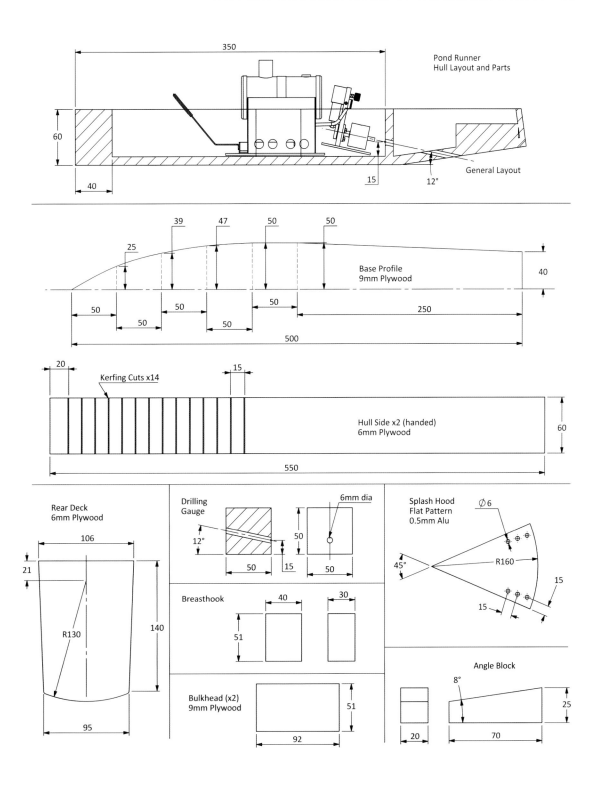

Fig. 2.78   Pond Runner boat drawings.

MAIDEN VOYAGE AND TIPS ON FREE STEAMING

Safety first: You will be using a fire in a public place. Be aware of the flames and how you handle the fuel tray, to be sure not to set light to anything by the lake. Also, check the fire is out when you have finished, and let the boiler cool down before handling. Keep spectators safe.

From experience, steaming time from cold for the simple boiler is approximately three minutes. Run time from one fuel load should be about fifteen minutes at 800rpm, by which time it can be expected that the water will be almost exhausted.

VOYAGE EQUIPMENT LIST

Be sure to pack the following:

Water
Solid fuel
Lighter
Work gloves
A syringe
Some cloths
A fireproof cloth such as a piece of fire blanket or a plumber's soldering mat
Spanners or screwdrivers to tighten loose parts
Safety glasses
Needle-nosed pliers (to handle hot components)
Recovery equipment (tennis ball on a string, or another boat!)

To prepare the boiler, remove the safety valve and fill the boiler two-thirds full with rainwater – this equates to about 88ml of water. Rainwater is the best as it is simply H_2O without any calcium or fluoride. If rainwater is not available, then frost from the inside of your freezer would also be a good choice, or condensed water from a humidifier. Filling is most easily done with a syringe through the safety valve hole.

Pack the fuel tray with solid tablets and light one end. Tilt the tray slightly to help the flames climb across the whole fuel tray, and then place the fire under the boiler.

Whilst raising steam, add some light oil to the cylinder port face, the cylinder pivot and the main bearing. Turn the flywheel by hand to run the oil through. It is also a good idea to position the cylinder about its exhaust stroke: this will block off the inlet port to allow pressure to build.

Wait for steam to hiss, and you may see condensate dripping from the engine. Now start flicking the flywheel to start the engine. Initially a mixture of condensed steam and oil will be expelled from the exhaust, but keep going and eventually the engine should run. Everything will be hot by now so be careful working around the engine.

Check the fuel level and top up the fuel tablets if you have used a lot to get steam underway.

Once the engine is running, place the boat in the water and set a heading for the maiden voyage. For this first voyage set the rudder for a fairly tight turn, so if the boat stalls it is not too far out. All being well, you can now experiment with different rudder settings and different headings to explore the lake.

Fig. 2.79 shows some ideas and fundamentals for free steaming.

Casting off towards any breeze is a good idea so that if the boat stalls it has a chance of drifting back to the lakeside. Take note of any reeds, weeds or low hanging branches that could cause issues, also any rocks, shallow areas or (as history has taught us) icebergs.

Voyage 1 is a good starting point – a small arc back to the lakeside. This loop can be increased in size (voyage 2) to go further into the lake.

If you want the boat to come back to the same place, then set off parallel to the lakeside (voyage 3) and it should sail a complete circle – but be aware that any currents or breeze may take you off course.

If you have another crew member with you, then you can sail directly across the lake and they can send it back, either in a slight curve or dead straight, as shown in route 4.

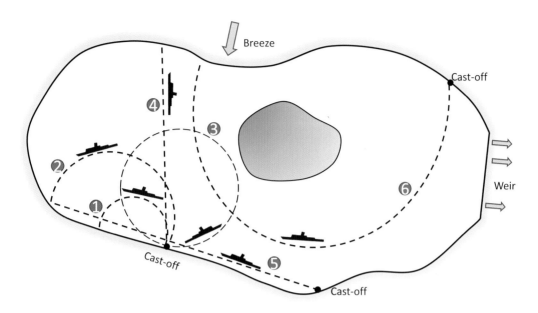

Fig. 2.79   Diagram of a hypothetical boating lake, giving some suggested sailing routes.

Another option is to sail straight but close to one side of the pond, as in voyage 5. Some captains like to walk alongside and make small adjustments with a stick to keep the boat sailing close by.

Finally, if there is an island in the lake and if you think you can set the rudder accurately enough, you could try circumnavigating it. This is a risky but exciting adventure, and best undertaken with a rescue strategy in place! Note how the start point and heading of route 6 is set so that the breeze is used to keep the craft offshore, rather than blowing it towards the island.

Experiments with the prototype Pond Runner indicate that steaming time should be about fifteen minutes, so keep an eye on the time and fuel levels as you go.

As a general rule with steam engines, if the engine stops suddenly on the lake, then the water has run out. If it gradually slows to a stop, then the fire has died down or gone out.

Before sailing a second time, inspect and remove any pond weed or debris from the propeller.

Check the hull, and empty any water in the bilge. Check the fuel and water levels. The water level can only be checked without pressure in the boiler, so extinguish and remove the fire, then lift the safety valve to remove any pressure before topping up.

PRECAUTIONS!

When you are working near the water, be aware that although your boat floats, nothing else does, including any tools you have with you and any bits you take off the boat; so servicing and maintenance is best done aside from the lake.

A word about solid fuel storage: solid fuel needs to be kept in an airtight box – a zip-lock bag or Tupperware should work. The reason is that over time solid fuel absorbs moisture, and if this happens, when it is heated it can pop and spit; this is something to be aware of if you are using old fuel tablets.

When you have finished sailing, it is best to let the solid fuel burn out in a safe place. Blowing it out often causes it to spit in your face. If it is an emergency, then use your fire cloth to get back in control, but if you must blow out the flame, put on your safety glasses, and be aware that it can re-ignite due to the heat of the fire tray.

Finally, don't pack things away until you are sure everything is safe and cool.

RESCUING A STRANDED BOAT

SAFETY NOTE: These rescue procedures apply only to a safe lake environment, not to rivers or the open sea.

If the boat has stopped in open water or is marooned somewhere, then the first thing is not to panic. Even if the fire is still burning, no harm will come to the silver-soldered boiler, even if it has run dry. Once retrieved you can let things cool down, refuel and sail again. The following are some ideas for recovery:

Sit and wait: Not very interesting, but a chance to eat your emergency banana, and with even the slightest breeze, your boat may continue moving and hopefully will beach in a location from which you can retrieve it. However, water currents may take over, and in a lake, these typically flow towards a weir, which is a significant hazard for a small boat. So if you're drifting towards the weir, a different strategy is needed.

Tennis ball: A tennis ball on a string or on a fishing reel is a favourite technique for model boaters. The tennis ball needs to be landed beyond the boat and then, as it is reeled in, it should catch on the boat and drag it to shore. Drag slowly to avoid taking on water or capsizing. Combining the tennis ball with a fishing reel gives the system more range.

Tensioned string: If you have a friend with you and the lake is not huge, you can use a ball of string to capture the boat. One person stays put and the other person walks round to the other side, unravelling a ball of string that is held between them. The tensioned string across the lake can then be used to catch on the boat and draw it to the side.

Wade in: If this is your rescue strategy, then take a towel. Wellington boots will help if the lake is very shallow, but expect to get wet and muddy if it is anything more than a paddling pool.

Swim: As a poor swimmer, I can't recommend this. Some people have retrieved their boat by swimming out to it, but besides drowning, you could get ill from the quality of the water. Even if you get your boat back you will be very wet and cold for the journey home.

Radio-controlled rescue boat: A fellow modeller might be able to help you out. I once suffered the humiliation of having my electric boat rescued by a model sailing yacht. The yacht sailed round the stranded boat with a piece of string, creating a loop to pull the boat back to shore. If you take your own rescue boat, some modellers use a fixed frame made of plastic plumbing tube, which resembles a forklift truck. The frame is used to capture the stranded boat and push it home. Alternatively, a strong magnet towed on a float, or suspended from a deck crane, can lock on to a metal plate on the ship's bow to tow it home.

Paddling boat: Another option is an inflatable dingy or canoe. This has the additional advantage of being able to rescue the boat from the water or a remote beached location.

Whatever you do, put safety first. It is important that this is a fun hobby, not a tragedy.

CHAPTER THREE

HARBOUR PILOT: THE ENGINE

The inspiration for this design came from a visit to the London Toy and Model Museum many years ago as a child. In amongst the spectacular Meccano models, clockwork toys and live steam models was a handsome patrol boat with a live steam motor. As we walked round the museum my eyes were drawn back to it and my memory of it is clear, although probably not very correct.

As I remember it, the hull had a vertical bow line to give a sense of presence on the water, and the sides were steep. It had a low, purposeful roofline and a short funnel behind the cabin. The hull sides were a long taper from the cabin aft, and the deck ran lower to the stern as well,

to produce a vessel with sleek lines. I have no recollection of the make or model of the boat, so what follows is an attempt to capture some of these features in a new design.

This build is more advanced than the Pond Runner, with more boiler fittings installed in a larger boat, and there is scope for radio control of the rudder, too. The hull is a more traditional construction of planking over a frame – the design theory for the hull is fully explained.

Also within the build chapters are some theoretical topics about boilers, boat design and model engine performance. These chapters should allow builders to design and construct their own model steamboat or make customizations to the plans.

Fig. 3.1   Harbour Pilot early morning sailing at the Lake Grounds.

THE LONDON TOY AND MODEL MUSEUM

The London Toy and Model Museum was opened in 1982 and occupied two town houses in Craven Hill, north of Hyde Park. The collection was founded by Allen Levey and David Pressland, both authors of books on the subject of toys, and avid bear collector Narisa Chakrabongse, who later married Allen and was herself a writer and publisher.

The museum featured toys primarily from the Victorian era and early twentieth century and included dolls' houses, model trains in various gauges, teddy bears, pedal cars, tricycles, tin toys, clockwork models and, of course, model boats. In the working toy category, notable manufacturers represented were Meccano, Marklin, Bassette-Lowke, Bowman, Mamod, Bayko and Hornby. The centrepiece of the museum was an extensive Gauge 1 train layout in the back garden, running live steam locomotives on sunny days.

The museum changed hands twice, and then finally closed in 1999, when the collection was separated and auctioned off.

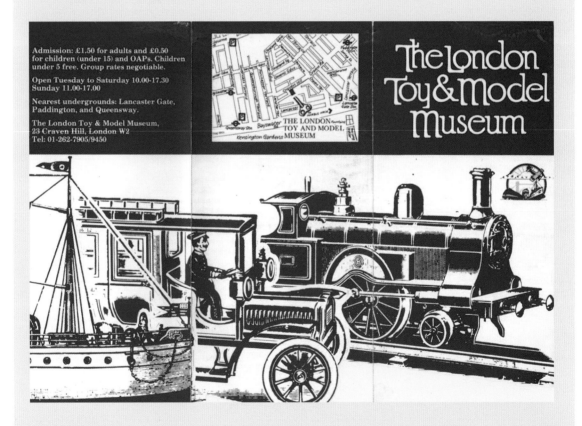

Fig. 3.2   London Toy Museum brochure. BRIGHTON TOY MUSEUM

THE ENGINE: GENERAL DESCRIPTION

The engine has a bore of 10mm and a stroke of 12mm. The piston and cylinder are both brass, but a cast-iron cylinder would also work. The overhung crank simplifies the crank build, and the single main bearing contains a rotary valve located on the main axle. The rotary valve admits steam to the top of the cylinder via a transfer pipe, and on the exhaust stroke the valve lets the steam exit through an outlet pipe, which can be connected to the smokestack. The flywheel is a marine-style one, which is smaller in diameter compared to a stationary engine.

The prototype engine runs between 500rpm and 1,400rpm on pressures of 10psi to 30psi respectively. Torque under 30psi of pressure was 8.6Nmm at 900rpm, proven to be enough to move a medium-sized model boat with a 35 to 40mm-diameter propeller.

One of the main problems with small engines is the condensation of the steam. The engine needs to be kept hot for the steam to do its work and get out to the smokestack before it condenses. Steps that can help reduce this condensation are insulation of the steam pipes, using the shortest pipe runs, lagging the cylinder, and superheating the steam.

Fig. 3.3   Harbour Pilot engine featuring a single cylinder with a rotary valve on the crankshaft.

that are needed to make a satisfactory part. The material is not important, but it should be 2mm thick or greater to allow for some countersunk holes on the underside.

ENGINE CONSTRUCTION

ENGINE BASE

A good place to start engine construction is with the base, which requires just cutting and drilling to complete it. Marking-out fluid can help with the placement of the drilled holes. Lines can be scribed with odd-leg calipers, and accurate centre punches are all

Fig. 3.4   Marking out the base for drilling requires nothing more than some measuring tools, a scribe and a centre punch.

PEDESTAL

Similar to the base, the engine pedestal is also a 2mm thick piece of metal. Again, the material is not important, and it just needs marking and drilling to complete it. If thicker or thinner material is used, the columns should be shortened or lengthened as necessary to place the cylinder at the correct height.

ENGINE COLUMNS

The base and pedestal are connected with four round columns made from 6mm brass. Each one is drilled and tapped 8BA in both ends, and working with brass helps make this less of a task. Each column should be the same length to ensure the plates are parallel when assembled.

Turning to length is fully described in Chapter 1, but you should start with the bar slightly over-long and face both ends in the lathe to get them square. Then remove them from the chuck and measure the length you have.

Now you can calculate what needs to be removed. With the part back in the chuck, bring up the lathe tool until it just touches. Zero the top slide and then take progressive cuts using the top slide until you reach final size.

THE FLYWHEEL

The flywheel is a simple turning job, and should be made from a heavy metal such as cast iron

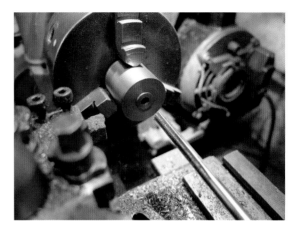

Fig. 3.6 Machining the flywheel. The centre hole, the shoulder and the end of the flywheel can be machined in one setting in the three-jaw chuck.

or steel. The three-jaw chuck can be used in the lathe to hold the metal blank while it is centre-drilled, drilled and reamed to a 6mm bore. A slow spindle speed should be used for the reaming. Also in this setting, the small 1mm shoulder can be machined, which will space the flywheel off the bearing block.

Finishing the outside of the flywheel is best done

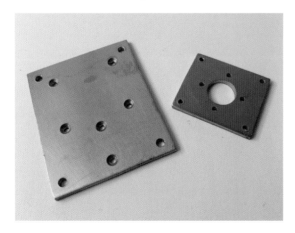

Fig. 3.5 The completed base and pedestal.

Fig. 3.7 A technique for holding a threading die square to the workpiece using the tailstock for support and the tool post to stop the holder rotating. The tailstock can be used to apply light pressure to get the die to engage.

Fig. 3.8   A threaded arbor for finishing the flywheel. It is important not to remove the arbor from the chuck after it has been machined to avoid losing accuracy.

Fig. 3.9   The flywheel edge being machined on the arbor. The flywheel can be gripped by the nut on the arbor and also by the grub screw of the flywheel.

on an arbor to ensure it runs fully true. A wobbling flywheel can be avoided by first machining a 6mm spindle in the lathe and adding an M6 thread on the end. The other end of the arbor should be finished with a nice square shoulder and a slight undercut to remove any radius in the corner. Both the turning and threading must be done without removing the arbor from the chuck to ensure it runs fully centred on the lathe axis. A neat and perpendicular thread can be cut with a standard die holder using the tailstock to hold it square and apply some pressure, whilst the chuck is turned by hand. The tool post can be used to stop the die holder turning, as shown in Fig. 3.7.

All this will mean that the arbor will have no runout, and so finishing the flywheel edge from this reference will give a perfect flywheel. Place the flywheel on the arbor and clamp it in place with a washer and M6 nut. Then take light cuts to take it down to final size.

THE BEARING BLOCK

The bearing block can be made from brass or bronze. It will also need to be soldered, so aluminium will not work here. A 16mm piece of brass bar needs to have a flat cut along it to a depth of 3mm. This can be done in the vertical slide on the lathe, or in the milling machine. Touch the cutter on the work to find a reference, and then take cuts until 3mm has been removed. Also in this setting, it is worth drilling and tapping the mounting holes so they are square to the newly machined surface. Finding the mid-point and the end can be done with an edge finder, and then the handle scales used to position a drill for the 1.8mm holes.

Fig. 3.10   The flat underside of the bearing block can be machined in the milling machine, or using the vertical slide in the lathe.

On the side opposite the flat, three holes should be drilled as shown in the drawing: note that they are off centre. The middle hole is for a connection to the cylinder head, and the outer holes for inlet and exhaust connections. These holes are best created holding the part in the drill vice with the flat face resting on a parallel.

To drill and ream the main axle hole the bearing block can be placed in the three-jaw chuck on the lathe with one jaw on the flat face: then the bar can be centre-drilled, drilled and reamed to 6mm. Drilling the axle hole last should ensure that any burrs from the steam port drillings are removed. For the reaming step it is best to turn the lathe by hand or use the slowest back gear speed, so that the minimum of material is removed. This hole needs to be a perfect fit with the axle for the valve to work at its best.

Fig. 3.11   Drilling and tapping the bearing-block mounting holes should be done in the same setting as the previous step – this way the tapped holes will be perpendicular to the flat face. You can also use an edge finder to position the holes accurately.

Fig. 3.12   The holes for the steam connections can be drilled by reversing the part in the vice so it is resting on the newly machined flat face.

THE BEARING STANDS

The bearing stands are simple round bars, turned to length and drilled through 2.3mm. They can be made of any available material. Aim for some accuracy in the lengths to ensure the axle ends up perpendicular to the cylinder bore in the final assembly.

THE CRANK DISC

The crank disc is made from a piece of steel bar turned to 18mm diameter, then centre-drilled, drilled and reamed with a 6mm hole and with a 1mm shoulder on one side to space it from the bearing block. The part should be finished to a thickness of 8mm including the shoulder.

To drill the off-set hole for the crank pin, a piece of packing can be used in the three-jaw chuck. The height of the piece of packing will determine the throw of the crank, and can be

Fig. 3.13   The position of the main bearing hole is determined by the machined flat on the block resting against one jaw of the three-jaw chuck of the lathe.

approximated with the following formula kindly shared by Marvin Klotz:

$$Packing\ piece = 1.5 \times e - r + \left(0.5 \times \sqrt{(4r^2) - (3e^2) + (2ew \times \sqrt{3}) - w^2}\right)$$

where:
e = eccentric off-set
r = radius of workpiece
w = width of jaws (the width of the face contacting the workpiece).

In this engine, the requirement is for a crank throw of 6mm, an overall disc diameter of 18mm (radius 9mm), and a jaw width on the chuck of 2mm.

Using the formula, that gives us:

$$Packing\ piece = 1.5 \times 6 - 9 + (0.5 \times \sqrt{(4 \times 9^2) - (3 \times 6^2) + (2 \times 6 \times 2 \times \sqrt{3}) - 2^2} = 7.96mm$$

Packing piece = 7.96mm

It should be noted that professional off-set drilling is done with the four-jaw chuck. The formula used here is really an approximation, but is accurate enough for this build. Also, a word of caution needs to be mentioned when using the three-jaw chuck like this, which is really outside its designed purpose. Take care to ensure that both workpiece and packing are secure. If you

are at all unsure you can always use this method to mark the hole position whilst turning the lathe by hand, and then finish the hole on the drill press.

Whichever you decide, this is a useful technique to be aware of, and with a slow chuck speed and light drilling pressure there should be no problem. In this setting the crank-pin hole can be drilled and tapped 8BA for the crank pin.

Fig. 3.14 Drilling and tapping the off-set crank-pin hole can be done using the three-jaw chuck and a packing piece of the right thickness.

Fig. 3.15 Cross-drilling the crank disc using a drilling guide in the drill press vice. The drilling guide must be of the same diameter as the workpiece, and care must be taken to set the correct position along the axis.

To finish, the part requires an 8BA tapped hole to take a grub screw to grip the axle. This can be done in the drill press.

THE AXLE

The main axle is a piece of 6mm silver steel. Before cutting to length, it may be helpful to leave the bar long. This makes it easier to hold the part securely when milling the valve flats.

The flats can be created on the milling machine or lathe, and should be made to a depth of 1mm each. The first flat can be cut in the correct location along the bar using the edge finder again, and with the rod held in a V block.

To get the second flat 180 degrees from the first, a piece of bar can be clamped to the first flat with a toolmaker's clamp. Then the bar can be rotated and a DTI (dial test indicator) used to check when the bar is precisely level. Then the second flat can be located and cut. To finish, the axle should be cut to length and the ends finished on the lathe.

Fig. 3.16 Milling the first flat on the axle can be done in the milling machine or lathe. Here it is shown held in a V block in the milling machine. The edge finder can be used to find the exact position for the flat.

Fig. 3.17 Setting the axle 180 degrees from the first machined flat can be done by clamping a piece of square bar to the first flat, and turning the axle 180 degrees. This rotation can be checked using a small level or a DTI.

THE CYLINDER

The cylinder is made from a suitably sized piece of brass, though cast iron can also be used. Most important is to get the bore of the cylinder parallel and square to the bottom face of the cylinder to avoid the piston binding. The bar should be held in the three-jaw chuck to have the bottom face squared off and the centre hole drilled and reamed to final size, all in a single setting. A D-bit can be used to ensure the hole is parallel to the very top of the cylinder. Also in this setting, the thick wall of the cylinder can be reduced as shown in the drawing, to allow for some cylinder lagging.

Next, the cylinder can be reversed in the chuck to have the port hole drilled and a $^7/_{32}$ × 32tpi thread added to the hole. The final outside diameter of the cylinder can then be turned to be a snug fit in the cylinder cladding, which is made from a 22mm domestic plumbing 'end feed' connector, from the hardware store.

For the engine to work at its best, the bore of the cylinder should be polished. This can be done by turning a wooden dowel to fit the bore and using metal polish to take out any machining marks.

The four mounting holes are best 'transfer-drilled' from the pedestal. Alignment is not critical here and can be done by eye; it just has to look right.

Fig. 3.18 The finished cylinder and cladding.

Fig. 3.19   Polishing the cylinder bore using a wooden dowel turned to be a wringing fit in the bore, and working the parts together with metal polish. It is worth taking steps to protect the lathe bed during this process.

Fig. 3.20   Transfer drilling the pedestal holes to the cylinder. Alignment is not critical here and can be done by eye.

THE PISTON

The piston is made from a piece of brass bar. Like the axle, machining from a longer piece of stock is useful for the cross-drilling of the gudgeon

pin. The piston should be made to suit the cylinder bore rather than to a specific dimension. The aim is for a sliding fit, but the piston can go from a tight fit to a loose fit in an instant, so care must be taken to find the precise point where a sliding fit occurs.

Fig. 3.21 shows how the material beyond the piston part was relieved first, to allow the cylinder to be trial fitted. A tight wringing fit is a good point to stop advancing the cutting tool and to make repeated passes at the same setting to take out any flex in the tool or workpiece. Finally, a piece of the finest wet'n'dry paper can be placed on a file and held to the piston to 'polish out' the tool marks until a sliding fit is found.

Next the underside of the piston should be hollowed out using a choice of drills, boring tools, milling cutters or D-bits, to follow the profile given in the cross-section drawing.

Cross-drilling the piston can be done in the pillar drill or lathe or milling machine. A central hole is needed, and this can be done in the drilling vice using a guide as with the crank disc, or it can be held in a V block and clocked centrally using an edge finder.

Finally, the piston can be returned to the lathe to be parted from the bar stock. The piston may not run perfectly true in this setting, but the outer diameter should not be touched, and the part should just be parted off from the bar to final length. Halfway through parting a small file can be used to chamfer the piston crown before completing the parting operation.

Fig. 3.21   Before machining the piston itself, some material is relieved beyond the piston, enough to allow a trial fit of the cylinder. For this reason, the material must stick out from the chuck equivalent to the cylinder bore length.

Fig. 3.22   The underside of the piston can be hollowed out using a combination of drills, milling cutters and D-bits.

Fig. 3.23   Cross-drilling the piston is done before the piston is removed from the bar stock; this is so it can be held more easily in the vice or V block.

CONNECTING ROD

The connecting rod should be drawn out and cut from a small piece of 2mm steel sheet. Take time to ensure the distance between the holes is correct. The width of the part above the big-end bearing area needs to be reduced so that it doesn't catch on the engine pedestal. This is just a job for some careful filing.

CRANK PIN

The crank pin starts life as a piece of $3/_{16}$in brass or steel hex. A 6mm length is turned to 2.2mm diameter and threaded 8BA. Use a sharp tool to add an undercut where the thread meets the remainder of the workpiece. This will allow the crank pin to 'pull up' square to the crank disc. To finish, the 3mm shoulder is turned to be a running

Fig. 3.24   The crank pin is a small turning task, best made from hex bar.

fit on the connecting rod big end, and then the finished screw can be parted from the bar stock.

STEAM FITTINGS

A piece of $^5/_{32}$in copper pipe is needed to connect the valve to the cylinder head. To get the length exact, assemble the bearing block on the base along with the pedestal and cylinder. Then form a piece of pipe over the cylinder head and down to the middle hole in the bearing block. Then it can be marked for cutting, as shown in Fig. 3.25.

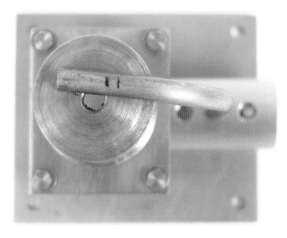

Fig. 3.25   The main steam pipe to the cylinder top will need to be cut to the correct length after forming. This should be just short of the top hole of the cylinder.

Fig. 3.26   Steam connections to the bearing block are all soft soldered in one setting.

Soft soldering is the easiest connection to the bearing block, and it is worth adding the inlet and exhaust pipes, to solder them all in one sitting. The exhaust pipe only needs to be long enough for a flexible connection to the smoke-stack. The inlet pipe is a little longer and will need to reach the regulator. This will need to be cut to an exact length with the whole steam plant assembled.

With the pipes soldered in place, the sim-plest connection at the cylinder head is a banjo and bolt. The banjo is just a brass collar, centre-drilled and then cross-drilled on one side only, to fit the pipe. Then it can be turned to final diameter and parted off. The bolt to hold the banjo can be made from a piece of 8mm ($^5/_{16}$in) hex brass. Turn the shank to 5.5mm and then thread $^7/_{32}$ × 32tpi to match the cylinder head. Centre-drill the threaded section to a depth of 10mm and then cross-drill on the drill press or mill. Finally return to the lathe and create an undercut region as shown, to allow the steam to exit the pipe and feed down the bolt into the cyl-inder. Part off from the bar stock to finish.

Fig. 3.27   The steam-feed banjo union and banjo bolt.

Fig. 3.28   The displacement lubricator assembly. This type of lubricator works by condensing some steam to displace oil into the steam pipe, to lubricate the inside of the cylinder.

THE LUBRICATOR

A lubricator should be considered a requirement if a superheater is to be used, as the dry steam will not provide sufficient lubrication. The simple superheater on this boiler will not dry the steam to this extent, but having a lubricator still adds benefit. Knowing how to make one is also a useful skill.

This design is a displacement lubricator, which catches some steam from the main engine feed and allows it to condense. The resulting water drops to the bottom of the oil tank, which lifts the oil up and into the steam feed to be taken to the engine. A small hole must be used to connect the oil tank to the steam feed to avoid too much oil being sucked into the engine.

The main body of the lubricator is a piece of round brass 11mm diameter, 25mm long, drilled through 7.9mm and tapped both ends $^5/_{16}$ × 32tpi. At one end it is cross drilled for the steam pipe. The steam pipe can be made from solid bar drilled $^5/_{32}$in for the main steam feed, or from a suitable piece of brass/copper tube. The steam pipe is drilled in the centre with a tiny drill, about 0.5mm if you have one. Slide the steam pipe though the lubricator body and point the small hole upwards. Then silver solder the assembly,

as it will be soft soldered to the main steam pipe during final assembly.

The filling cap and drain plug can be made from any piece of hex or round brass. They can be ornate or plain, fitted with a T-handle, or knurled as you please. At the top of both threads, a square shoulder should be machined to take a fibre washer to make a good seal.

FINAL ASSEMBLY

Bolt the main bearing to the engine base with two long 8BA counter-sunk screws. Check the orientation here because the pipe connections are not symmetrical: the pipes are biased towards the flywheel end of the base. The columns are next, and they are screwed to the base of the cylinder with some 8BA counter-sunk screws from the underside.

The engine pedestal can be screwed to the cylinder base with four 8BA nuts with washers.

Wrap some insulation round the cylinder and hold it in place by sliding on the lagging. Proper insulation is available from model engineering

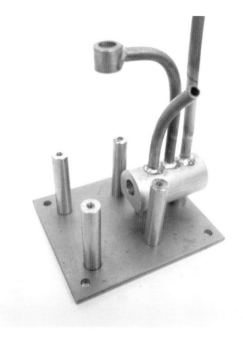

Fig. 3.30   Assembling the cylinder lagging and cladding.

Fig. 3.29   Engine part assembled.

suppliers, but if you like you can use some string – anything to help keep the cylinder warm.

Attach the connecting rod to the piston with the wrist pin. Ensure the wrist pin is short enough not to scratch the cylinder bore. Oil the piston and slide it into the cylinder.

Attach the crank disc to the axle with a small grub screw. The relationship of the crank pin to the valve flats is important and is best given by the drawing. The crank pin should be between the valve flats, but if it is 180 degrees out, the engine will run backwards.

Slide the axle into the bearing with a little oil. Check it spins freely, and then add the flywheel. To ensure the flywheel grub screw doesn't mark the crankshaft, a small piece of soft metal, brass or copper, should be placed in the grub-screw hole first. This way it will be possible to remove the crank for servicing without scratching the valve block bore.

Fig. 3.31   Adding a brass plug to the grub-screw hole. This is a good idea on any engine but important on this design so that the axle can be removed at a later time, without scoring the inside of the valve body.

Fig. 3.32   *The assembled engine.*

Slide the cylinder/piston assembly into place under the steam pipe but over the columns, and add the crank pin.

Secure the top of the engine with four more 8BA bolts with washers into the columns.

Check that the engine spins freely, and then connect the steam pipe to the top of the cylinder.

The engine can now be tested on compressed air. The crank direction should be clockwise when viewed from the crank end, or anticlockwise viewed from the flywheel end. This is important as most propellers have a right-handed thread and we want the engine rotation to act as a tightening force on the thread. As a consequence, we will need to specify a left-handed propeller, which sounds very specialized, but they are, in fact, easy enough to source. For reference, a left-handed propeller turns anticlockwise when viewed from the stern of the boat.

POWER COUPLING

Another part to make for the engine is the coupling to the propeller shaft. In full size boats this would be a universal joint or a flexible union. With small steam engines we need a coupling with minimal losses and something tolerant of any misalignment of the shafts. One of the simplest ideas is to have two discs coupled with a drive pin. The drive pin can be fitted with a small piece of rubber or some heat-shrink to reduce noise when running.

If you have purchased the propeller shaft and propeller, then an M4 thread is likely to be on both ends of the shaft. Therefore, turn up a piece of aluminium the same diameter as the flywheel and add an M4 thread in the centre. In the drill press, mark and drill for the drive pin. The exact location is not critical because the next step is to transfer-drill this hole to the flywheel, which will ensure that both holes sit on the same radius. Now the hole in the drive disc can be tapped 8BA.

Make the drive pin from a piece of 3mm rod. Turn a small shoulder on one end and thread 8BA. This should screw into the drive disc and pull up square to the surface.

Fig. 3.33   *Power coupling disc. The exact position of the drive pin is unimportant, as long as it is transfer-drilled to the flywheel. However, care should be taken to ensure the pin is perpendicular to the disc face.*

RUNNING AND CHECKING PERFORMANCE

If there is access to compressed air in the workshop then the engine can be tested on pressures up to 30psi. At this pressure the speed should be significant; if it is not, and if the engine is struggling at lower pressures such as 10psi, then it is likely there is friction in the motion somewhere. It is true to say that on very small engines, friction is a great enemy. In fact, sometimes a loose-fitting, poorly made and rattly engine can be seen to turn very freely and work very fast on low pressures because the friction is so low. However, the same engine will have no useful output: it will leak and waste steam under load, and is not what we are aiming for.

Instead we just need an engine that has no tight spots when turned by hand. If there are, then try moving just some parts of the engine, such as the piston in the bore or the axle in the bearing, to identify the cause. Also look closely at the connecting rod for any strange movement that could indicate a skewed crank pin.

It is worth checking for debris trapped in the valve and cylinder, which could cause friction.

The rotary valve assembly is quite sensitive to debris. Try turning the axle in the bearing without the flywheel fitted so you can feel tight spots more easily. If it needs cleaning, remove the flywheel and slide the crank out and clean with a rag and compressed air.

Once the engine is running on air, then just a good running-in session with lots of oil may be all that is needed to get the engine freed up.

ENGINE PERFORMANCE

Something interesting about steam engines is that they can produce their maximum torque from zero rpm. The reason is, the engine torque is a factor of the steam pressure and the cylinder area, and these are independent of engine speed. For example, a steam locomotive starting from a station can use *all* the pressure available in the boiler to get the train moving. The flow rate of the steam is controlled by the regulator, and this is important to avoid wheel slip, but the pressure at the cylinder is limited only by the boiler pressure.

Understanding this relationship between pressure, flow rate and engine rpm is best done using a hypothetical example. Let's say we have a stationary engine running 'off load' and because there is no load on the output, the only pressure we need acting on the piston is enough to overcome the engine's internal friction. To keep the engine running steadily, the regulator is set to restrict the flow rate to the cylinder. The pressure required to run the engine like this might be only 35psi, and so the regulator is set so that the time taken for the cylinder pressure to reach 35psi each cycle means the engine is running at the required 120rpm.

Now if we add a mechanical load to the engine, the torque, and hence the pressure, needed to keep things running will increase. Let's say it now takes 45psi of cylinder pressure to move the loaded engine. If we don't touch the regulator so the steam flow rate remains the same, then 45psi will take longer to build up in the cylinder than the 35psi previously required: the result is a slower engine speed, but delivering more torque.

To counter the load on the engine, the regulator could be opened to allow a faster steam flow rate, meaning the pressure to move the loaded engine takes less time to accumulate each cycle, bringing the engine speed back up.

In summary, the pressure required to drive the engine at any speed is a factor of the piston area and the load on the engine. The regulator controls the steam flow rate to set the rpm. It is, nonetheless, interesting to plot engine speed against pressure and torque to generate some performance curves to make sure there is enough power for a given task.

To measure rpm at a given pressure a simple mechanical rev counter can be used. Fig. 3.34 shows a Meccano fixture that allows the operator to count engine revolutions of a model engine, even when the engine is running so fast it is a blur.

In this design the worm gear is meshed to a

*Fig. 3.34
Meccano rev
counter featuring
a 57:1 reduction
ratio. Each turn
of the gear wheel
represents fifty-
seven turns of the
engine, enabling
the engine speed
to be calculated
over time.*

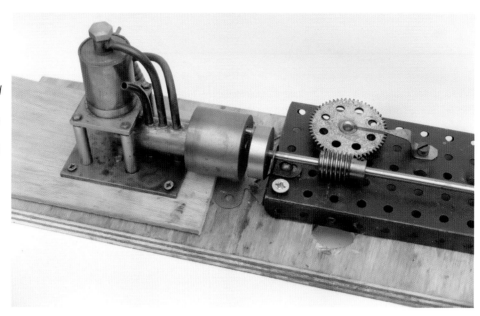

fifty-seven-tooth gear. This means that for every fifty-seven turns of the engine the large gear will make one turn, which can be seen and counted. Counting a total of ten turns and timing the duration for this to happen, will allow the operator to calculate the engine speed. The main thing about the mechanical rev counter is that it should introduce as little friction as possible to avoid affecting the results. With this in mind, the Meccano system shown was assembled to run loosely, with some oil to help reduce friction.

The engine featured here was tested at 10psi, 20psi and 30psi. At 10psi ten turns of the counter wheel took 51 seconds. Each turn of the counter wheel means fifty-

seven turns of the engine. So it follows that at 10psi, the engine turned 570 times in 51 seconds:

$$\left(\frac{570}{51}\right) \times 60 = 670 \text{rpm}$$

Engine speed is therefore 670rpm.

Calculating the results for the other pressures gave the graph shown in Fig. 3.35.

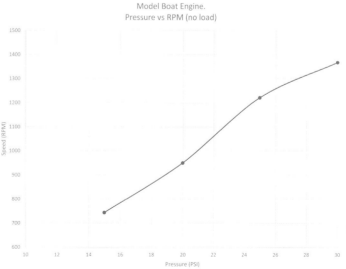

*Fig. 3.35 Speed versus pressure output
graph from the Meccano rev counter.*

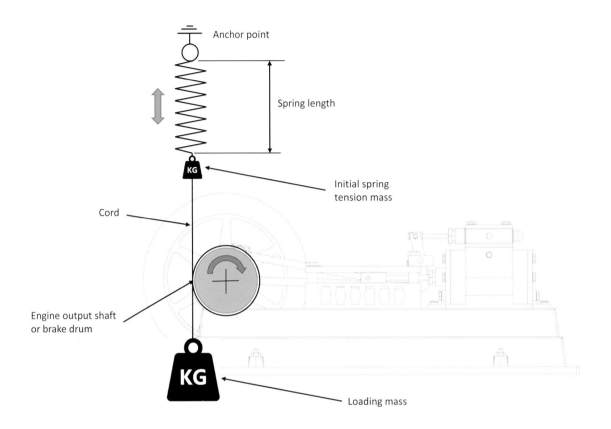

Fig. 3.36   A schematic of a torque brake. The spring must be calibrated for this to work, and some trial and error is expected to create a torque load on the motor that is measurable, but which doesn't stall the motor.

The other parameter to measure is engine torque. This can be done using a simple rope brake as a dynamometer, see Fig. 3.36.

With this apparatus, the engine torque can be considered to be the weight of the mass (Mw), less the spring balance reading (Ms), multiplied by gravity to get a result in Newtons (N):

$$(Mw - Ms) \times g$$

This result must then be multiplied by the radius of the brake wheel to give torque (T) in Newton metres (Nm) or Newton millimetres (Nmm):

$$(Mw - Ms) \times g \times r = T$$

Furthermore, if we multiply the torque by the angular velocity in radians per second (rad/s), we introduce a unit of time, and this allows us to calculate a value for engine power in watts (W).

Our final engine power equation therefore reads:

$$(Mw - Ms) \times g \times r \times 2\pi \left(\frac{rpm}{60}\right) = Power \ (W)$$

WHAT IS A RADIAN?

Measuring angles in degrees comes from Babylonian times. The Babylonians had a base 60 number system, so 360 degrees worked well for them. However, for metric calculations radians are a better fit. A radian is the angle we get inside a circle when the arc on the circumference is the same length as a radius.

We know the circumference of a circle is $2\pi r$. Therefore if we divide the circumference by the radius, we will know how many radians are in 360 degrees:

$$Radians\ in\ a\ circle = \frac{Circumference}{r} = \frac{2\pi r}{r} = 2\pi$$

Therefore, we can say there are 2π radians in a full circle. Now we know this, and the fact that the measured engine speed was in revolutions per minute, it follows that:

$$\frac{2\pi \times rpm}{60} = angular\ velocity\ in\ Rads/sec$$

To understand how the rope brake works it is best to consider the situation when the engine is stationary. In this case, all the weight of the mass will be taken by the spring balance. So the first term in the formula goes to zero: that is to say, the spring balance reading and the weight are equal. So (Mw–Ms) = 0, and so the formula tells us the engine is producing zero torque, which is correct.

When the engine is running, we can expect the friction between the rope and the brake wheel to lift the weight. This will reduce the spring balance reading. The more the weight is lifted by the engine, the lower the spring balance reading will be, and the greater the difference between Mw and Ms and hence the greater the calculated torque. Some of the terms in the formula are constants, such as gravity and the radius – so it is the increasing difference between Mw and Ms that we are watching.

Fig. 3.37 shows the Meccano rev counter fitted with a rope brake on the axle. The mass of the weight needs to be set so that it can be lifted, but not spun round by the engine. A few experiments with a beaker of water can be used to allow the weight to be 'tuned' to the situation. Similarly, the

Fig. 3.37   Harbour Pilot motor connected to the torque brake.

extension spring will need to be soft enough to react to the torque from the engine, which we can expect to be quite low as it is a small model. In this example the spring force was reduced further by providing a 2:1 ratio of leverage between the spring and the rope brake.

MEASURING MASS

A calibrated spring gauge is not necessary to measure weight or mass. A normal extension spring can be used, as long as the chosen spring has been characterized with a few weights of known mass. The requirement is to load the spring with various weights, and measure the extension each time to find a linear spring rate value in Newtons/mm or kg/mm.

However, there is an additional complication with extension springs. There may be an initial tension holding the coils fully closed. Therefore, we need to first add some weights to open the spring coils just slightly. This will create a reliable datum to start the measurements. Then more weights can be added with length measurements taken as before.

To measure a spring, hang it from a secure location. Add some weight until the coils just open, and measure its length. Calculate or measure this weight and note it down. Then add some more weights to stretch the spring and record the new length and the total weight.

The spring rate (K) will be the final load (L_2) minus the initial tension load (L_1), divided by the spring extension (l):

$$K = \frac{(L_2 - L_1)}{l}$$

Taking several measurements with increasing weights should give a linear relationship that can be plotted on a chart. Take care not to exceed the spring's elastic limit as we should only use the linear part of the spring curve for this measurement. In fact, in engineering, springs are only ever used up to 80 per cent of their extension (or compression) for best reliability.

The challenge with the friction brake set-up is to ensure that the engine and measuring equipment are well matched. If the engine is too powerful, it may end up swinging the weight around, and if the weight is too heavy, the engine may stall. There are a number of variables to play with, not only the weight being used, but also the radius of the brake wheel.

The surest way to match the engine and weight is to go with a small brake-wheel diameter so the engine is not easily over-powered. Then use an 'anchored' string (one without a spring at the top) and add water to a beaker to find the weight needed to slow the engine down.

Now you know this weight, you can find a spring that is stretched generously under this weight, but not beyond its elastic limit. If necessary, a lever can be used to get the spring to behave as needed. For this build, the resulting graph is shown in Fig. 3.38.

To plot the curves, a series of measurements can be taken with increasing weight on the brake rope for a given steam pressure. RPM can also be recorded to produce curves for each steam pressure. As expected, the curves show a decrease in rpm as the torque increases. This is symptomatic of the engine under load. For a fixed pressure, the more torque that is needed, the slower the speed gets.

The curves also show that the higher PSI enables higher torque. This can be seen if you read off the curves for a fixed speed. At 1,000rpm for example, using 20psi we can only produce 1.6Nmm of torque. Increase the pressure to 25psi, and 1,000rpm equates to 4.8Nmm of torque. Finally, at 30psi the engine produces 6.8Nmm of torque. This confirms a relationship between increased steam pressure and increased torque. Maximum torque is also greater at 30psi, seen by the fact that the curve is further to the right of the chart.

Engine torque spreadsheet

$$Power = (M_w – M_s) \times g \times r \times (2\pi \times (rpm/60))$$

Spring rate   0.0145 Kg/mm
Spring length   85 mm

PSI	Brake Mass (Kg)	Spring l (mm)	Spring Ext (mm)	Spring force (Kg)	$M_w – M_s$ (Kg)	G m/s	Radius (mm)	Torque (Nmm)	Time for 10 revs	RPM	Rads/s	Power (mW)	
20	0.118	87.57	2.57	0.037265	0.080735	9.81	2	1.58402	34	1005.882	105.3333	166.8502	
20	0.21	89.87	4.87	0.070615	0.139385	9.81	2	2.73473	35	977.1429	102.3238	279.8283	
20	0.308	93.78	8.78	0.12731	0.18069	9.81	2	3.54514	36	950	99.48147	352.6755	
20	0.4	96.1	11.1	0.16095	0.23905	9.81	2	4.69016	40	855	89.53332	419.9257	
20	0.498	97	12	0.174	0.324	9.81	2	6.35688	43	795.3488	83.28681	529.4443	
20	0.594	99.91	14.91	0.216195	0.377805	9.81	2	7.41253	51	670.5882	70.22221	520.5245	
20	0.688	102.68	17.68	0.25636	0.43164	9.81	2	8.46878	58	589.6552	61.74712	522.9226	
20	0.826	-------	-------	-------	-------	9.81	2	-------	-------	-------	-------	-------	Stalled
25	0.118	87.74	2.74	0.03973	0.07827	9.81	2	1.53566	27	1266.667	132.642	203.6926	
25	0.21	89.78	4.78	0.06931	0.14069	9.81	2	2.76034	28	1221.429	127.9047	353.0603	
25	0.308	93.05	8.05	0.116725	0.191275	9.81	2	3.75282	31	1103.226	115.5269	433.551	
25	0.4	95.93	10.93	0.158485	0.241515	9.81	2	4.73852	34	1005.882	105.3333	499.1245	
25	0.498	99.09	14.09	0.204305	0.293695	9.81	2	5.7623	35	977.1429	102.3238	589.62	
25	0.594	101.76	16.76	0.24302	0.35098	9.81	2	6.88623	40	855	89.53332	616.5468	
25	0.688	104.26	19.26	0.27927	0.40873	9.81	2	8.01928	43	795.3488	83.28681	667.9005	
25	0.826	107.2	22.2	0.3219	0.5041	9.81	2	9.89044	53	645.283	67.57232	668.3201	
30	0.118	87.27	2.27	0.032915	0.085085	9.81	2	1.66937	26	1315.385	137.7436	229.9447	
30	0.21	90.14	5.14	0.07453	0.13547	9.81	2	2.65792	27	1266.667	132.642	352.5519	
30	0.308	92.88	7.88	0.11426	0.19374	9.81	2	3.80118	28	1221.429	127.9047	486.1888	
30	0.4	95.88	10.88	0.15776	0.24224	9.81	2	4.75275	30	1140	119.3778	567.3725	
30	0.498	98.72	13.72	0.19894	0.29906	9.81	2	5.86756	32	1068.75	111.9167	656.6773	
30	0.594	102.1	17.1	0.24795	0.34605	9.81	2	6.7895	34	1005.882	105.3333	715.1607	
30	0.688	103.97	18.97	0.275065	0.412935	9.81	2	8.10178	38	900	94.2456	763.5576	
30	0.826	107.14	22.14	0.32103	0.50497	9.81	2	9.90751	47	727.6596	76.19857	754.9382	
30	0.9	109.2	24.2	0.3509	0.5491	9.81	2	10.7733	50	684	71.62666	771.6585	

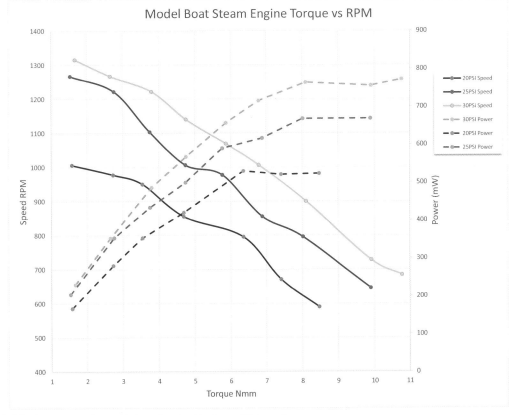

Fig. 3.38   Torque and speed data for the Harbour Pilot engine.

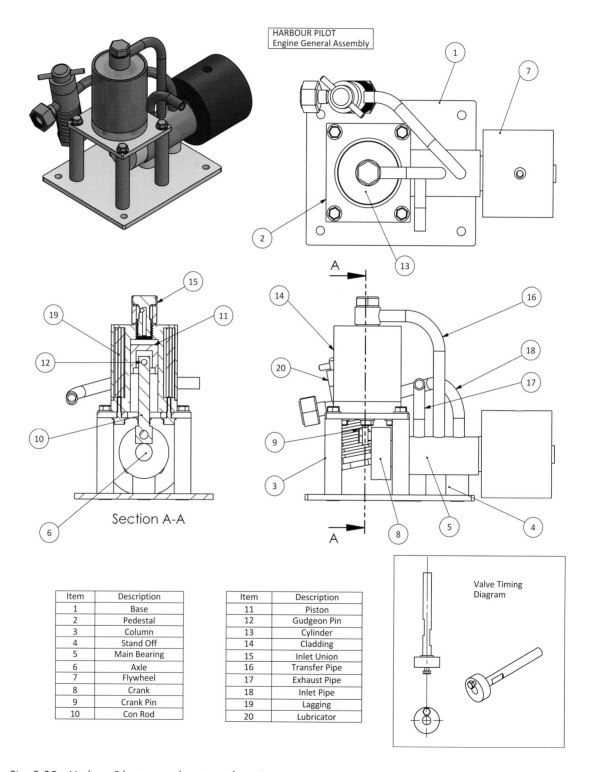

HARBOUR PILOT
Engine General Assembly

Section A-A

Valve Timing
Diagram

Item	Description
1	Base
2	Pedestal
3	Column
4	Stand Off
5	Main Bearing
6	Axle
7	Flywheel
8	Crank
9	Crank Pin
10	Con Rod

Item	Description
11	Piston
12	Gudgeon Pin
13	Cylinder
14	Cladding
15	Inlet Union
16	Transfer Pipe
17	Exhaust Pipe
18	Inlet Pipe
19	Lagging
20	Lubricator

Fig. 3.39   Harbour Pilot engine drawings, sheet 1.

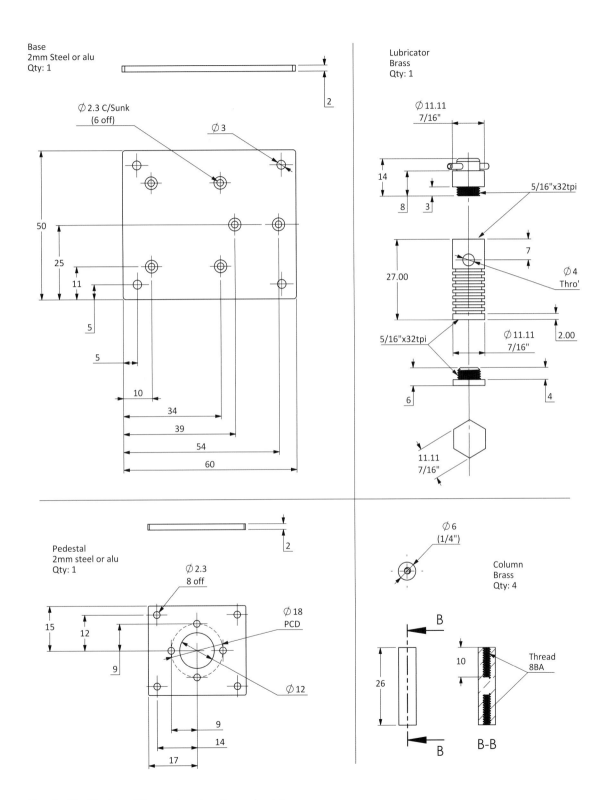

Fig. 3.40   Harbour Pilot engine drawings, sheet 2.

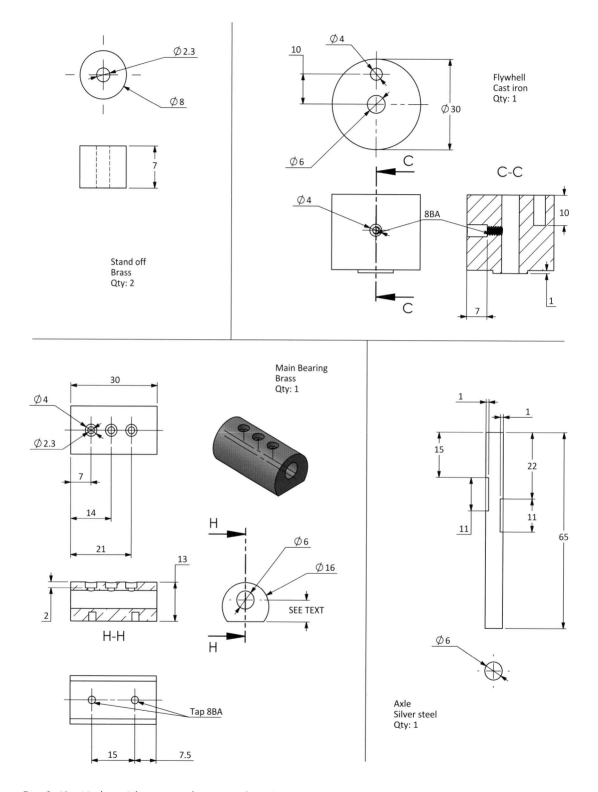

Fig. 3.41   Harbour Pilot engine drawings, sheet 3.

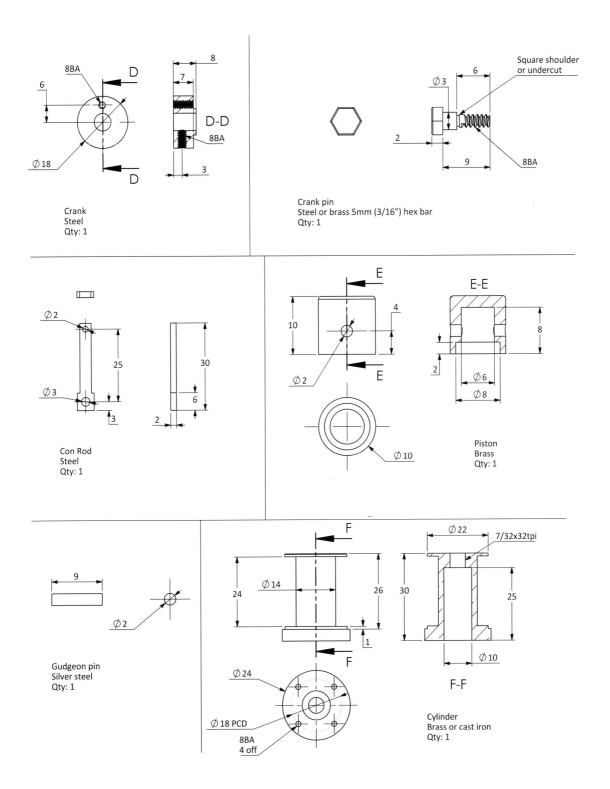

Fig. 3.42 Harbour Pilot engine drawings, sheet 4.

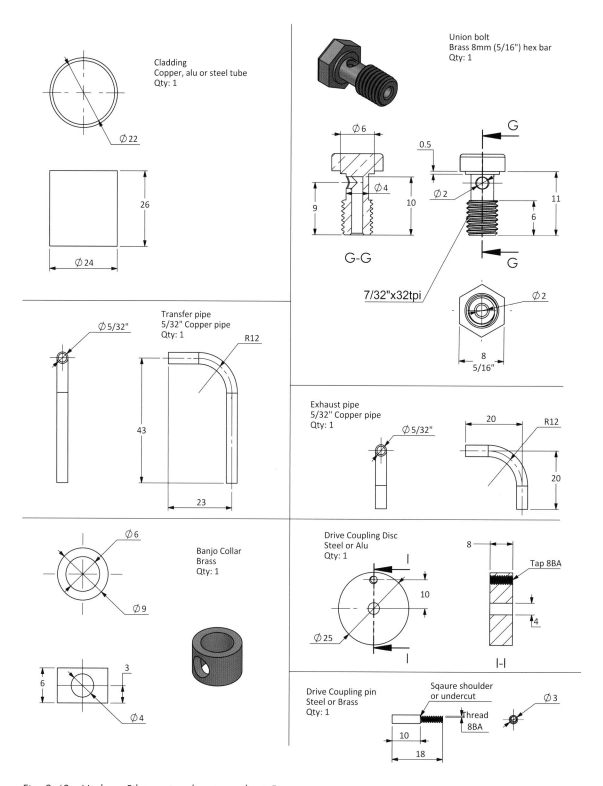

Cladding
Copper, alu or steel tube
Qty: 1

Ø 22

26

Ø 24

Union bolt
Brass 8mm (5/16") hex bar
Qty: 1

Ø 6

Ø 4

9

10

G-G

0.5

Ø 2

G

11

6

7/32"x32tpi

Ø 2

8
5/16"

Transfer pipe
5/32" Copper pipe
Qty: 1

Ø 5/32"

R12

43

23

Exhaust pipe
5/32" Copper pipe
Qty: 1

Ø 5/32"

20

R12

20

Ø 6

Banjo Collar
Brass
Qty: 1

Ø 9

3

6

Ø 4

Drive Coupling Disc
Steel or Alu
Qty: 1

I

10

Ø 25

8

Tap 8BA

4

I-I

Drive Coupling pin
Steel or Brass
Qty: 1

Sqaure shoulder
or undercut

Thread
8BA

Ø 3

10

18

Fig. 3.43   Harbour Pilot engine drawings, sheet 5.

CHAPTER FOUR

HARBOUR PILOT: THE BOILER AND FIREBOX

GENERAL DESCRIPTION

The boiler is of a horizontal design to maximize heating surface and keep the centre of gravity low in the boat. The pressure vessel is made from copper with bronze bushes, silver soldered throughout. A number of copper spikes are included on the boiler underside to increase the efficiency and achieve the required heating surface in a shorter design. A central stay helps support the end plates and serves to mount the boiler on the firebox.

A safety valve is vital for a safe working boiler, and the instructions show a suitable design that can be set to open at the correct pressure based on spring force. The recommended maximum working pressure is 30psi.

The burner is just a simple tray designed to hold Sterno gel fuel. This fuel is readily available and is sold primarily to the catering industry as a method of keeping buffet food warm. It is not massively powerful, but it burns in a controlled manner and creates enough heat to produce steam as long as it is shielded from any breeze.

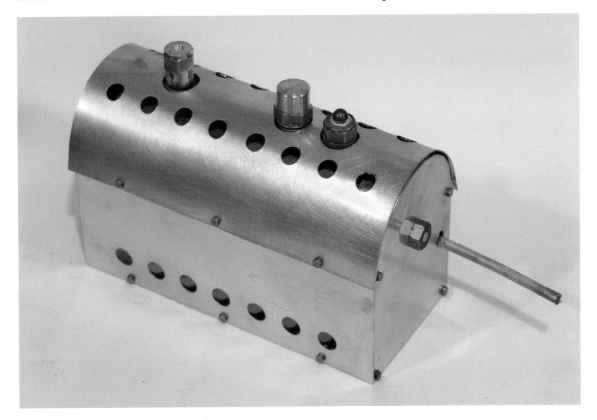

Fig. 4.1   Harbour Pilot boiler assembly.

Another advantage for a model boat system is that it can also be contained in a lower profile housing than most other fuels, lowering the centre of gravity of the boiler. From a safety point of view it is quick to light, doesn't spill easily, and doesn't spit as solid fuel can.

A steam dome on top of the boiler is located next to the mandatory safety valve. A condenser

UNDERSTANDING STEAM

Steam is not a gas, but a vapour, and as such its behaviour depends on its temperature and pressure. One thing to understand is that the boiling point of water increases as pressure increases. At sea level, water boils at 100°C, but at the summit of Mount Everest it boils at around 70°C due to the lower air pressure.

The reciprocal is also true – the higher the boiler pressure gets, the higher the boiling point of the water. This is how a pressure cooker works. It provides additional pressure to make the water boil at a higher temperature, thus cooking the food faster.

As a result of this relationship, we cannot simply state that a certain amount of energy is needed to produce a certain amount of steam because it will depend on the pressure we are talking about. Instead 'Steam Tables' are used, which are a matrix of conditions a boiler designer can look up. The definitions are as follows:

Wet steam: Steam containing water in the form of mist.

Saturated steam: Steam that exists at the same temperature as the water from which it was formed. This would be 100°C at sea level.

Superheated steam: Steam heated to a temperature higher than its boiling point. This steam is also known as dry steam.

A superheater: Wet steam is passed back through the fire to add further heat to the steam. The benefit of doing this is an increase in the energy content of the steam, and the fact that the steam can then release some of its energy and do work, whilst still remaining above the water vapour point. This reduces the amount of condensation expected in a given situation.

Another topic we should mention is latent heat. You will often find that a steam engine will run on compressed air as well as steam. However, the power output on steam is much greater because the steam contains much more energy. The difference is that the air is just a compressed gas, and the only energy you get out is what you put in to compress it in the first place. Steam, on the other hand, contains hidden energy called latent heat (latent from the Latin *latere*, meaning hidden). Latent heat occurs when more energy is added to a system without a change in temperature. In the case of steam, it is a significant amount of energy. For example: ignoring pressure, it takes 419KJ (kilo-joules) of energy to heat 1kg of water from 0°C to boiling point. However, it takes a further 2,256KJ to turn the water into steam.

When steam is put to work, all this energy can be released.

is designed to sit on the steam dome and take the exhaust steam to add some realism to the model, and also to retain the water/oil mix from the exhaust and prevent it from entering the water.

The simplest steam models of yesteryear used to have the steam outlet from the boiler directly connected to the engine with a single pipe. Not only was this simple, but the wet steam from the boiler would help lubricate the engine. However, it is well known that small boilers benefit greatly from even a modest amount of superheating. So a superheater is included here, and as a consequence a lubricator is needed, as dry steam will not lubricate the engine satisfactorily.

Other boiler fittings include a regulator, to provide a control for cruising speed, and a non-return filling nozzle to top up the boiler without having to first release all the pressure.

Steaming time from cold with this boiler should be about five minutes, with the safety valve lifting at six minutes. Run time on 100ml of water will be about eight minutes with the engine running at full speed.

PRESSURE VESSEL DESIGN AND SAFETY

BOILER MATERIALS

Copper is the best material for the pressure vessel. Brass has been used by toy makers in the past, but over time the zinc can 'leach out' and you may be left with a slightly porous and compromised boiler. This process typically takes many years, but it also depends on the quality of the brass, so to be sure, copper is recommended.

Thin material is better for heat transfer than thick metal. This boiler design can be described as externally fired. It is a simple pot above the heat source. Internally fired boilers, like the type found on locomotives, can have thick-walled tubes, but for external firing and at the pressures we are using, something about 22 gauge or 20 gauge will be best. There are calculations included in

this chapter that you can use to prove if a piece of thin-walled copper is going to be safe enough.

Externally fired boilers are sometimes called 'pot' boilers, and they don't have the best efficiency because of their external firing. However, there are a number of steps worth taking to keep this inefficiency to a minimum. We know from science that heat can be transferred by convection, radiation and conduction.

Convection is the movement of heat due to hot air rising and cold air falling, but convection will not occur in windy conditions. Without a decent boiler housing any breeze will take heat away from the fire, so a boiler housing with vent holes is essential. Typical toy housings used to leave the top of the pressure vessel exposed for aesthetics and easy access to the boiler fittings, but further efficiency can be gained by enclosing the whole pressure vessel.

Radiation is part of the electro-magnetic spectrum, and is the heat you 'feel' from an open fire. Insulating the firebox helps contain this radiation and can give significant benefits.

Conduction is the heat travelling along solid paths. We need to maximize conduction through the pressure vessel into the water by maximizing the heating surface. With a pot boiler this can be done in a number of ways, including fire tubes, water pipes and heat exchanger pins. The following table gives some ideas as to how to maximize heat transfer in a small externally fired boiler, and also highlights the benefits and downsides of each design.

Taking all these points into consideration, the boiler specified for this build has some heat exchanger pins: more work to solder, but easy enough to build, and experiments have shown it is worth the extra effort for a decent gain in efficiency.

BOILER SAFETY AND PRESSURE CALCULATIONS

The best material for a small model boiler is copper, and basing a design round a piece of thin-walled, solid-drawn copper tube is a good

Ways of Maximizing Heat Transfer

Boiler Type	Image	Benefits	Problems
Simple pot boiler	Fig. 4.2 	Simple to build.	Low efficiency.
Pot boiler with added fire tubes	Fig. 4.3 	Increases heating surface by typically 50 per cent.	Reduces water capacity. Reduces space for boiler fittings and steam collection. Central stay not possible.
Pot boiler with water tubes	Fig. 4.4 	Increases water capacity for longer run time. Increases heating surface by typically >50. Central stay still possible.	Manufacturing problems, forming tight bends in the water tubes. Increases pressure vessel heights.
Pot boiler with heat exchanger pins	Fig. 4.5 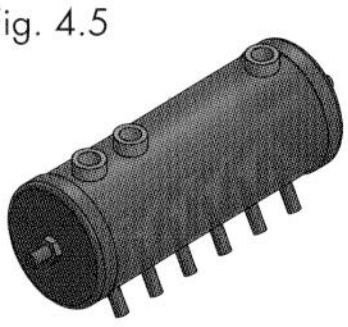	Increases conduction into the water. Increases heating surface.	More soldering joints.
More complex design with lower boiler drums	Fig. 4.6 	Large increase in heating surface. Increases water capacity for longer steaming time.	More complicated to build. More soldering joints. Increase in overall boiler height.

starting point. Copper is easy to work with and conducts heat well.

Even a small boiler can hold a significant amount of energy, and so it is important that it is designed right and built well, to be safe. Some rudimentary calculations are shared here in case the builder has different material to hand or has the idea for a different boiler design. If you are building the boiler exactly to the plans, then feel free to skip to the build section.

The main body of the boiler is made from a 1¾in-diameter piece of 20g copper tube with a wall thickness of 0.9mm. In order to calculate how strong this is, the following formula can be

THERMAL CONDUCTIVITY AND HEAT TRANSFER

The thermal conductivity of copper is very good, second only to diamond and silver. A material's thermal conductivity is the number of watts conducted per metre thickness of the material, per degree of temperature difference between one side and the other. The result is a value in W/mK (watts per metre Kelvin, or watts per metre Celsius can be used if you prefer).

Copper has a conductivity of 385W/mK: this means that a 1m length of copper would need 385W of heat applied at one end, to generate a 1°C temperature difference along its length. A high number here indicates that a lot of power is needed to maintain the 1°C temperature difference, because the copper conducts heat so readily. An insulator would need a very low amount of power, since adding heat to one end would soon heat it 1°C above the other end because it is difficult for the heat to escape along the part.

Assigning conductivity to materials using this standard test allows us to compare their thermal properties. However, this is not the full story. In boiler design we are more concerned with the rate of heat transfer – that is, how quickly/efficiently we can get the heat from the fire into the water, rather than pure conductivity. To understand this, we need to take into account the thickness and area of the material. Both these properties affect the rate of heat transfer, and so does the temperature difference between the two zones.

The rate of heat transfer is affected by four factors, summarized in the following formula:

$$\frac{Q}{t} = \frac{kA\Delta T}{d}$$

Where
Q = amount of heat transfer
t = time
k = material thermal conductivity (385W/mK for copper)
ΔT = difference in temperature between each side of the part ($T_{hot} - T_{cold}$)
d = distance the heat must travel (thickness of the boiler shell)

As the formula shows, the rate of heat transfer is proportional to area and inversely proportional to thickness. For the boiler to work at its best we need to maximize the surface area and minimize the thickness. A hotter fire will also help, as this will increase the ΔT term, which is the difference between the hot fire and the cold water. This understanding comes from the second law of thermodynamics, which states: 'Heat will always flow from a hotter to a colder body.'

The greater the difference in temperatures, the more heat will flow to reach an equilibrium.

So a thick-walled copper boiler would have the same conductivity as a thin-walled vessel because it is the same material, but the thickness would mean a slower heat transfer giving a longer steam-up time, using more fuel in the process.

So the best boiler for our purpose would be one that maximizes area whilst minimizing thickness to give the greatest efficiency – *but this* must come second to safety, of course.

used, which comes from thin-walled pressure-vessel theory:

$$T = \frac{P \times D}{2\sigma}$$

T = tube thickness
P = working pressure
D = boiler diameter
σ = maximum tensile stress for copper

Working pressure is normally measured in psi (pounds per square inch) for steam engines, and therefore it makes sense to use imperial units for this calculation.

σ for copper is about 30,500psi. But where safety is concerned in engineering, there is always a factor of safety applied. A factor of ten is normal for a working boiler such as this, so for the calculations we should use:

$$\sigma = \frac{30500}{10} = 3050\text{psi}$$

We can rearrange the formula to find the maximum working pressure for the given piece of copper tube:

$$P = \frac{(2T \times \sigma)}{D}$$

and we should convert to imperial units:
T = 0.9mm = 0.0354in
σ = 3,050psi
D = 1¾in = 1.75in

Putting these numbers into the formula, we get:

$$P = \frac{(2 \times 0.0354 \times 3050)}{1.75} = 123.5\text{psi}$$

So the proposed working pressure of 30psi is 25 per cent of the maximum pressure, which itself is actually a tenth of the real tensile stress of copper. Properly made, the boiler will be plenty strong enough.

THIN-WALLED PRESSURE VESSEL

Thin-walled pressure theory is an area of engineering science concerned with vessels that have a diameter-to-thickness ratio of greater than 10. Thin-walled calculations ignore the stresses in the thickness of the shell, as this is insignificant to the result. For example, a 50mm tube with a wall thickness of 2mm has a ratio of:

$$\frac{50}{2} = 25$$

Therefore, thin-walled theory can be applied. For the same wall thickness, if the diameter were much smaller, say 18mm, then the ratio would be:

$$\frac{18}{2} = 9$$

This would be unsuitable for thin-walled pressure vessel theory.

For a cylindrical component, hoop stress calculations are one of two stresses in the shell. If the shell could be divided into small square tiles, each tile would have a hoop stress and longitudinal or axial stress on it.

Fig. 4.7 Diagram showing hoop and longitudinal stress. In a cylindrical, thin-walled pressure vessel, the hoop stress is always twice the longitudinal stress.

However, the hoop stress is always twice the longitudinal stress, and so for maximum stress calculations only the hoop stress needs to be considered.

Regarding the end plates, they are typically made of a thicker material than the shell because they are flat and lack the inherent strength of a hoop, especially after the heat of soldering. As a rule of thumb, 'with a small pot boiler such as this, the next gauge up can be used (18 gauge)' (*Model Engineer's Handbook 3rd edition*, Tubal Cain).

It is good practice to add some stays to support the end plates, and for stay calculations we can assume there is no strength in the plate itself, so all the pressure must be taken by the stays.

We can calculate the pressure on the end plate by multiplying the working pressure by the area. The area of each end plate is given by the formula:

$$\text{Area of a circle} = \pi \times r^2$$

r = radius, which in this design is 0.875in

Therefore:

$$\textit{End plate area} = \pi \times 0.875 = 2.405\text{in}^2$$

If our maximum working pressure is 30psi (pounds per square inch). Then we can multiply this pressure by the area to find the total force on the end plate:

$$2.405 \times 30 = 72\text{psi}$$

If we use the same tensile strength for copper as before (3,050psi), then the area of the stay must be:

$$\frac{72}{3050} = 0.0236\text{in}^2$$

Then convert to a radius by rearranging:

$$\text{Area of a circle} = \pi \times r^2 \rightarrow r = \sqrt{\left(\frac{\text{area}}{\pi}\right)} = 0.0866"$$

0.0866in radius or 0.173in diameter

So the stays must be 0.173in (4.4mm) diameter at their thinnest point. This is typically at the root of any thread that may be on the stay. For this boiler design, threads of $^3/_{16} \times 32$tpi are specified, which have a core diameter of 4mm. This is slightly undersized but makes use of the taps we have, and with an overall safety factor of 10, is still acceptable.

The final design for this model is therefore a piece of 1¾in 20-gauge copper tube cut to length, with 18-gauge flat end plates supported by a stay with a minimum diameter of 4mm.

SPECIFYING THE BOILER

Matching the boiler to the engine is vital to get a boiler that produces enough steam at a rate to keep the engine running at the required speed. In simple terms the water capacity of a boiler determines the running time, and the heating surface determines the rate of steaming. The water capacity is not too much of a concern because a top-up pump can be used to top up the boiler under pressure, and on a small boat like this, it is important not to make the boiler too big and heavy. However, we do need to be sure the boiler can produce steam equal to, or greater than the rate that the engine consumes it. To be able to estimate a boiler size, we have to agree some parameters:

• Working pressure to be 30psi, a reasonable number for a small boat
• Maximum engine speed (from bench tests) 1,400rpm
• Swept volume of the engine each revolution is 0.942cc (cylinder area × crank stroke)

The 'rate of steaming' requirement of the boiler is the cylinder volume multiplied by the engine speed. This engine is single acting, so just one cylinder volume per revolution.

$$1400\text{rpm} \times 0.942\text{cc} = 1318\text{cc/min of steam}$$

So the boiler must produce more than 1318cc of steam every minute to keep the engine running at the maximum speed.

To estimate the boiler size steam tables are used, which are tabulated parameters of steam including boiling temperatures for various pressures, and also expected volumes of steam from a given volume of water. They also contain scientific data on energy and enthalpy, but for our purposes, the column showing how much steam can be expected from a given volume of water at a certain pressure is the key bit of information.

For this calculation we need to consult just one line from the table, which explains how steam behaves at 30psi. It makes sense to use SI units on this calculation so that our measurements come out in mm or cm. 30psi is roughly 2 bar of pressure. Be aware that this is 2 bar of gauge pressure or 3 bar of absolute pressure, depending on which table you are referencing.

Gauge pressure	Boiling temperature	Steam m^3/kg	Steam cc/g
2 bar	134.7	0.5875	587.5

The steam table tells us that we can get 587.5cc of steam from one gram of water at 2 bar gauge pressure. So how many grams of water must we turn into steam every minute to keep the engine running?

$$\frac{1318}{587.5} = 2.24\text{cc of water}$$

Empirical tests give an approximate rule for simple externally fired pot boilers – that they will 'evaporate 1cc of water per minute, for every 40 square centimetres of heating surface.' (*Model Boilers and Boiler Making* Chapter 3, K.N. Harris.)

Therefore it follows that:

$$40 \times 2.24 = 89\text{cm}^2 \text{ of heating surface needed}$$

Our main boiler diameter is 4.45cm, and only half of this should be considered the heating surface, as the upper half is not in contact with the fire. Half the circumference is therefore:

$$\frac{(\pi \times d)}{2} = \frac{(\pi \times 4.45)}{2} = 6.99\text{cm}$$

If we then divide our calculated heating surface by this circumference, we will get the length of boiler we need:

$$\frac{89.6}{6.99} = 12.8\text{cm } or \text{ 128mm long}$$

This would be the minimum requirement to keep the engine running flat out. In reality, with the engine under load we can expect a slower speed, but this simple calculation is a good reference point for a boiler design. It is also worth remembering that some enhancements to increase heating surface can be added to the design, which will make a more compact boiler. In this case there should be room for a number of copper spikes known as heat exchanger pins. These work in the same way as a heatsink you might find in a computer. If we include three rows of nine spikes, each one 4.8mm in diameter and 12mm long, the additional heating surface is a useful 4.8cm².

So it would not be unreasonable to shorten the boiler to 120mm, which should still support the engine working hard. In a situation where boiler space is limited, the size can be reduced further, but only if a lower maximum engine speed can be ascertained.

BOILER SUMMARY

Material: Copper
Working pressure: 30psi
Test pressure: 60psi
Diameter: 44.5mm (1¾in)
Length: 120mm
Heating surface: 88cm²
Steaming rate: 1318cc/min max
Fittings: Safety valve, filling valve, steam dome, superheater and regulator

Lubricator: Displacement
Steam pipe internal diameter: 2.5mm min

BUILDING THE BOILER

Start by making the flanged end plates from 18-gauge (1.2mm) copper. Cut two 60mm diameter discs. These can be just roughly cut by hand as we can true them up later, on the lathe.

To make the flanges a former is needed; this should be turned from aluminium, or steel or hardwood to a diameter of the boiler shell outside dimensions (44.45mm). A generous radius should be added to the help the copper flange form without cracking. To hold the blank copper discs to the former, a clamping plate is used. This can also be steel or aluminium or hardwood, and turned to a smaller diameter of 40mm to allow for the forming process. The clamping plate, former and copper blank should all be drilled in the centre, 4.8mm holes for the clamp plate and copper blank, and 4.0mm for the former, which should then be tapped with a $^3/_{16}$in × 32tpi thread.

Once both blanks have been prepared, they should be annealed in the brazing hearth. To

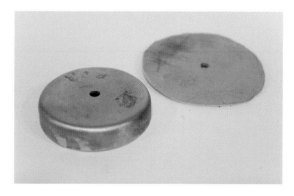

Fig. 4.9   Finished flanged plate and second blank. Several annealing steps should be expected to form the copper without cracking. The example shown was annealed five times.

anneal, just heat to glowing red and leave to cool or quench in water to speed things along. Then load each blank on to the former and progressively form the edge flange with a plastic-faced hammer. The annealing and forming steps will need repeating to get the final shape without the copper cracking or rippling. In this build, five annealing steps were used for each end plate.

Finally, the formed end plates can be trimmed on the lathe, holding them in the reverse jaws and using a boring tool to take light cuts and trim any

Fig. 4.8   Boiler end plate forming equipment. The former was turned to match the external diameter of the boiler tube. Both the clamp plate and former were drilled centrally as the boiler featured a longitudinal stay.

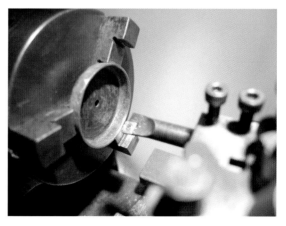

Fig. 4.10   Trimming the flanged end plate on the lathe using the external jaws of the three-jaw chuck and boring tool. Light cuts, a sharp tool and some oil will help when machining copper.

Fig. 4.11 Using a wrap of paper to help cut a tube end square.

fixed steady to support the workpiece. If you are cutting and filing the tube, wrapping a piece of paper round will provide a 'square' edge to work to.

To mark out the boiler tube for drilling, a piece of paper cut to the circumference of the boiler shell and then folded in half will allow the location of the top fittings and middle row of heat-exchanger pins on the bottom to be found. The two outer rows of pins are 35 degrees from the centreline, which equates to an arc length of 13.5mm. Mark a line 13.5mm from the centreline to find their positions.

To ensure that the lines drawn along the boiler length are parallel to the axis of the tube, a

unevenness off the edge of the part. Copper is quite 'chewy' to machine, but a sharp tool, light cuts and some oil should help.

With the end plates complete, trial fit them to the copper tube and measure the overall length. This length will vary from build to build because it depends on the radius of the flanged end plate. Trim the boiler tube to get the total length with the end caps to be 120mm. The boiler shell can be trimmed by cutting and filing, as the edge will be covered by the flanged ends and not visible; or it can be trimmed on the lathe with use of the

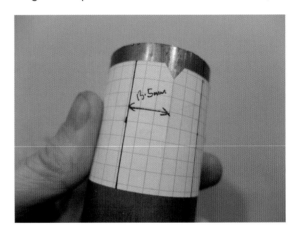

Fig. 4.13 Marking the boiler circumference in four separate places: the top, the bottom and 13.5mm either side of the bottom centreline, to drill for the heat exchanger pins.

Fig. 4.12 Trimming the boiler tube to length using the fixed steady in the lathe. Alternatively, the end can just be filed.

Fig. 4.14 Using a straight-edge to make parallel lines on the boiler. Any straight-edge will work – a piece of angle metal or a wooden batten.

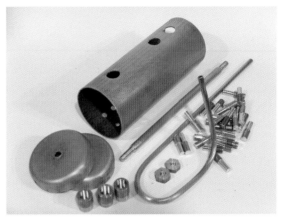

Fig. 4.15 Boiler parts ready for soldering. Parts are the main boiler tube, two end caps, steam-feed pipe, central stay, heat spikes, bushes and end nuts.

piece of angled metal placed on a flat surface is ideal. Rotate the boiler shell to place the marks just made along the edge of the angle, and then scribe a line against the edge. Jenny calipers can be used to mark off the location of all the holes along the length of the barrel.

Centre-punch and drill out the holes to final size, starting with a 3mm drill and working progressively upwards to create circular holes without deforming the copper.

The stay for the boiler should be based on the overall length of the pressure vessel. Fit the end caps, measure the length, and subtract twice the end plate thickness. Then machine up a copper, threaded stay, whose unthreaded length is equal to the number just calculated. Thread both ends $3/_{16}$in × 32tpi. If in doubt, make the threaded lengths over-long; they can be trimmed after final assembly to get them just right.

The heat exchanger pins significantly increase the heating surface of the boiler; they work in the same way as a simple computer heatsink. They are machined from 5mm ($3/_{16}$in) copper rod. The eighteen outside spikes are all the same, but the nine in the middle row are shorter to help the vessel sit lower to the fire. Turn a 4mm diameter shoulder on each pin. Trial fit the spikes in the drilled barrel. Any that are too tight can be further reduced on the lathe. Any that are too loose can

be centre-punched where they sit in the barrel. The centre-punch burr will help create a 'gripping' fit.

The three boiler bushes are all the same dimension and should be made from bronze.

The steam take-off pipe is a piece of $5/_{32}$ copper tube bent in two places using the barrel as a guide. The pipe should reach up into the steam dome and then out of the bottom of the barrel. It can then be routed to the front and bent in a 'U' shape to return parallel to the boiler edge.

The final parts before silver-soldering are some nuts to go on the stays to hold everything together. These can be bought or made from bronze hex bar, or even round bar, drilled and tapped $3/_{16}$in × 32tpi.

SOLDERING THE BOILER

Clean all the parts to be joined with abrasive, and then dust off or wash off any debris. Mix some of the tenacity flux with clean water into a thick paste, and apply it to each part as you slide it into position. Put the end plates and central stay through first, and secure them with the end nuts, with flux on all mating surfaces. Locate the bronze bushes in the boiler top, then flux and insert all the copper spikes. Place the whole assembly in the hearth with the copper spikes uppermost.

Fig. 4.16 Pressure vessel ready for silver soldering. All joints must be fluxed thoroughly.

Brazing is a simple operation. The biggest mistake for the novice is adding the silver-solder rod before the work is hot enough; so spend some time working the flame all round the job before focusing on the first area to be joined. Dip the rod in the flame and in the flux to create a flux-coated rod, and then work from one end of the boiler to the other, soldering as much of the end plate as you can access, along with a small amount of solder on each spike. Use some barbecue tongs to rotate the workpiece so you can access any unsoldered areas on the topside. Don't forget to solder the stay nuts where they touch the end plate and the stay thread.

While the work is cooling, the pickling bath can be prepared. Citric acid is a much safer alternative to the traditional stronger acids, and is a very effective pickle given a bit more time. It can be purchased from a brewery supplier in crystal form. It works best if mixed in hot water – two teaspoons per litre, in a Tupperware container large enough for the boiler. If necessary, scrub the boiler with abrasive cloth and then return to the pickling bath until it is clean.

BOILER FITTINGS

STEAM DOME

The steam dome is made from brass or bronze 12mm (½in) hex bar. It is best machined from the lower end first so it can be reduced, threaded and counterbored to the drawing. Once parted from

the bar stock it can be reversed in the chuck to have the top of the dome formed.

EXHAUST AND CONDENSER

Wherever you sail your boat, the water will be home to some wildlife and we should be sure not to pollute it. In bygone days, people would use castor oil in the steam so that it was biodegradable, but this will still leave an unsightly slick on the water.

The proper solution is to take the steam exhaust and feed it into an oil trap. The model is designed to have a collection tank up at the bow to trap the oil/steam mix from the exhaust. But before the exhaust enters the oil trap, it passes over the steam dome, where steam is allowed to escape up the funnel, and any condensate is left to drain off to the tank. This 'dome top' condenser is a brazed assembly made to be a push-fit over the steam dome, with entry and exit take-off connections as shown on the drawing.

Fig. 4.17 Condenser assembly designed to fit the steam dome. This is a short length of tube with a steam inlet and a drain outlet. Steam is allowed to escape upwards, and any condensate, including any oil, drains off to a storage tank.

The collection tank can be made from a metal tube soldered to a baseplate, or it can just be a plastic pot of the right size. At the time of this build I was learning to use a 3D printer, and so the one shown is a 3D printed part, but there is no need for the design to be this extravagant!

Silicone tube can then be used to connect the exhaust system components.

SAFETY VALVE

The safety valve is important to ensure that the working pressure of the boiler remains safe. Credit for this design goes to Tubal Cain, as it comes from his book *Building Simple Model Steam Engines*, although he attributes the design to an earlier model engineer called LBSC. Permission to use a version of this valve was kindly given by Special Interest Model Books.

The design is similar to that found on many toy boilers, including Mamod and Willesco. The valve requires a stainless spring, which is sold in long lengths by model suppliers. In this design the spring is $3/_{26}$ OD, $1/_8$in ID, with a wire gauge of $1/_{32}$in. Also required is a bronze ball $5/_{16}$in in diameter.

The body of the safety valve is a piece of 11mm ($7/_{16}$in) hex brass or bronze, with a spigot turned and threaded to $5/_{16}$in × 32tpi. The component is then parted off from the bar stock, leaving a hex body as shown in the drawings.

A piece of scrap brass is then used in the chuck to create a $5/_{16}$in × 32 tapped hole to hold the valve for the centre drilling. With the valve body screwed into the threaded arbor, it can be centre-drilled and drilled through 2.5mm diameter. The centre drill should be used to create a tapered seat for the bronze ball.

Next a piece of steel rod has 8BA threads cut both ends, or a piece of 8BA studding could be used if available.

The bronze ball should be drilled and tapped 8BA using the three-jaw chuck in the lathe and screwed to one end of the rod with some thread lock.

Finally, the part is assembled with a length of

Fig. 4.18   Safety valve assembly. This design is adapted from one detailed by Tubal Cain and presented in his book Building Simple Model Steam Engines *published by Nexus Special Interest Books.*

the spring and a washer and two nuts. To ensure the bronze ball is seated well and making a tight seal in its seat, a sharp tap on the top with a small hammer will help it find the best position.

Setting the safety valve can be done with a hydraulic pump during the boiler pressure test, by finding the pressure at which the water leaks through the valve. If such a pump is not available, then the spring force can be set based on some test data from the author's build. This valve had already been set hydraulically so that it leaked just before 30psi.

To set the spring force mechanically, a simple method of measuring the spring force is needed, and Fig. 4.19 shows something made from Meccano. A wooden jig could also be used. The main requirement is that the arm is very loose on the pivot to ensure the device is sensitive enough. The safety valve needs to be mounted upside down on the jig and secured with a tool-maker's clamp.

This equipment can now be used to equate the 30psi pressure to a spring force in the valve. The simple lever is used to press on the safety valve and a water-filled beaker is the weight. The beaker contents and position should be varied to

Fig. 4.19 *A suitable Meccano jig for measuring and setting safety-valve spring force. Spring force was set to 440g.*

find the setting which *just* starts to press the safety valve spring. At this instant the downward force of gravity acting on the beaker of water must equal the spring force of the safety valve, whilst taking into account the leverage of the system.

On the author's build, the weight of the beaker of water plus the weight of the arm of the tester was measured on the kitchen scales and totalled 130g. The beaker position was 149mm from the pivot, and the safety valve was 44mm from the pivot. The ratio of the distances was calculated as:

$$\frac{149}{44} = 3.38$$

This was then multiplied by the weight to get the spring force:

$$3.38 \times 130 = 440g \text{ spring force}$$

So it should now be possible with similar equipment to set the safety valve to the same spring force. The spring force increases with the amount

of compression, so it is important to take the measurements when the spring is just starting to compress.

FILLING CAP/ GOODALL VALVE

To fill the boiler manually with a funnel nothing more is needed than a simple filling cap. This could be a piece of brass turned and threaded to fit the boiler bush and sealed with a fibre washer. The housing could be hex, or round with flats, or knurled.

However, to give the option of filling the boiler under pressure, a valve known as a Goodall valve can be added. The Goodall valve is named after Deryk Goodall, who applied the simple design to model steam locomotives back in the 1980s. It is actually an alternative implementation of a Schrader tyre valve. Fitting a Goodall valve to the boiler allows the operator to top up water whilst under pressure, using an adapted plant sprayer.

Fig. 4.20 *A completed Goodall valve. A Goodall valve is a simple non-return valve that allows the user to top up the boiler whilst under pressure, using a suitable pump. A suitable pump can be made from a plant spray bottle.*

A drawing for a suitable valve is given in the plans, and the only special part that is needed is a piece of silicone tube. This tube acts as a one-way valve, and silicone will easily stand the heat of the boiler. The hole in the top of the valve needs to be a press-fit on to the filling tube, so once a piece of stiff filling tube has been found, the hole can be drilled to suit.

A plant sprayer makes a suitable pump, which can be connected to the Goodall valve by pressing and holding the tube on to the fitting, whilst pumping the sprayer.

STEAM REGULATOR

The regulator is attached directly to the output of the superheater, and is fixed to the rear bulkhead of the firebox. It features a simple screw-down needle to give a degree of control over the steam flow rate to the engine. It is a brass housing with a stainless-steel needle with a handle on the top. The housing is a silver-soldered assembly of a piece of square bar and two pieces of $\frac{1}{4}$in round bar. To begin, the square bar should be centred in the four-jaw chuck with enough protruding to create the top shoulder with a diameter of 7.9mm ($\frac{5}{16}$in).

There are two hole diameters on the inside to create a shoulder for the regulator to close against. Drill the smaller hole first to the correct depth, and then the larger hole to take the thread. Drilling to a precise depth is not easy – it can be done either by drilling and then measuring the depth with a thin rod and then adding depth in increments; or, depending on the depth of the hole and the length of the drill, you can mark the drill or make a collar to clamp on the drill, or just position it in the chuck to create a drill of the right length. The part should also be externally and internally threaded in

this setting: $\frac{5}{16}$in × 32tpi externally down to the outside shoulder, and $\frac{3}{16}$in × 32tpi internally, to the inner shoulder.

On the drill press the part can be drilled on each side to take the inlet/outlet spigots. Drill the 2.5mm holes first, which should break through into the centre hole; then open out the start of the hole to create a shallow $\frac{1}{4}$in feature to hold the inlet and outlet spigots.

The inlet and outlet are both made from $\frac{1}{4}$in brass bar threaded externally with a $\frac{1}{4}$in × 32tpi die, and drilled through 2.5mm. Before removing them from the chuck use a centre drill to create an internal chamfer for the steam pipe to locate in.

The main body and two spigots should now be silver soldered together, ensuring that the longer spigot is at the bottom of the assembly, as it will also be used to hold the regulator to the rear firebox cover.

The regulator needle is just a piece of stainless-steel rod threaded $\frac{3}{16}$in × 32tpi, and with the end machined to a point in the lathe using the top slide set over at an angle. The part should then be cut to the length on the drawing, and the handle and handle boss can be silver-soldered to the top of the needle.

Fig. 4.21 The steam regulator is a simple screw-down tap with a needle point to give a degree of control over the boat speed.

Fig. 4.22 A threading tap with the end ground flat, for threading up to a shoulder.

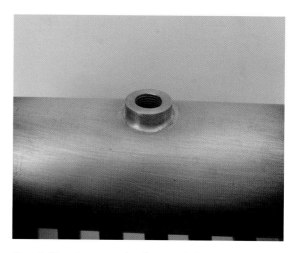

Fig. 4.23 An example of a good, filleted, silver-soldered joint.

The nut on the top of the housing is known as a gland nut, and graphited yarn can be 'packed' underneath it to create a steam-tight seal. The nut is a piece of hex bar drilled through 5mm, and then counter drilled 7mm to leave a shoulder at the end. A D-bit should then be used to create a flat bottom to the counter bore, and a $5/_{16}$in × 32tpi thread added inside. It may be necessary to grind the end of a tap square, to get the thread to reach the shoulder.

TESTING THE BOILER

It is important to test the boiler for leaks and to ensure that all joints are safe. The first check is a visual inspection of the solder joints, where you should see neat fillets of silver. The fillets should flow down to a smooth blend with the copper parts.

To pressure test, water should be used as it will not compress and store energy as air can. The best equipment is a simple pump and pressure gauge as shown in Fig. 4.24.

The usual test procedure is to pump up to twice working pressure (60psi for this build) and leave the vessel to hold that pressure for ten minutes. If all is well the gauge will not change. If pressure has dropped, do the test again with the vessel on a paper towel to try to detect where the leak is.

If you need to buy a pump, then one of the best and most economical options is a plant spray bottle. These simple devices can easily pump 200psi,

Fig. 4.24 Hydraulic test pump shown holding the test pressure of 60psi.

and so all that is needed to test the boiler is a suitable piece of hose attached to the nozzle. (*See* Chapter 2 for a suggestion on how to make hose unions.)

If remedial work is needed, then the water must be emptied from the boiler and all the joints refluxed before reheating and attending to the leaking joint.

If a gauge is available but not a pump, then the boiler can be tested by filling with water and heating. Heat should be applied gradually because the pressure can climb quite suddenly, but it is a work-around for anyone without a pump. A gauge is necessary for a valid test, but you can repurpose a gauge from a foot pump and connect it to one of the boiler bushes with a suitable adaptor and/or length of hose.

BUILDING THE FIREBOX AND BURNER

THE FIREBOX

The firebox housing is made from two end plates held between some stand-offs. Each end panel is different: one has an opening to allow for the burner, the other is closed but with a hole for the steam feed pipe.

The best material for the firebox is brass. Steel can be used, but it may soon rust. If steel is used, then high temperature barbecue or exhaust paint is a good way to protect it. The end plates need some stiffness, so 0.8 to 1mm brass is advised.

To start the end panels, a rectangle of 75 by 64mm should be cut with square corners. Then the holes can be marked and centre-punched. The firebox opening can be milled or just chain-drilled and filed to final shape.

The top curve can be cut with shears and then filed smooth.

Before making the side panels and stand-offs, take a measure of the pressure vessel length across the nuts. If this is 130mm or less, you can just make the stand-off lengths to the plans and use washers if your pressure vessel is slightly short. If your pressure vessel is longer, you will need to adjust the firebox length accordingly. This will affect the stand-offs, side plates and heat shield.

The side panels are simple cutting and drilling jobs, and thinner material can be used here as the parts are just covers and not structural. Something 0.5mm should be easy to work with. The best tool to drill the vent holes is a step drill. Start by marking and centre-punching the hole locations, and then pilot drill with a 2.5mm drill. Open out to 4mm, and use the step drill to increase the diameter to final size. Any burr on the reverse side can be removed using the step drill again with light pressure against the next size step up, to tidy the hole.

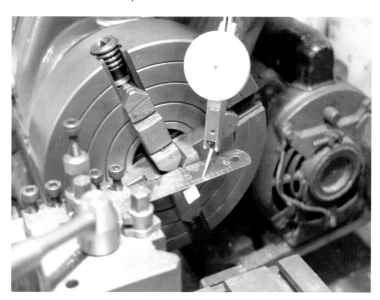

Fig. 4.25   One method to centre square stock in the four-jaw chuck. The stock does not need a centre-punch, rather the deflection at each corner is measured by the DTI. Adjustments are made until all four corners give the same reading on the DTI.

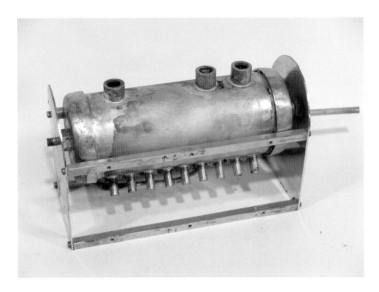

Fig. 4.26   Test fit of the pressure vessel in the firebox frame.

The square stand-offs are made from $^3/_{16}$in brass set up in the four-jaw chuck to run centrally. There are a number of ways to do this, but with square stock, where there is no centre marked, the set-up shown in Fig. 4.25 can be used. This consists of a flexible strip (an old hacksaw blade without teeth is ideal) set to run over the top of the bar stock. Then a DTI can be used to read the deflection on each corner of the workpiece as the chuck is turned by hand. Adjustments are made until all four corners read the same.

When using this process, it is worth mentioning that when one corner is high, both of the chuck jaws on each side must be tightened. If you get to the situation where two corners are the same but high, then just the jaw between these corners must be tightened. This process has to be done a total of eight times to create the stand-offs, so you will get better at it!

Once each end of the work is centred, it should be centre-drilled, drilled and tapped 8BA.

The square stand-offs are also drilled on the side and tapped 8BA. These can just be marked and drilled and tapped, or if you have made the firebox side plates, you can transfer-drill the holes from the side plate to get an exact fit. The lower

two stand-offs also have holes to mount the firebox to the base.

It is now possible to assemble the two end plates and four stand-offs, and check that the frame stands square.

The pressure vessel can now be assembled in the firebox using any spacers required to ensure a good fit, and oriented so the topside bushes are vertical. Check the hole placement on the rear cover against the steam feed pipe location.

The firebox heat shield can be brass, but aluminium adds some contrast to the assembly and is less springy when it comes to forming the curve. Whichever material is used, 0.5mm is a good thickness, to make the curve easier to form. The shield is designed to be slightly longer than the firebox body, to give a neat appearance.

Before drilling the three holes for the boiler fittings it is worth checking the exact location on your pressure vessel and adjusting their position accordingly. When all the drilling is done, the part can be gently curved by hand around a piece of round bar or tube. It will have a tendency to fold where the vent holes are, so pay particular attention to this area and try to form the curve as evenly as possible. If the part does fold slightly along the line of holes, then this is most noticeable if the material is shiny, as the reflection amplifies the condition. Buffing the part with abrasive to achieve a brushed finish will help disguise this.

THE BURNER

The burner is designed to burn Sterno fuel and is made from a piece of folded brass sheet, soldered at each corner, and with a short handle made from 3mm rod. The base can be made from 0.5mm brass sheet or similar, marked, cut and drilled for the handle. Then it should be folded where shown. One method to get everything folded nice and square is to cut a block of wood

Fig. 4.27 Folding the burner tray round a wooden former.

to be used as a former. Sand the block so that it is the correct size for the inside of the tray, and all four sides can be formed against the block.

Folding with this gauge of brass can be done holding the work in the vice and then forming by hand. To sharpen the fold, a wooden block hit with a hammer can be used.

The handle is a piece of 3mm rod. Stainless steel is a good idea here, as it is a poor conductor of heat. Reduce a short section at one end and thread 8BA, then bend to the plan. Again, bending can be done in the vice, but care must be taken not to damage the thread. A wooden dowel can be drilled in the lathe and glued in place to create a handle.

BOILER ASSEMBLY

We will need to mark and cut the superheater to an exact length, to get it to fit the regulator position. To do this, assemble the firebox ends with some stays and the pressure vessel. Also put a nut and cone into the regulator inlet. Hold the regulator next to the superheater to mark it for the first cut, but make sure it is overlong by a few millimetres at this stage.

Now offer up the regulator assembly, pushing the superheater pipe into the union cone: note how much it needs to move to get it to the right location, and then shorten the superheater accordingly. When the superheater is correct, remove the pressure vessel and silver solder the cone in place – not forgetting to put the nut on the pipe first!

Two other parts are suggested in the drawings. One is a base for the firebox with an extended front section so the burner tray can sit on it when it is withdrawn from the firebox. This can be of any metal. The other is a pair of simple springs that help the burner tray to stay in place during rough seas. The brass springs provide a small amount of friction against the burner tray sides to help it hold its position.

Fig. 4.28 Test build to fit a superheater to the regulator. Careful shortening of the steam pipe is needed to get everything to fit exactly.

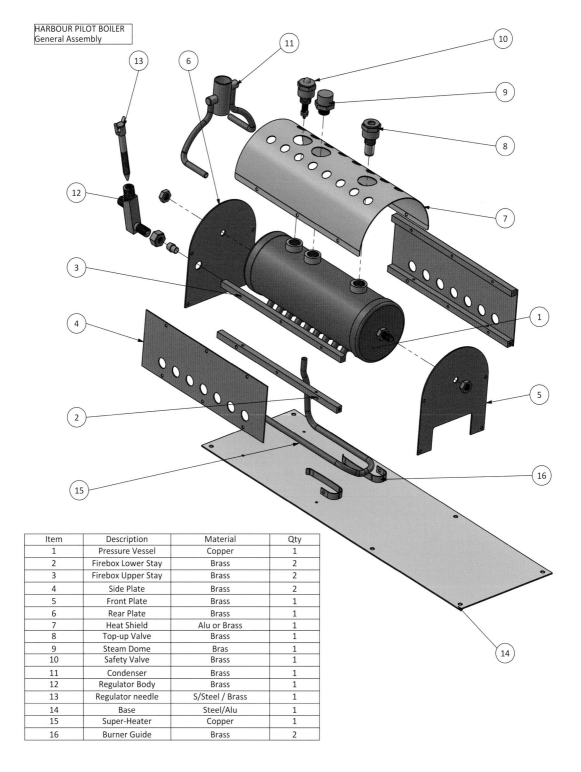

Item	Description	Material	Qty
1	Pressure Vessel	Copper	1
2	Firebox Lower Stay	Brass	2
3	Firebox Upper Stay	Brass	2
4	Side Plate	Brass	2
5	Front Plate	Brass	1
6	Rear Plate	Brass	1
7	Heat Shield	Alu or Brass	1
8	Top-up Valve	Brass	1
9	Steam Dome	Bras	1
10	Safety Valve	Brass	1
11	Condenser	Brass	1
12	Regulator Body	Brass	1
13	Regulator needle	S/Steel / Brass	1
14	Base	Steel/Alu	1
15	Super-Heater	Copper	1
16	Burner Guide	Brass	2

Fig. 4.29   Harbour Pilot boiler drawings, sheet 1.

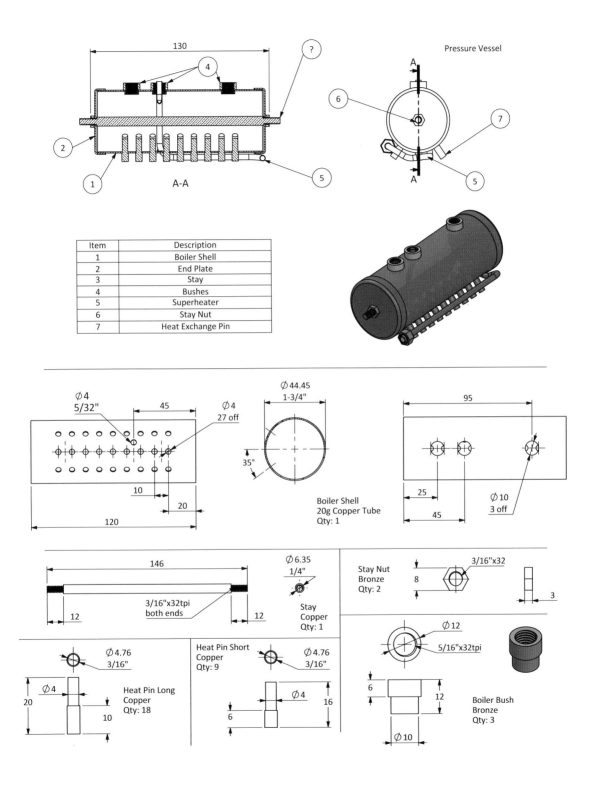

Item	Description
1	Boiler Shell
2	End Plate
3	Stay
4	Bushes
5	Superheater
6	Stay Nut
7	Heat Exchange Pin

Fig. 4.30   Harbour Pilot boiler drawings, sheet 2.

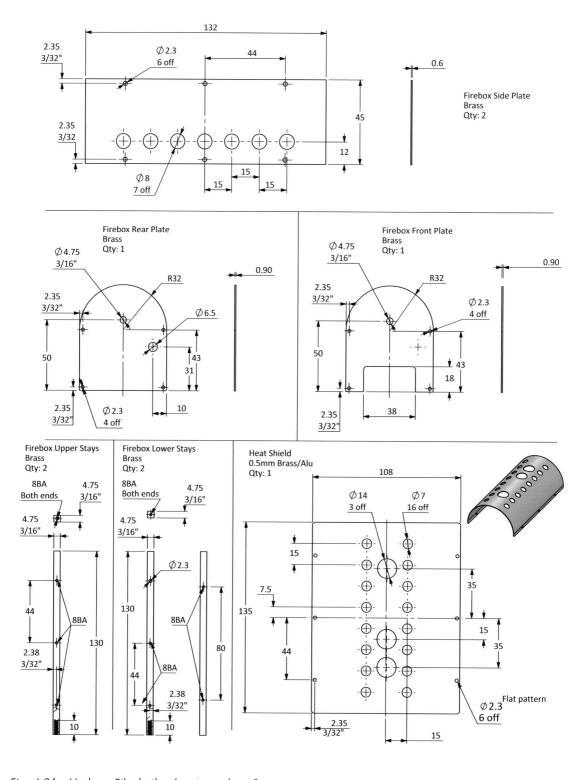

Fig. 4.31   Harbour Pilot boiler drawings, sheet 3.

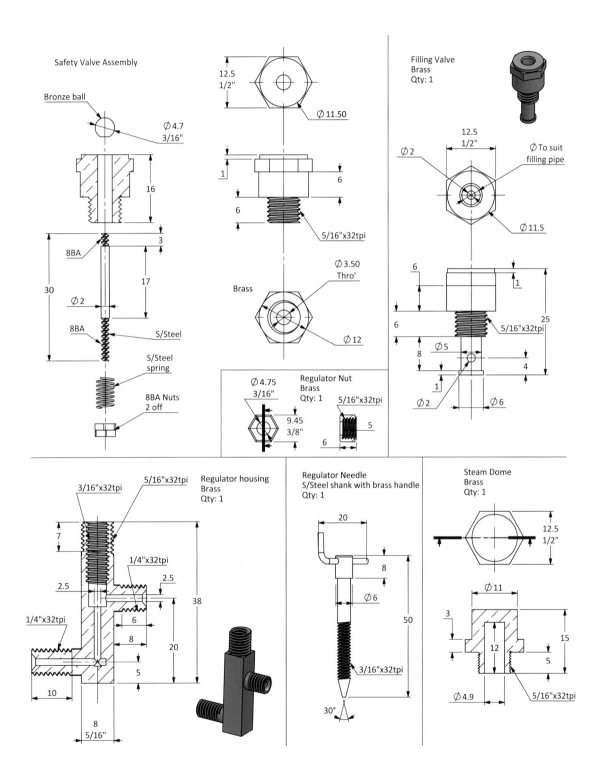

Fig. 4.32   Harbour Pilot boiler drawings, sheet 4.

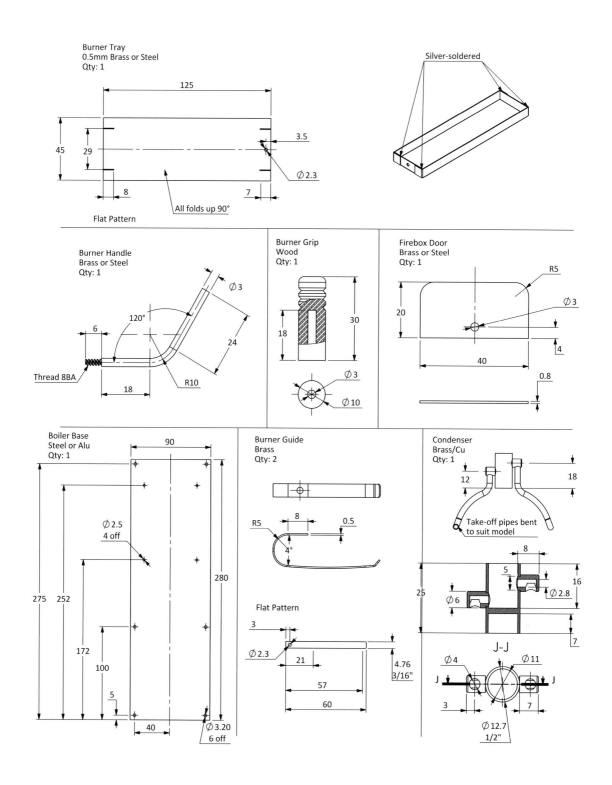

Fig. 4.33   Harbour Pilot boiler drawings, sheet 5.

CHAPTER FIVE

HARBOUR PILOT: HULL CONSTRUCTION

The hull construction for the Harbour Pilot uses the traditional method of planking over a wooden frame. More specifically it uses sheet timber to create a skin over a frame of bulkheads and a keel. An alternative construction would be to use individual planks, as you would in a full-sized boat, but this is more of a fine modelling skill than the working toy boat being considered here. With sheet timber, compound curves (surfaces curved about more than one plane) are difficult, and with this in mind, the design of the frame uses straight-edges, to work more easily with the sheet timber. Where the side panel joins the underside planking of the hull is known as the 'chine' of the boat. This can be sharp or rounded, but again, for a sheet-timber build a sharp chine (known as a hard chine) is the best.

THEORETICAL HULL DESIGN

Hull design is a complex subject and is as much an art form as it is an engineering discipline. As such there is a degree of judgement needed to create a design. A typical hull will have complex curves that are difficult to draw in 3D, and so 2D views and a range of cross-sections are used to illustrate the hull form. An easier starting point can be had by copying a hull from full-size plans, or copying images of a boat in a dry dock. However, if a scratch-built model is proposed, the following text aims to provide the necessary knowledge for the model builder.

The first thing to understand is that a boat hull can be a displacement type or a planing design. A displacement hull properly ballasted

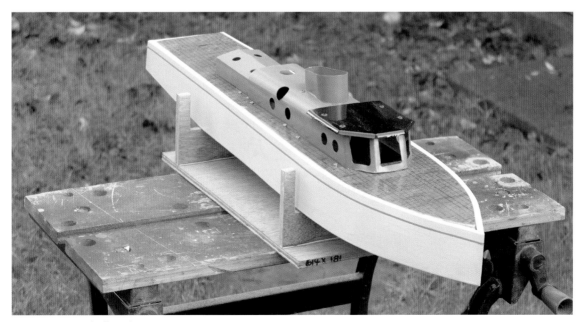

Fig. 5.1   Boat hull and superstructure.

will be stable and remain afloat regardless of the vessel's speed. A planing hull requires movement to give the best performance. A jet-ski is a good example of a planing hull: the craft is barely buoyant when stationary in the water, but once moving, generates a lifting force enough to carry a rider. Planing hulls require a certain amount of speed, more speed than we can expect from the small steam engine, so the following notes are more applicable to displacement hull design.

Fundamentally we need to match the hull to the steam plant. If the hull is too small the weight of the steam plant will sink the boat; if the hull is too big, the engine will struggle to move it. We therefore want the boat to be as small as possible but without the risk of sinking. We can arrive at some approximate hull requirements by considering three factors:

• Water displacement, to ensure the boat will float.
• Some dimensional coefficients, to understand the hull's form and proportions.
• Centre of gravity/buoyancy, to ensure it is stable.

WATER DISPLACEMENT

Archimedes discovered that in order to float, a hull must displace water equal to the total weight of the craft. If we know the weight of the finished boat including fuel and cargo, we should be able to calculate the volume of water we need to displace:

The weight of the steam plant fully fuelled = 2kg
Predicted weight of the hull = 0.5kg
Total weight = 2.5kg

So we need to displace 2.5kg of water to get the boat to float. 1 cubic centimetre (cc) of water = 1 gram, so we need to displace a volume of 2,500cc of water.

HULL COEFFICIENTS

To understand the shape we can develop to displace this water volume but ensure the boat is streamlined, there are a number of coefficients used by designers. These coefficients are ratios of the boat's form compared to datum prisms or shapes based on the overall length, width and draught of the hull. Three of the most useful coefficients are:

Block coefficient: A measure of the overall fullness of the hull.
Prismatic coefficient: A measure of the 'fineness' of the hull.
Midship plane coefficient: To determine the cross-sectional hull form.

Note that although we are designing a complete hull, these coefficients are concerned only with

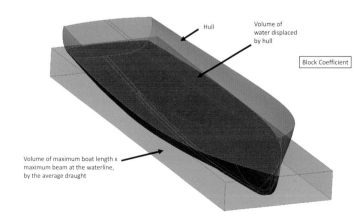

Hull
Volume of water displaced by hull
Block Coefficient
Volume of maximum boat length x maximum beam at the waterline, by the average draught

Fig. 5.2 Visualization of a hull block coefficient. This is the volume of the submerged part of the hull divided by a theoretical cuboid, which is the length of the boat at the waterline, multiplied by the width at the midplane, multiplied by the average draught of the hull.

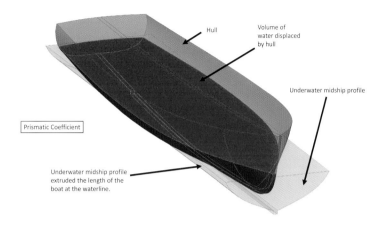

Fig. 5.3   Diagram of a hull prismatic coefficient. This is the volume of the submerged part of the hull divided by a volume made up of the midship section, multiplied by the hull length at the waterline.

Prismatic Coefficient

Hull

Volume of water displaced by hull

Underwater midship profile

Underwater midship profile extruded the length of the boat at the waterline.

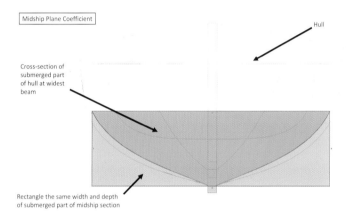

Midship Plane Coefficient

Hull

Cross-section of submerged part of hull at widest beam

Fig. 5.4   Diagram of the midship plane coefficient of a boat hull. This is the submerged area of the midship section divided by a rectangle with the same width and depth as the submerged section.

Rectangle the same width and depth of submerged part of midship section

the submerged volume. This is the volume that determines how the boat moves through the water.

The block and prismatic coefficients both use the volume of the submerged part of the hull as a starting point, which is the displacement volume just calculated.

For the block coefficient this number is divided by a theoretical cuboid, which is the length of the boat at the waterline, multiplied by the width at the midplane, multiplied by the average draught of the hull.

The prismatic coefficient is the same displacement volume, divided by a volume made up of the midship section, multiplied by the hull length at the water line.

The midship plane coefficient works on area instead of volume. It is the submerged area of the midship section divided by a rectangle with the same width and depth as the submerged section.

Each of these coefficients has a formula:

$$Block\ Coefficient = Cb = \frac{\nabla}{(L \times B \times D)}$$

Where:

∇ = displaced volume of hull
L = length of the hull at the waterline
B = width of the ship's beam at the widest point
D = mean draught of the hull

$$Prismatic\ Coefficient = Cp = \frac{\nabla}{(A_m \times L)}$$

Where:

∇ = displaced volume of the hull
A_m = immersed area of the midship section
L = length of the hull at the waterline

$$Midship\ Plane\ Coefficient = Cm = \frac{A_m}{(B \times D)}$$

Where:

A_m = immersed area of the midship section
B = width of the ship's beam at the widest point
D = mean draught of the hull

It is also true that Cb = Cp × Cm

Note that ∇ is used in hull design to denote volume, rather that 'V', which is used for velocity.

The maximum that any of these coefficients can be is 1, which would be a rectangular block. In reality the closest hull form to this is a flat-bottomed barge with parallel, vertical sides. This would have a midship plane coefficient of 1, but would likely have prismatic and block coefficients of perhaps 0.8 or 0.9 due to the taper at the bow.

The prismatic coefficient is a useful tool to visualize how blunt or graceful a hull is going to look; this is because it is an indication of the rate at which the hull cross-section changes along the length. A short, blunt hull will have a higher rate of change and therefore a higher prismatic coefficient. We can see this if we put some hypothetical numbers into the formula:

$$Cp = \frac{\nabla}{A_m \times L}$$

If we fix a vessel's displaced volume to be 1,000m³ and the cross-sectional area to be 15sqm, we can compare a vessel whose length is 100m to one of 75m:

100m vessel:

$$Cp = \frac{1000}{(15 \times 100)} = 0.67$$

75m vessel:

$$Cp = \frac{1000}{(15 \times 75)} = 0.88$$

This demonstrates that a lower prismatic ratio means a sleeker and more slender hull design.

Finally, in the table opposite is a very useful list of typical coefficients kindly provided by Mohammud Hanif Dewan, director of education at LMTI and PhD researcher on Maritime Education and Training. Mohammud runs a huge online resource for learning about maritime architecture and hydrodynamics. These numbers are derived through many years of experimentation and research by engineers, and can be used as a guide for model boat design.

CENTRE OF GRAVITY VERSUS CENTRE OF BUOYANCY

First, we should define these terms:

The centre of gravity of a boat: This is the location of a point where we could, in theory, balance the boat. For a simple hull this can be assumed to be on the centreline of the hull, approximately half way along the length, but at a height somewhere above the water depending on the cargo and superstructure.

The centre of buoyancy: This is the centre of gravity of the displaced mass of water created when the boat floats. This is easier to understand looking at Fig. 5.5.

Any floating vessel will always have a centre of gravity above the centre of buoyancy because it is floating with part of its mass above the waterline. So we need a solution that makes a stable boat despite the high centre of gravity. In full-scale ship design this is the only way you can build a huge cargo boat with containers stacked high on the deck that still remains seaworthy in rough waters. The term used to describe a 'top heavy' boat that is still stable is called 'metastability'. It is worth understanding this to ensure

Typical Hull Coefficients

Type of vessel	Block coefficient	Prismatic coefficient	Midship area coefficient
Crude oil tanker	0.82–0.86	0.82–0.9	0.98–0.99
Product carrier	0.78–0.83	0.80–0.85	0.96–0.98
Dry bulk carrier	0.75–0.84	0.76–0.85	0.97–0.98
Cargo ship	0.60–0.75	0.61–0.76	0.97–0.98
Passenger ship	0.58–0.62	0.60–0.67	0.90–0.95
Container ship	0.60–0.64	0.60–0.68	0.97–0.98
Ferries	0.55–0.60	0.62–0.68	0.90–0.95
Frigate	0.45–0.48	0.60–0.64	0.75–0.78
Tug	0.54–0.58	0.62–0.64	0.90–0.92
Yacht	0.15–0.20	0.50–0.54	0.30–0.35

the hull is matched to the steam plant for a successful build.

As mentioned, boats have a centre of buoyancy below the centre of gravity. The easiest way to visualize this is to look at a hull with a rectangular cross-section. In Fig. 5.5 the centre of gravity is the centre of mass for the entire boat hull. The centre of buoyancy is the centre of gravity of the displaced water volume.

It is clear to see that when the boat is level the downward force from the weight of the boat and upward buoyancy force are in line and the boat is stable.

If we tilt the boat, as shown in Fig. 5.6, we need to know if the boat will

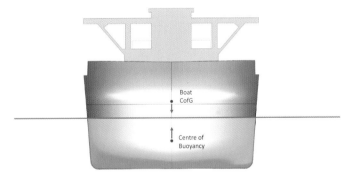

Fig. 5.5   Diagram of the centre of buoyancy and the centre of gravity of a level vessel.

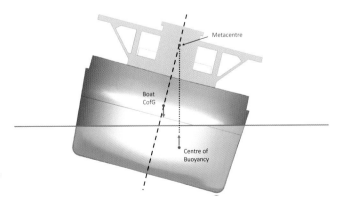

Fig. 5.6   Diagram of the reaction forces of a tilted hull. Note how the centre of buoyancy has moved because the shape of the submerged volume of the hull has changed. In a stable vessel this movement is quick to create a responsive reaction force.

now self-right, or turn over. The centre of gravity of the boat is still in the same place, but the centre of buoyancy has moved because of the change in shape of the displaced water.

To see which way the boat will now tip, we add a vertical line up from the centre of buoyancy. Where this line crosses the centre of gravity of the boat, we mark a point called the 'metacentre'. For as long as the metacentre is above the centre of gravity, the buoyancy force will self-right the boat. If it is below, the buoyancy will add to the tipping direction and the boat will capsize.

So a stable hull will resist capsizing until the greatest angle of lean. One reason a flat-bottomed hull is so stable is because as the boat tips, the centre of buoyancy moves very quickly in the same direction to create a stabilizing force on the hull.

How does this help our hull design? With the boat empty on a calm day, it makes little difference. But if our centre of gravity is high, as can be the case with a boiler of water above a fire, we must ensure the buoyancy reaction can cope with it under reasonable conditions.

The variables that we have to adjust the metacentre height are the width of the hull and the depth of the hull in the water. Both these factors affect the shape of the displaced water and the way this shape changes as the boat rolls. If the hull is narrow the boat may need ballast to help it sit low enough to be stable. A wider hull can afford to sit higher.

THOMAS SIMPSON AND SIMPSON'S RULE

Thomas Simpson was born in England in 1710. He was a self-taught mathematician who published a number of books on mathematical subjects including calculus, probability, geometry, algebra and trigonometry. However, 'Simpson's Rule', although named after Thomas Simpson, was in fact devised by Isaac Newton as part of his work on differential and integral calculus, a fact acknowledged by Simpson in one of his papers.

SIMPSON'S RULE

It is also important to mention 'Simpson's rule' in this chapter. Simpson's rule is a mathematical method that has calculus as its foundation, but uses simple arithmetic to allow a boat designer to quickly approximate areas and volumes formed by curved geometry.

Simpson's rule works on the principle that the area under any curve can be closely approximated by dividing it into equal sections and applying a weighting factor to the line lengths, and finally multiplying the answer by the section spacing divided by three. This sounds more difficult than it is.

The only conditions are that the curve must not reverse, there must be a straight reference plane

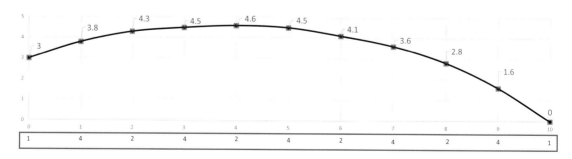

Fig. 5.7   A made-up example of a hull curve at the waterline. Simpson's rule can be used to approximate the area under the curve.

opposite, and the number of sections is an even number.

Simpson's rule is most easily understood with a simple example. Take a moment to study the curve in Fig. 5.7. The curve shows a shape that could represent the waterline profile of half a boat when viewed from above. Working out the area of this shape and then multiplying it by two would give the total area of the waterline of the vessel.

Simpson's rule requires that the curve is divided into an even number of sections using an odd number of dividing lines (called 'stations'). These stations must be equally spaced along the x-axis. In this case, the curve has been divided into eleven stations and the space between each one is five squares.

Along the x-axis are two sets of numbers. The upper row is the number of the station – this is just a sequential pattern to keep a note of where we are with the calculation. The number below (in a blue box) is the Simpson's multiplier. It can be seen that the multipliers have a pattern, with both end ones being 1 and then a number sequence of 4, 2, 4, 2, 4, 2, 4, 2, 4 for the remaining stations. Written out, Simpson's rule is:

$$Result = \frac{h}{3} \times \left((S0 \times 1) + (S1 \times 4) + (S2 \times 2) + (S3 \times 4) \ \ldots\ldots + (Sn \times 1) \right)$$

Where:
S = the station value
h = station spacing

So you can see that you will multiply the value at each station by the Simpson's multiplier, add them all up and then multiply the answer by one-third of the station spacing, which is given the notation 'h'. If we put the numbers from Fig. 5.7 into the rule, we get:

$$Area = \frac{h}{3} \times \big((3 \times 1) + (3.8 \times 4) + (4.3 \times 2) + (4.5 \times 4) + (4.6 \times 2) + (4.5 \times 4) + (4.1 \times 2) + (3.6 \times 4) \\ + (2.8 \times 2) + (1.6 \times 4) + (0 \times 1) \big)$$

So the approximate area under the curve is 177.6 squares. If you have the patience to count the squares manually, you should get a number very close to this. Multiplied by 2 gives 355.2 squares for the total area of the waterline on this theoretical vessel.

Here is a second example if you want to try it for yourself.

This is a profile that could be the midship plane of a vessel (inverted). Just half the curve is shown here, and then we can double the result to find the total area. The station spacing this time is four squares. There are five stations to calculate (0 to 4).

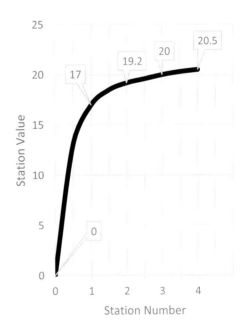

Fig. 5.8 A second curve to run calculations on.

Here is a table of data to keep things neat, which the reader is welcome to fill in.

Table of Data

Station	Value	Simpson's multiplier	Area x Simps
0		1	
1		4	
2		2	
3		4	
4		1	
Totals			

See if you can get an answer of about 275 squares for the half profile.

One of the most useful things about Simpson's rule is that if the stations are line lengths (as in this example) the result will be an area, but if the stations are areas, the result will be a volume!

This means Simpson's rule can be applied to each bulkhead in a hull design to find their areas; then it can be applied to all the areas to find the volume of displaced water in the hull.

We can take this data a step further to calculate the centre of buoyancy for the vessel. Let's take another example, a hull divided into eleven stations.

In this example the midplane has been taken as the zero point. Any reference can be used, but the midplane is a good datum, as we can reasonably expect the centre of buoyancy to be nearby.

The 'arm' column in the table is just the distance of each station from the midplane. You can see by looking at these numbers, that the planes are evenly placed at 70mm centres. The moment is then calculated, which is just the arm distance multiplied by the station area.

Calculating the Centre of Buoyancy

Station	Area (mm²)	Simpson's multiplier	Area x Simps	Arm (mm)	Moment Area x Arm
0 – bow	0	1	0	350	0
1	2,137	4	8,548	280	589,360
2	3,505	2	7,010	210	736,050
3	4,403	4	17,612	140	616,420
4	4,638	2	9,276	70	324,660
5	4,638	4	18,552	0	0
6	4,607	2	9,214	–70	–322,490
7	4,397	4	17,588	–140	–615,580
8	3,496	2	6,992	–210	–734,160
9	2,369	4	9,476	–280	–663,320
10 – stern	1,401	1	1,401	–350	–490,350
Totals	**35,591**		10,5669		**–559,410**

To find the longitudinal centre of buoyancy we divide the total moments by the total area:

$$\frac{-559410}{35591} = -15.71\text{mm}$$

This tells us that the longitudinal centre of buoyancy is 15.71mm from the midplane (station 5), and the minus sign means it will be 15.71mm towards the stern.

If possible, we should try to put the centre of gravity of the loaded boat over this location, so it sits level in the water.

In the case of a hull design, the moments we are calculating are the distances from a common datum multiplied by each station area, where the station area is an indication of the mass of displaced water for that section of the hull.

Once the centre of buoyancy is known we can take steps to balance the position of the steam plant about this point to set the trim of the boat.

SELECTING A PROPELLER

One last thing to look at before we start on the Harbour Pilot design is the propeller. Most boat propellers are two-, three- or four-bladed. There are many parameters, but for modelling purposes, and so as not to over-complicate things, the diameter, pitch and number of blades can be

JUST A MOMENT

Moments are forces multiplied by distances and are used in engineering and science to calculate torque and bending deflections. Most people intuitively understand moments as they are the fundamental principle behind leverage, but some may be unfamiliar with the science of them.

We can witness moments in action if we look at how a spanner undoes a nut. For a first scenario, let's say we have a short spanner, 100mm in length. The spanner is pulled by a mechanic who weights 75kg, and he puts all his bodyweight on to the spanner. The moment (or torque) applied to the nut is the force times the distance. To get our answer in Newton-metres (Nm) the force should be in Newtons and the distance in metres. To convert the mechanic's weight into Newtons we multiply by gravitational acceleration, which is a constant 9.81m/s_2.

$$Force~(N) = 75\text{kg} \times 9.81 = 735.75\text{N}$$

$$Dist~(m) = \frac{100}{1000} = 0.1\text{m}$$

$$Moment~(torque~at~the~nut) = F \times Dist. = 735.75 \times 0.1 = 73.6\text{Nm}$$

The mechanic cannot push any harder, but if we give him a longer spanner (300mm) he should be able to produce more torque.

$$Moment~(torque~at~the~nut) = F \times Dist. = 735.75 \times 0.3 = 220.7\text{Nm}$$

In both situations the mass of the mechanic is the same. He pushes with the same level of effort, but generates more torque thanks to the greater leverage or greater 'moment' of the system. Moments are always calculated as a force multiplied by a distance and have the units 'Nm'.

used to broadly describe a propeller. The diameter is quite simply the circle scribed by the tip of the blades. The pitch is the forward motion you would get from the propeller for one turn, in the same way as a nut travels along a thread each turn. For example, if a propeller has a 50mm pitch, it will (in theory) move the boat 50mm forwards for every turn. In reality, because the water is a fluid, there will be a percentage of slip between the propeller and the water; however, this is ignored for the purposes of describing a propeller's pitch.

PROPELLER EFFICIENCY

To understand why a larger diameter propeller is more efficient we need look at the situation in terms of energy. Physicist Isaac Newton observed that every action has an equal and opposite reaction. In the case of a boat, we use the propeller to throw water out the back and the opposing force moves the boat forward. The more water we throw and the faster we throw it, the greater the force pushing the boat forward.

Algebraically, the propeller thrust is the mass of the water multiplied by the acceleration applied to it.

$$Thrust = M \times a$$

Where:
M = mass of water in kg
a = acceleration in m/s^2

However, the kinetic energy formula to support this process is:

$$Kinetic\ energy = \frac{1}{2} M \times V^2$$

Where:
M = mass of water in kg
V = velocity of the water in m/s

This energy equation brings another level of understanding to the situation. It shows that the required kinetic energy is proportional to the mass; but proportional to the *square* of the velocity. This means reducing the velocity (using a slower propeller) will have a much greater effect on the energy input than reducing the mass (the amount of water). The equation tells us that if we want to save energy, we can reduce either the mass or the speed of the water, but that reducing the speed will have a much greater effect.

To put another way, a smaller propeller acts on less water, so it has to speed the working fluid up more to generate the same thrust. Half as much water moving twice as fast generates the same thrust, but takes twice as much power.

As a result, the largest blade area we can fit into our boat and without stalling the engine, the more water we can move but at a lower speed using less energy. Less energy means a greater efficiency.

To select a propeller, the simplest starting point is to choose a diameter to fit in the boat. The largest diameter that is reasonably possible gives the best efficiency, but taking into account the gap between the propeller and the underside of the hull, which should be about 12 per cent of the propeller diameter. For example, if you are fitting a 40mm propeller to your boat, you should look to maintain a gap of 4.8mm from the propeller tip to the hull.

If you are buying a propeller, the pitch is not always specified, so you would pick a diameter to fit the hull and purchase something with a thread to fit the propeller shaft. Keep in mind that a fine pitch is like a low gear, giving more torque and providing good acceleration but with a limited top speed. A larger pitch is like a high gear, giving slower acceleration but a higher top speed. The problem with too much pitch is that the motor may have difficulty turning the propeller fast enough for it to work.

Unfortunately, calculating what propeller pitch is optimum for a given boat requires information that may not be available, such as the resistance of the hull to push through the water. To make matters worse, this drag varies, depending on the speed. As already mentioned, many model propellers sold in shops don't specify a pitch, though it is possible to approximate it with some careful measurements. This is more difficult with smaller propellers as the margin for error is less, but the process is given here, in case it is useful.

The propeller diameter can be measured tip-to-tip if the propeller has an even number of blades. For odd numbers, a measurement from the hub axis to tip (the radius) can be used. The other thing to note at this stage is where the propeller is at its widest. This is typically 70 to 75 per cent out from the hub, but you need to measure how far this is from the hub centre.

With the propeller lying flat on a reference surface, four measurements are now taken. First, measure the width of the propeller at its widest point (w), ensuring that this is the width parallel to the reference surface not parallel to the blade

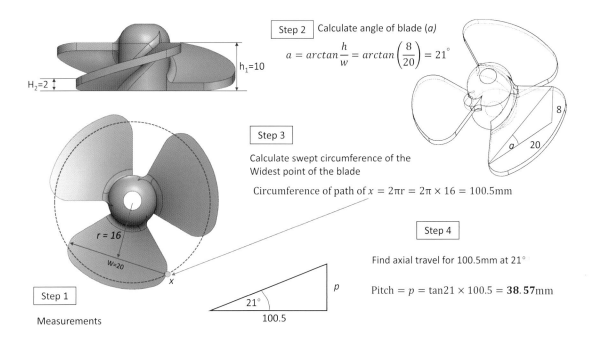

Step 2 — Calculate angle of blade (a)

$$a = \arctan\frac{h}{w} = \arctan\left(\frac{8}{20}\right) = 21°$$

$h_1 = 10$

$H_2 = 2$

Step 3

Calculate swept circumference of the Widest point of the blade

Circumference of path of $x = 2\pi r = 2\pi \times 16 = 100.5$mm

Step 4

Find axial travel for 100.5mm at 21°

Pitch $= p = \tan21 \times 100.5 = \mathbf{38.57}$mm

$r = 16$

$W = 20$

x

$21°$

100.5

p

Step 1

Measurements

Fig. 5.9   A schematic showing one method to measure the pitch of a propeller.

surface. Then measure the height of the propeller's leading (h_1) and trailing edge (h_2) at the widest point. Finally, estimate the radius from the propeller axis to the point where the width was measured (r). This is shown in Fig. 5.9.

From these measurements, we can calculate the angle of the blade from the reference surface using trigonometry:

$$\text{Tan } a = \frac{8}{20} \therefore a = \arctan\left(\frac{8}{20}\right) = 21°$$

Now we can calculate how far this angle will drive the propeller forwards for a whole turn.

The calculation we just made was for a section of the propeller blade 16mm from the hub. We can work out the swept circumference of this point using the following formula:

$$Circumference = 2\pi r = 2\pi \times 16 = 100.5mm$$

The final step is to work out how far the 21-degree angle would push the boat for a 100.5mm swept distance. Although this swept distance is a helix, we can straighten it out to show it as a triangle with the vertical given the notation p for pitch.

The tan of the angle multiplied by the horizontal distance gives:

$$\tan21 = \frac{p}{100.5} \therefore p = \tan21 \times 100.5 = 38.57mm$$

So this propeller has a pitch of approximately 38mm.

In reality the simplest approach to propeller selection is to try three or four propellers and run some back-to-back tests to find the one that best matches the engine performance. On the whole we are looking for the largest diameter, though a low-power engine may not be able to turn this. So experimenting with a few different designs is really the best way forwards.

A suitable test system for comparing propeller performance is shown in Fig. 5.10 and Fig. 5.11. This is a simple pivot arm with the engine mounted on it, and a counterbalance to give a level start position. With the engine mounted vertically, any propeller should provide a lifting force on the beam, which can then be levelled by adding weight. After the test, the added weight can then be measured, and any adjustment made for the leverage of the system. This mass multiplied by gravity will give the motor thrust in Nm or Nmm.

For a given supply pressure, the expectation is that a small propeller can be turned faster, and a large propeller will be slower, but which one gives the greater lift is the knowledge to be gained from this test. The most lift generated for the given pressure, is the best matched propeller for the engine.

Fig. 5.12 shows eight propellers that were tested for comparison. These were a mixture of

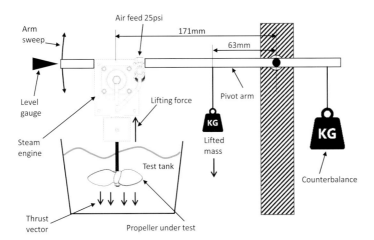

Fig. 5.10 Propeller characterization system diagram. This test equipment can be used to measure the static thrust of a propeller.

Fig. 5.11 The physical implementation of the propeller characterization test system.

3D-printed and purchased parts of various diameters, pitches and blade counts. The test was conducted at 25psi rather than the maximum 30psi, to allow for running under less-than-optimal conditions. The table on the following page gives the results.

The data showed that the highest thrust value was provided from the Graupner two-blade design; however, the diameter was actually too large to fit in the space available. The data also showed that the best results came from the propellers with a larger pitch (faster helix) and the greatest diameters. With this in mind two more propellers were designed and printed (9 and 10). With four and five blades, both these propellers had the same surface area, and so the four-bladed one was made larger in diameter accordingly.

Although these propellers both produced good thrust, they also dropped the RPM. And although engine speed was not specifically measured during the test, there was a concern that a slow engine would more easily stall. By chance, during the test, a leaf landed in the water tank and when it mixed with the propeller the speed reduction was noticeable. This would be the same with any pondweed out on a lake; so in the end, propellers 2, 4 and 6 were selected for open-water tests.

The open-water tests were necessary because

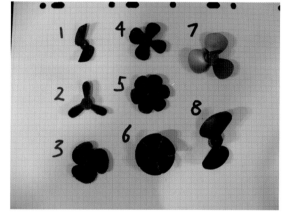

Fig. 5.12 A selection of propellers that were characterized on the test jig.

the static thrust test only really indicated starting force, not cruising performance. There was also a question about the whirlpool created in the test tank and how this might affect results.

The open-water test showed propellers 2 and 6 to be about equal in terms of vessel speed, with propeller 6 running with a lower engine RPM, due to its larger surface area. It is likely that propeller 6 was running more efficiently, but with more risk of a stall if any obstacle touched the propeller. The final choice was propeller 2.

It is worth stating that if you have built a scale

Comparative Testing for Eight Propellers

Propeller	Description	Diameter (mm)	Pitch (mm)	Lifted mass (g)	Thrust (Nmm)	Comments
1	2-blade straight leading edge	35	30	18	84.68	
2	3-blade	35	14	50	235.21	Fast helix
3	3 wide blades	35	60	15	70.56	
4	4 blades	35	30	33	155.24	
5	6 blades	35	70	21	98.79	
6	5 blades	35	35	53	249.32	Large area prop.
7	Gold 3-blade	40	25	63	296.37	
8	Graupner 2-blade	45	50	111	522.17	Too larger dia.
9	5-blade home-designed	38.5	80	67	315.18	Low RPM
10	4-blade home-designed	43	80	69	324.59	Low RPM

model with scale power output, you should be prepared to go smaller on the propeller, because although your model is true to scale, the water viscosity is a constant and will be the same as for a full-sized boat.

If you are scratch building a metal propeller, then a straightforward method to follow is to create separate blades and solder them to a boss. Use the first blade as a template to make the others so they are all similar. Then use some hex bar for three or six blades, or square bar for two or four blades. Drill the boss for your propeller-shaft thread, and twist the blades so they all create the same thrust.

Be aware that simple angle blades are not as effective as more complex forms. A full-sized boat propeller will change in section, profile, area and curvature from its root to the tip. If you enjoy CAD and have access to a 3D printer then you may want to print a selection of more detailed propellers for testing.

Note: If you want to print an exact copy of the propeller selected here, there is a link to the .STL file given at the back of this book.

PRACTICAL BOAT DESIGN

The earlier text looked at some hull theory relevant to model boat building. Now we must take some of that learning and apply it to the hull design for the Harbour Pilot. We also need to know how to sketch out a design using two-dimensional views to create the desired 3D structure.

Hull design is part of an engineering discipline called maritime or naval architecture. It is a very involved subject, taking many years of study and practice to master. For modelling purposes however, we just need to be able to draw a hull we like the look of, and check its displacement and stability against the proposed steam plant/cargo.

Part of the complexity in this area of engineering comes from the fact that hulls have compound curves – that is, surfaces that are curved along more than one plane. This means that calculating the volume of a hull, or the displacement, is not possible using simple geometry.

CREATING A STREAMLINED SHAPE

The hull coefficients described previously are one of the tools to help estimate the displacement of

SCREWS OR PADDLEWHEELS?

One of the problems with the paddlewheels seen on early ships was that of 'paddle immersion'. Immersion would vary as a ship rolled on the waves, and a decrease in fuel supplies during a voyage would result in a loss of performance. It was thought that a screw-driven boat would overcome both these issues.

Screw propellers underwent much experimentation in the late 1700s, and early ideas included James Watts' 'spiral oars', which he proposed but never implemented on his boats.

The earliest successful implementations came from two independent inventors: John Ericsson, a Swedish engineer, and Francis Pettit Smith from Britain. Both suffered rejection from the British admiralty, who thought a screw-driven boat would be unseaworthy and difficult to steer. However, Francis continued to experiment and file patents for his designs. His early propellers were wooden and consisted of a blade with two complete turns on a cylindrical hub. Fortuitously, one of his early propellers got broken at sea and as a result the boat suddenly went twice as fast. Inspection showed the broken propeller now had just one complete turn and Francis revised his patent accordingly.

In 1839 he set up the Propeller Steamship Company and built the steamship SS *Archimedes*, recognized as the first successful implementation of a screw propeller. Shortly after, he advised Brunel to use a screw on his SS *Great Britain*, with further success.

Ericsson sailed his prototype screw-driven ship to the USA, where the US Navy was more open to the idea than the British admiralty. Later he went on to design the USS *Princeton*, the first screw-propelled warship of the US Navy.

A final blow was dealt to paddle power in 1845, when a tug-of-war between paddle steamer HMS *Alecto* and the screw-driven ship HMS *Rattler* resulted in the paddle boat being dragged backwards at 2.5 knots.

a hull to help create a streamlined shape with the correct displacement. However, hull design is best described as a 'design spiral', meaning that it is an iterative process, and the final design may require the initial attempt to be fine-tuned as parameters are calculated.

To start the design, it is useful to make a note of any fixed criteria, such as the width needed to accommodate the steam plant, or the maximum length, perhaps to allow the boat to be transported on your bicycle to the lake. In addition we should have in mind a hull form, such as flat-bottomed, V or round.

For this build, the width of the hull around the steam plant will need to be a minimum of 140mm for access to stoke the fire and provide space to operate the controls. As a rule of thumb, the most graceful boats have a length of six times their beam, but we can go less than this for small boats and a compact design. For this model, we can set a target length of 700mm, which will allow access to withdraw the firebox and room for the propeller shaft. Finally, we will specify this as a V hull, which gives manufacturing advantages because we can still make a streamlined design whilst not needing any compound curves.

The displacement needed to keep the boat afloat is just the total mass converted into a water volume. This is calculated in cubic millimetres, as we will work in millimetres on the drawing:

The weight of the steam plant fully fuelled = 2kg
Predicted weight of the hull = 0.5kg
Total weight = 2.5kg

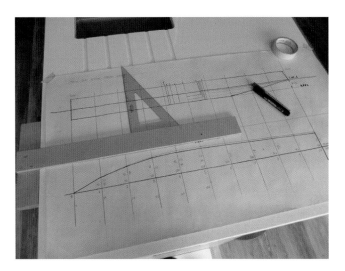

Fig. 5.13   A simple drawing bench set-up in the kitchen.

So we need to displace 2.5kg of water to get the boat to float.

1000mm³ of water = 1 gram, so we need to displace a volume of 2,500,000mm³ of water. At this point it helps to start making a drawing. The final drawing should have a side view, a plan view and section views at regular intervals throughout the length of the hull, which can be used to design bulkheads.

LAYING OUT A BOAT DESIGN

The best way to lay out a boat design is using a large piece of paper, taped down to a table or bench with masking tape. Wallpaper is a good choice here, as it provides plenty of length to draw on. Parallel lines will need to be drawn, which can be done with a T-square; this can be bought, or you can just make a T-square out of two pieces of wood screwed together at 90 degrees.

On the paper, two horizontal lines should be drawn. The upper one will be the loaded water line (LWL) of the side elevation, and the lower one the centreline of the plan view (plan CL).

Divide a 700mm length into ten sections (each 70mm), with vertical lines going down the page. These lines are known as stations, and they should be labelled from 0 to 10. The sixth line (station 5) should have the text 'MS' for 'midship' added.

On the right-hand side of the page draw a vertical line, which will be the centreline of the cross-section views: label this 'CL'. Finally, a 45-degree diagonal line should be added where this centreline crosses the centreline of the plan view. This initial framework is shown in Fig. 5.14.

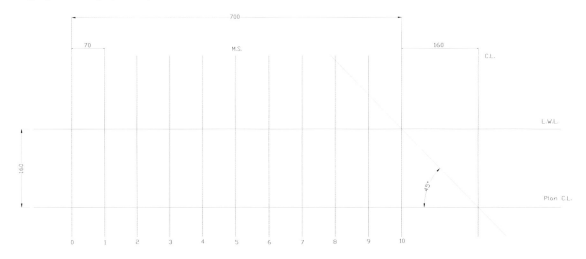

Fig. 5.14   Hull design, step 1: initial drawing framework for hull design.

The block coefficient is a good way to now calculate a midship plane area, but we will need to decide on a suitable coefficient first. Without any coefficient the depth of the submerged part of the hull will simply be the displaced volume divided by the area. This would be:

$$\frac{2500000}{(700 \times 140)} = 25.5mm$$

Although this block would float, it would be shaped like a house brick, with no streamlining. In order to take into account the shape of the hull and how it might increase the submerged depth, we can assign a block coefficient. For a shallow V hull this might be of the order of 0.65, but this is somewhat based on experience. Therefore it is necessary to go with a 'best guess' at this stage and then work the design through, to see it the numbers add up. Remember:

$$Block\ Coefficient = Cb = \frac{\nabla}{(L \times B \times D)}$$

Where:
∇ = displaced volume of the hull
L = length of the hull at the waterline
B = width of the ship's beam at the widest point
D = mean draught of the hull

So for the proposed hull we can estimate the expected waterline position using:

$$0.65 = \frac{2500000}{(700 \times 140 \times D)}$$

$$\therefore D = \frac{2500000}{(700 \times 140 \times 0.65)} = 39.24mm$$

This means the hull will sit an average of 39.24mm 'into' the water. Above this waterline we will need some 'freeboard', which is an amount of hull above the water to help the ship ride any waves without water breaching the sides; but for the time being, we are working on the submerged volume, which will have a depth of 40mm (to the nearest round number) from the loaded waterline down to the keel.

SKETCHING OUT A MIDSHIP SECTION FOR THE HULL

This depth can now be used to sketch out a midship section for the hull. We know the width (140mm), the submerged depth (40mm), and that it should be a shallow V. So it is time to draw a midplane section that gives the shape we like the look of. Traditionally, this section view would be positioned in the middle of the side elevation view on the vertical line marked MS. However,

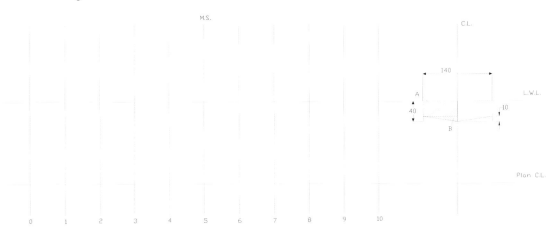

Fig. 5.15   Hull design, step 2: midship section added to the plan.

for clarity we can place it on the right-hand side, centred about the vertical centreline (CL) – *see* Fig. 5.15.

Looking at the midplane sketch, we can work out the area using simple geometry. Half the plane can be divided into a rectangle (A) and a triangle (B). Working out each area and adding them up and then multiplying by two (for the other half of the midplane) will give the total midplane area:

$$Rect\ A = 70mm \times 30mm = 2100mm^2$$

$$Triangle\ B = \frac{70 \times 10}{2} = 350mm^2$$

$$Total\ area = (Rect\ A + Triangle\ B) \times 2$$

$$Total\ area = (2100 + 350) \times 2 = 4900mm^2$$

We can also work out the rectangle that encloses the midship section, a rectangle of the width of the widest points, and the full submerged depth. This rectangle area is:

$$140mm \times 40mm = 5600mm^2$$

The midship plane coefficient is the ratio of these two areas:

$$Midshop\ plane\ coefficient = \frac{4900}{5600} = 0.87$$

We can also check the prismatic coefficient:

$$Prismatic\ Coefficient = Cp = \frac{\nabla}{(Am \times L)}$$

Where:
∇ = displaced volume of the hull
Am = immersed area of the midship section
L = length of the hull at the waterline

$$Cp = \frac{2500000}{(4900 \times 700)} = 0.72$$

All this looks quite reasonable. The midship plane coefficient of 0.87 means that we have a nice, full cross-section to house the steam engine and boiler. The prismatic coefficient of 0.72 means the hull should be fairly sleek, which is ideal for the modest power-plant.

Back on the drawing board it is now a good idea to draw out the sections along the hull and work out the displacement against the target of 2,500,000mm³.

THE HULL IN THE PLAN VIEW

However, before we do this, we need to know how the hull looks in the plan view, because this will dictate the width of each of the sections. We have already set a target block coefficient of 0.65. The difficulty is now sketching a waterline profile that meets this ratio, because the hull form changes along its length and tapers down to the keel. This is where some uncertainty will creep into the design.

The best way to proceed is to draw a shape we like the look of and work through the rest of the process. If the shape chosen has a lower block coefficient, then we can expect the boat to sit lower in the water than the 40mm calculated. We can either live with this, or we can redraw the waterline profile making it wider, and then recalculate.

Use the 45-degree line to drop construction lines down from the cross-section view and then across to set the width on the plan view at the MS line. Also take some horizontal lines from the cross-section view so we can start sketching a side elevation. Fig. 5.16 shows the top and side elevations on the drawings.

The curve on the plan view should reach the designated beam width of 140mm at the midplane and close to a point at the bow. The width at the stern will typically be a little less, and a slight taper from the midplane to the stern looks good. In this case, the sketch pulled the midplane forwards. The midplane is always the cross-section of the hull at the widest point, and the freehand sketch resulted in this being at station 3 rather than station 5.

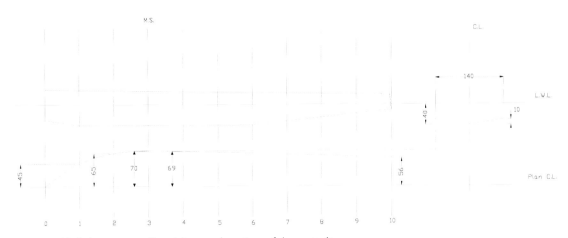

Fig. 5.16 Hull design, step 3: adding a plan view of the waterline.

The sketched plan profile can be copied using the dimensions given in the drawings – and note that a straight line was used from station 5 to the stern. The final sketch in this example gave the Harbour Pilot a stern width of 112mm.

On the side view there needs to be some clearance for the propeller and rudder, and this was achieved by lifting the keel at the stern from station 6, resulting in a 6-degree rake.

WORKING OUT THE HULL DISPLACEMENT

The outline of the hull is now complete, but we need to know the cross-section areas at each station to work out the displacement. Using projection lines and the 45-degree construction line, take each station in turn and project the height from the side elevation and the width from the plan view to see the shape on the cross-section view. Note that on the cross-section views, only half the profile is shown. This is just to make the drawing clearer, and is acceptable because the sections are symmetrical about the boat centreline. Traditionally, sections forward of the midship plane are drawn on the right of the centreline, and sections aft are drawn on the left.

From the plan and side views the area of each station can now be calculated. Then we can use Simpson's rule to approximate the displaced volume.

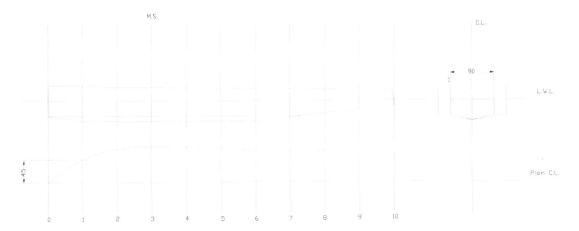

Fig. 5.17 Hull design, step 4: projecting the first bulkhead from the side and plan views.

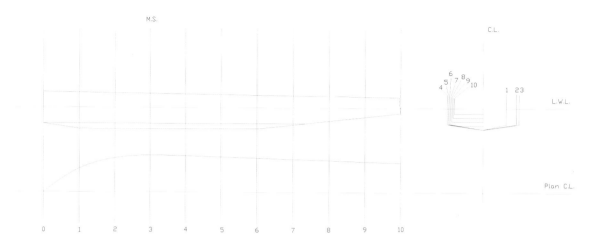

Fig. 5.18 Hull design, step 5: projecting all the bulkheads from the side and plan views.

Calculating the Area of Each Station

Station	Area	Simpson's multiplier	Result Area × Simps
0–bow	0	1	0
1	3,150	4	12,600
2	4,550	2	9,100
3–MS	4,900	4	19,600
4	4,830	2	9,660
5	4,678	4	18,712
6	4,526	2	9,052
7	4,023	4	16,092
8	3,016	2	6,032
9	2,035	4	8,140
10–stern	1,120	1	1,120
		Sum of results	110,108

This summed result must now be multiplied by the station spacing divided by 3.

Station spacing = 70mm:

$$\left(\frac{70}{3}\right) \times 110108 = 2569186 mm^2$$

The target displacement was 2,500,000 so we are quite close – in fact within 3 per cent of the target.

If this number were to come out a lot lower than the target displacement, the vessel might still float but it would sit lower in the water than drawn. If this were a problem, it is a matter of working out how far you are away from the target, and redrawing the design to compensate.

For example, if your answer were 10 per cent down, then you could redraw your waterplane profile aiming for a 10 per cent bigger area. This could be done by using Simpson's rule to calculate the current area, and then going from there. This is over-simplifying things because the relationship is not linear, but it would get you closer.

In this case the estimate is larger, so the vessel might sit higher. This might be viewed as a good thing, but in fact it reduces our stability. It might be all right, but our options are either to redraw the hull to correct the situation, or to be prepared to add ballast to the finished boat if needed.

The amount of freeboard (how much of the hull sticks above the water) can be determined largely from appearance, but also with consideration to the expected sailing conditions. A steep-sided hull such as this design needs more freeboard than a heavily flared hull, which will displace much more water as the boat is loaded or tipped. To give the boat a streamlined profile the deck was sloped by 10mm front to back with a resulting freeboard of 30mm at the bow.

Before drawing in the propeller shaft position, we need to see where the steam plant will fit, and to determine the height of the engine output shaft. At the same time we should start to draw in the open section within the hull, which will create the engine room for the steam plant. Ultimately this will create some bulkhead templates that we can cut from sheet timber to create the frame. Calculating the centre of buoyancy for the proposed hull may help decide on a position for the engine.

To find the longitudinal centre of buoyancy we divide the total moments by the total area.

$$\frac{-5107620}{36828} = 138.68mm$$

This tells us that the longitudinal centre of buoyancy is 138mm behind the midplane (station 3), which means towards the stern. If possible, we should try to put the centre of gravity of the steam

Calculating the Centre of Bouyancy

Station	Area (mm^2)	Simpson's multiplier	Area × Simps	Distance from midplane (mm)	Moment Area × distance
0–bow	0	1	0	210	0
1	3,150	4	12,600	140	441,000
2	4,550	2	9,100	70	318,500
3–MS	4,900	4	19,600	0	0
4	4,830	2	9,660	–70	–676,200
5	4,678	4	18,712	–140	–654,920
6	4,526	2	9,052	–210	–950,460
7	4,023	4	16,092	–280	–1,126,440
8	3,016	2	6,032	–350	–1,055,600
9	2,035	4	8,140	–420	–854,700
10–stern	1,120	1	1,120	–490	–548,800
Totals	36,828		110,108		–5,107,620

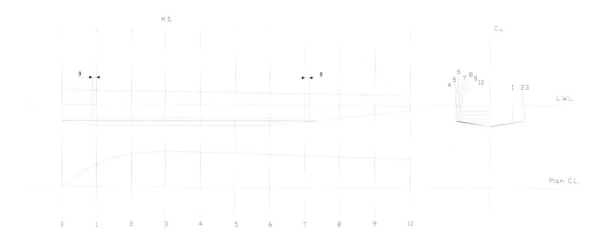

Fig. 5.19 Hull design, step 6: keel profile and floor position.

plant over this location, so the boat sits level in the water.

The proposed keel profile is shown in blue in Fig. 5.19, the side elevation. This sets the height of the floor in the engine room, which in turn affects the width we can have. We want the floor to be as low as possible for our lowest centre of gravity, but be aware that setting the floor too low would result in a very thin and weak keel and a very narrow engine room. Some judgement needs to be used to find the keel's best height.

Note how the proposed keel profile also inter-

acts with the bulkheads already drawn. At the front the keel is full height between stations 0 and 1 to create a strong connection to the planking at the bow. Behind the engine room the keel jumps up to support the control room at the stern. The position of this feature is aligned with the bulkhead at station 7, but with an allowance for the bulkhead thickness of 9mm.

Note that station 7 is the watertight bulkhead between the engine and control rooms, and that station 1 has no cut-out either. So only bulkheads 2, 3, 4, 5 and 6 contain the engine room. Cut-

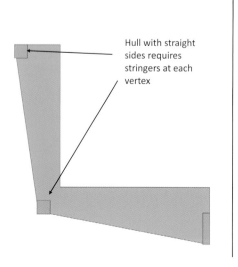

Hull with straight sides requires stringers at each vertex

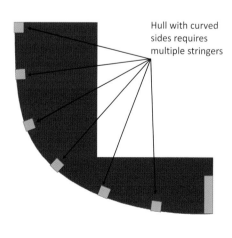

Hull with curved sides requires multiple stringers

Fig. 5.20 *The number of stringers will depend on how curved the boat sides are. A boat with straight sides will only need stringers at the corners. A curved hull will need more support.*

outs for stations 8 and 9 will depend on what you need to put in the control room, but if in doubt make the cuts as generous as you can, as it is difficult to enlarge them once the hull is assembled.

On the top view, sketch in a shape that represents the steam plant, and find a position that allows access to the firebox and leaves some room for a coupling to the propeller shaft. One idea is to cut the steam-plant footprint from card and then slide it about on your drawing to better visualize things. Do the same to the side view – the height of the steam plant should be on the keel, plus an allowance for a floor in the engine room. Then use the 45-degree line to project these profiles to the cross-sectional views to check everything works. It will be necessary to reduce the engine-room width towards the bow because of the curve of the hull, but of course the floor should be the same level throughout.

Now the position of the output shaft of the engine is known, look for a suitable position and angle for a propeller shaft that allows for a proportionately sized propeller. The longer the shaft is, the shallower the angle can be, but leave room for a rudder too.

It should now be possible to copy the bulkheads and keel profiles on to wood and cut them out to start the hull build – but before we do, the last job is to add some notches in the bulkheads for the stringers. Stringers run fore and aft, and are curved strips that support the planking. You can add as many as you like, but as a minimum there should be one at the 'chine', which is where the side planking meets the underside planking, and typically there is also one at the top just under the deck. A hull with a more curved cross-section will need more stringers for support than one with a hard chine (see Fig. 5.20).

HARBOUR PILOT BOAT BUILD

Now we have the plans for the Harbour Pilot drawn up we can start the build, but it is prudent just to review them from a practical standpoint, to make sure we can manufacture it correctly.

The build principle is closely aligned to full-scale wooden boat construction, where the hull is constructed upside down on a frame. In our case, the keel will form the frame. Another consideration is access to the steam plant: we really need to be able to remove the entire deck in order to work and maintain the engine systems. With an electric or clockwork boat we could glue all the frame parts to the underside of the deck, including the bulkheads and the keel, and this would help make the structure strong. However, being able to remove the deck is preferable with the steam plant.

With this in mind, the following modifications are suggested. First, it will be useful to make the upper stringer stick up above the bulkheads so that the deck panel can locate inside it. As a consequence, the deck panel will need to be smaller by the thickness of the stringer on both sides. In this case it was proposed to make the stringers from 6mm plywood, so the deck must be redrawn 6mm narrower on both the port and starboard sides.

At the stern, the transom will also be used to locate the deck, so it will be redrawn 6mm taller in its centre section, resulting in a 12mm notch for the upper stringer.

A third change is to add a triangle of wood up at the bow to give the upper stringer something to adhere to where it is stressed the most. The planned part would be 9mm thick, and so it must be that the keel up at the bow needs to be reduced in height by this amount. Lastly, the keel is best constructed overlong at the bow so it can be sanded to be an exact fit to the assembled frame.

Finally, a manufacturing issue is that of trying to drill a hole for the propeller tube, which has to be at the correct angle and the correct location, along the centreline of the hull. A typical shaft tube is 6mm diameter, and trying to drill this through the 9mm thickness of the keel is likely to go wrong.

Instead it is proposed to cut the keel section in half, to place the propeller shaft exactly, and

Fig. 5.21 Creating a propeller shaft housing in the keel. By cutting the keel to accept a propeller shaft at this stage of the build, the position can be more easily controlled than drilling for the shaft after the hull is complete.

then rejoin the keel using support plates on each side. Consequently, the width of the parts for bulkhead number 8 must be modified accordingly, to accommodate the support plates.

The final drawings for the hull parts, including these changes, are given at the end of this chapter.

HULL CONSTRUCTION

Each time a part is drawn out it is good practice to ensure that a centreline is marked on it. The boat has a centreline, but not really any edges that we can use as a datum, so having a centreline on all the parts helps align everything during construction.

Another important point is to use a waterproof adhesive throughout the build, so your boat doesn't spring apart on the lake.

Take some 9mm plywood and cut out the keel profiles, and bulkheads 1 and 7. Cut the keel braces from 6mm plywood. Assemble and glue all the parts and place them upside down on the bench to ensure they are aligned and square as the glue dries.

Cut out a deck profile, in accordance with the plans, from 6mm plywood, including the 6mm reduction just discussed. This deck panel will be removable in the final boat to give access to the

steam plant. For this reason it will not be glued to the frame, but will serve as a 'former' to help guide the frame parts to the correct shape.

Trace the nose of the deck on to a piece of 9mm plywood, and cut it out. This part will be the bow support plate, and it can be put on one side for the time being.

Take the deck panel and drill it to take three mounting screws; position these where the deck cut-outs will eventually be made. Screw the deck to a supporting plank, and cover it with clingfilm so that no glue will stick to it.

As designed, the upper stringers are made from 6mm square wood, but we will add another 6mm to the top side, to enable it to hold the deck in place. So cut two strips of 6mm plywood, 12mm wide and 750mm long. Take one of these strips, place it against one side of the deck, and carefully form it to follow the deck profile from stern to bow. Hold the strip where necessary by using tacks into the supporting plank. At the bow mark, cut and sand the leading edge to the correct angle to align with the hull centreline.

Then fit the second upper stringer using the same process, and once again, spend some time finishing the bow end to be a neat fit with the first strip.

Fig. 5.22 Forming the upper stringers around the deck profile. The deck needed to be removable in the final model, so it was covered in clingfilm to stop glue adhering to it.

Fig. 5.23   Gluing the bow support plate to the upper stringers.

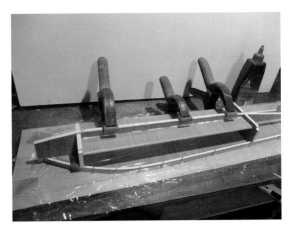

Fig. 5.24   Attaching the engine-room floor to the hull frame. It is important to take measurements to ensure it is central.

Now take the bow support plate (the part previously traced from the deck nose profile), and glue it in place between the upper stringers.

When the keel sub-assembly is dry, it should be glued in place on the model. At the same time, the transom plate can be glued at the back. To help with the placement and gluing of the bulkheads, the engine-room floor is assembled next. This is just a rectangle of 6mm plywood, but it is important to take the time to ensure it is centred about the keel.

Next, each of the bulkhead halves can be cut and glued in place against the keel, floor and upper stringers.

The lower stringers are more curved than the upper ones. In full-sized boats, curved frame members are formed by steaming the wood and then clamping it to a former. However, on our model boat we can make life easier by laminating two wood strips together. So take two wood strips 3 × 6mm and glue them together on the frame. Work your way towards the bow and secure the laminated stringer to the bulkheads with gaffer tape or small pins.

As a general point, when cutting wood for the stringers, it is better that the stringers are larger and stick out from the bulkhead profile. It is much less work to sand the stringers to match the bulkheads than the other way round.

Fig. 5.25   The bulkheads assembled in the frame.

When the glue is dry, inspect the frame and sand any parts that are not flush. The stringers, deck and keel will all need forming to match the angles on the bulkheads, and at the front the bulkheads themselves will need to be shaped towards the bow. The best tool for this is just sandpaper on a block so you can transfer the angles from one part to the next. Try to do as much of the sanding as possible whilst the frame is on the support plank, although it will be necessary to remove it to sand the bow to final shape.

PLANKING

Before starting the planking, you may want to float-test your frame, to check trim and overall sea-

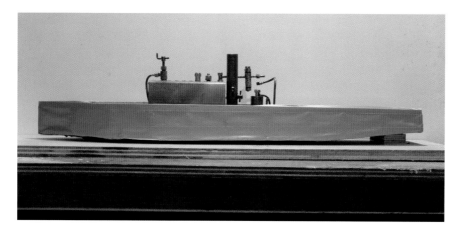

Fig. 5.26 For float testing before doing any planking, a temporary hull skin can be made from gaffer tape (note the early prototype boiler housing shown in this image).

Fig. 5.27 The first planking panel in place and sanded back to the hull frame.

The best wood for planking the rest of the hull is modelling ply, sold by model shops and available in nice thin sheets. For this build 1.5mm ply was used, and a single sheet of 300 × 1,200mm was found to be more than enough to cover the hull. Each piece of wood should be cut over-sized to cover one of the hull lower sections, and it can then be glued in place and held with tacks or small dressmaker's pins. Any small holes can be easily painted over. The planking should be allowed to stick out on all sides for trimming.

Once the glue has dried the plank can be trimmed with a modelling knife, and then sandpaper used to make the edge flush with the adjoining surfaces. This process is repeated for the second side. The following photographs should give a feel for the construction steps.

worthiness with the boiler and engine on board. If you do, then gaffer tape can be wrapped over the frame to create a temporary skin for a float-test.

The planking starts at the stern. The raised section that contains the propeller is made from 6mm ply. It is not curved, so doesn't need to be thin ply, but more importantly, because the 6mm panel is sanded to match the bulkhead profiles, it should provide a support edge for the back of the underside panels.

The side planking will be added last, so next to go into place is the underside planking. There are no dimensioned drawings for the planking panels, as they are very much taken from the frame geometry and sanded to be an exact fit.

Fig. 5.28 The first underside plank fitted.

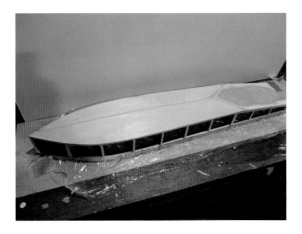

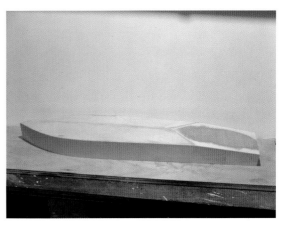

Fig. 5.29   The second underside plank added and sanded back to the frame.

Fig. 5.30   The side planking complete.

The superstructure parts are all made from aluminium, or at least a metal of your choosing. These parts will get hot, so wood is not advised, or you might end up with a Viking funeral. 0.5mm aluminium is a good choice because it is easy to work and doesn't spring back much after folding. Another option might be the metal from a biscuit tin. The plans for the superstructure are very rudimentary, reminiscent of a tin toy with 2D profiles riveted to form a 3D structure. If you have fine modelling skills, then feel free to elaborate on the design.

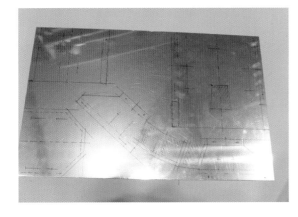

Fig. 5.31   Marking out the superstructure panels. The drawings for all the superstructure parts have a scale bar that can be used to copy the drawings at full scale if needed.

Mark out each part as accurately as you can. The drawings given are not full scale, but there is a scale bar on each of them if you want to scan them in and reproduce them full size. Then you can stick the paper to the metal using a glue stick, and use it as a guide, similar to the process used in dressmaking. Thin metal can be cut using strong scissors (sometimes called Kevlar scissors) or tinsnips.

Drill any holes before bending so you can use the pillar drill on the flat pattern. Thin metal can easily catch on a drill, a problem that is worse with larger drill sizes, so take care to properly secure the metal before you drill. A step-drill is ideal for the larger holes because it reduces drill changes and is less likely to catch. If you use a step-drill, note how the edge of the next step up can be used to deburr the hole to create a neat finish. Thin sheet needs support to avoid distortion, so place scrapwood under the part for each hole drilled.

All the folds can be made just using thumb pressure in the vice.

TIPS AND SEQUENCING

The following tips and sequencing are advised to make the best of this slightly tricky job.

The wheelhouse roof has some curved edges to make it look more substantial. These can be

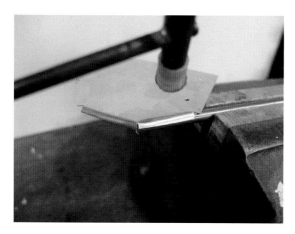

Fig. 5.32 Forming the edge of the wheelhouse roof over a piece of 8mm steel bar. Work from the centre outwards to ensure access to each edge in turn.

created by gently hammering the metal over an 8mm bar held in the vice. Use a plastic hammer to avoid marking the work, and form the middle sections first because doing them after the outside sections makes access much harder. The four holes in the roof are best transfer-drilled from the wheelhouse.

The wheelhouse windows should be drilled in the lower corners before folding, but not cut. Cutting out the windows will make it harder to get a neat fold. So drill the window corners and also a small chain of drilled holes along the window

bottom edge; then fold the part and cut window sides with some shears or scissors. The lower tabs for mounting under the deck are best folded with the wheelhouse in place on the deck so that the fit can be made snug. We can come back to this later.

The wheelhouse roof can now be positioned centrally on the wheelhouse sides and held with a small clamp for drilling and riveting.

The engine cover has more rounded corner folds. The fold line on the plans is the start of the fold, so clamp the part along this line against a 20mm piece of bar and then fold down the sides by 90 degrees.

The rear cover has three folds of various angles, and a smartphone with a spirit-level app is good for approximating these. The wooden blanking panel at the end can also be used as a template for the angles.

Fitting the superstructure to the deck needs to account for the final boiler and engine position, which may vary from build to build. The plans give the suggested deck cut-outs, but it is more likely that these will need adjusting for the folded metal parts.

Start by cutting a small opening in the deck just large enough for the boiler and engine to stick through. This can be marked by eye and then cut using a coping saw. Then place the deck on the hull.

Fig. 5.33 Locating the central engine cover to mark the deck for cutting. It is important that the regulator and engine top line up with the holes in the cover. The other covers can be positioned relative to the central engine cover as their position is not critical.

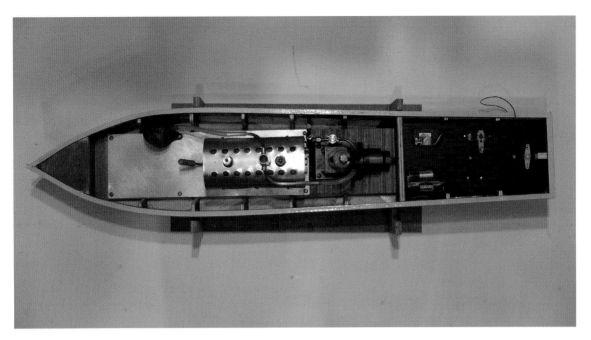

Fig. 5.34 The complete hull layout of the Harbour Pilot showing all the key components including the steam plant, radio equipment and condenser circuit.

The only part of the superstructure with a critical position is the middle engine cover, which needs to have the safety valve aligned with the funnel, and the hole in the side aligned with the regulator. Slide the cover fore and aft to find the best position. If necessary open out the funnel cut-out slightly so the regulator sits cleanly in the side hole, and then mark the deck to record this position. Measure the final width of the cover, and measure this out on the deck.

You should now have a rectangle you can cut that will fit with the engine cover. Transfer-drill the mounting holes in the lower tabs into the deck, and secure with small nuts and bolts.

The wheelhouse can go on next. Use the same process to slide it fore and aft to find the best position, mark the deck, and then measure the width of the wheelhouse and mark this on too. The cut-out for the wheelhouse is rectangular, and the deck area below the windows is not removed. Next offer the wheelhouse into place: mark where the lower tab hangs below the deck, and then fold on this line.

The rear cover can be installed using the same process. The intention is that the cut-out in the deck stops before the control room at the stern, so that this can be a relatively watertight area for radio-controlled equipment. Finally, the wooden end panel can be sanded to fit the rear opening and glued in place on the deck, and secured to the rear cover with some small woodscrews.

The superstructure can be painted, or left as raw aluminium. A good paint to use is model enamel. There is a huge range of colours and it is a durable finish. Wood can be painted with primer first, and if any transfers are used, then a finishing coat of clear varnish will help them stay put.

SAILING THE BOAT

Refer back to the Pond Runner chapter for some tips on sailing your steam launch. There are some important safety considerations for both the fire and the water, as well as some navigation tips.

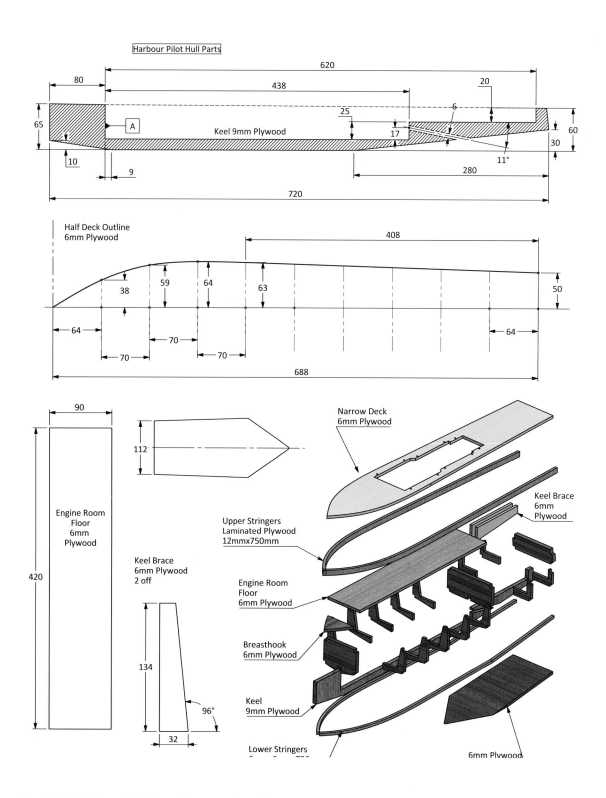

Fig. 5.35   Harbour Pilot boat drawings, sheet 1.

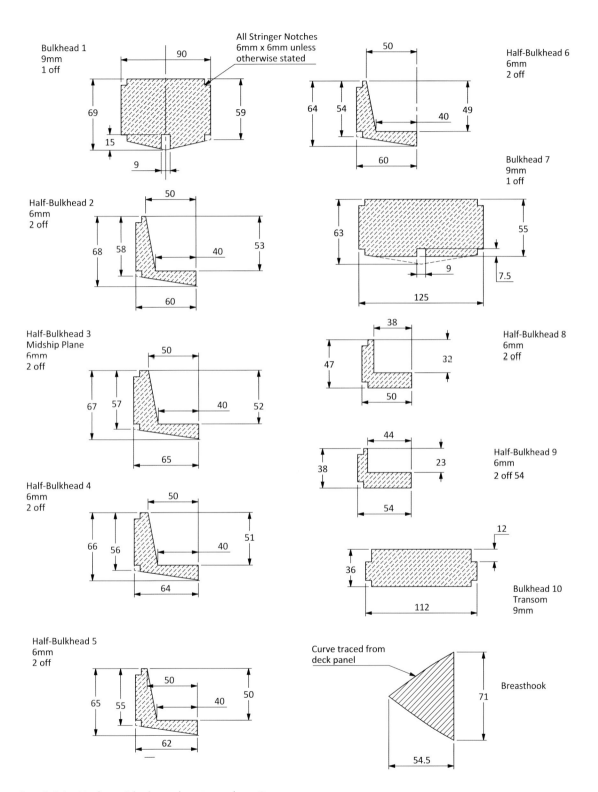

Fig. 5.36 Harbour Pilot boat drawings, sheet 2.

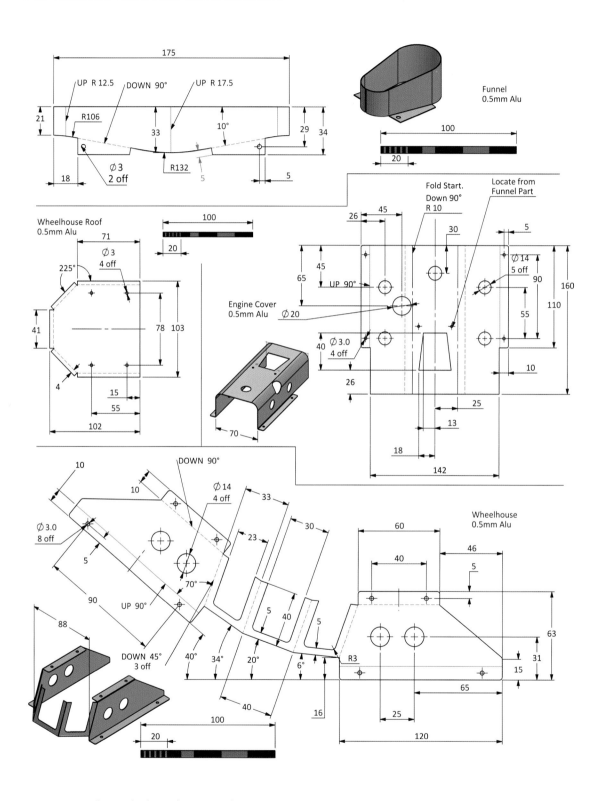

Fig. 5.37 Harbour Pilot boat drawings, sheet 3.

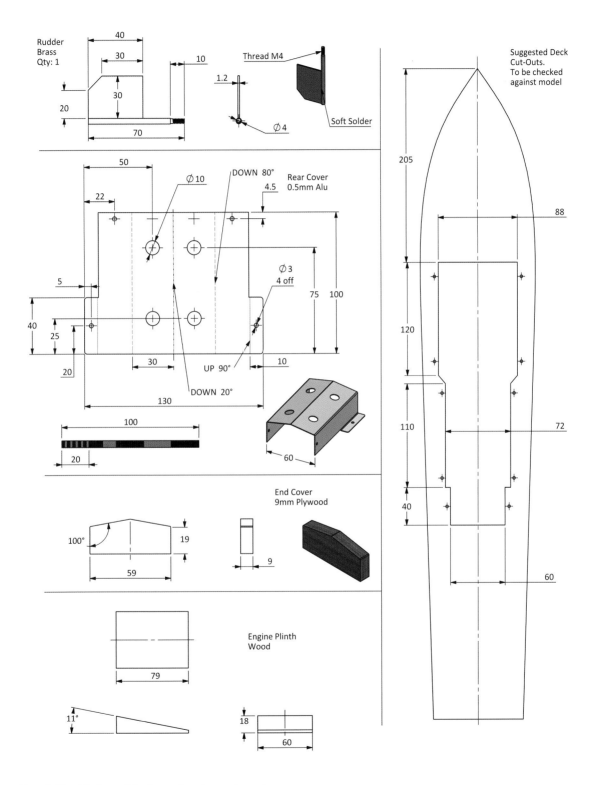

Fig. 5.38   Harbour Pilot boat drawings, sheet 4.

CHAPTER SIX

PADDLE STEAMER: A VINTAGE VESSEL

Paddle steamers can have a large paddlewheel at the stern or a pair of smaller wheels, one each side of the hull. The single large stern wheel is a design most associated with the USA, notably on the Mississippi river. Port and starboard wheels were more generally seen around the globe.

Although paddle steamers have been reduced to tourist attractions these days, they retain one benefit over screw-driven vessels in that they have a shallower draught and are therefore less likely to ground in shallow water. This might be worth bearing in mind, depending on your chosen sailing location.

The most handsome paddle steamers feature a long, elegant hull; however, the model given here is relatively short for practical reasons, and more closely resembles a paddle tugboat.

This build gives the opportunity to explore another hull construction method. This time the sides are laminated and formed on a jig to create a rigid outline. Then the underside of the hull is a panel, curved from bow to stern to make a more streamlined hull and to make room for the rudder.

This boat is powered by the boiler from the Harbour Pilot, but is coupled to a 2-cylinder development of the simple oscillating engine used on the Pond Runner. Having 2 cylinders gives more power strokes per crank revolution, meaning the engine will be less likely to stall under load. Even with 2 cylinders, a reduction gear will be necessary to increase the torque output from the engine, enough to turn the paddlewheels in the water without risk of stalling.

In the paddle steamer, the torque at the paddlewheel shaft is reduced through the diameter

Fig. 6.1   Paddle steamer model on the water.

GEARS AND TORQUE

Gears allow engineers to balance speed and torque in rotary motion. They can be considered to be a rotary version of the 'lever', which trades distance for a multiplication in force. A reduction gear will decrease rotary speed but increase the torque (strength) of the motion. Likewise, a high gear ratio will give a faster output but with lower torque. The correct gear for a mechanism will depend on the application.

If a drive system is viewed in terms of energy, it can be said that the power in the system is limited by the output of the engine, whether it is a steam engine, sterling engine, petrol or diesel engine, or an electric motor. However, although this power is fixed, it can be delivered differently with the use of a gearbox to provide more strength or more speed, or a compromise between the two.

Just a few gears can make a significant change in speed/torque. In 1992 Arthur Ganson took just twelve reduction gears, each one with a ratio of 50:1, and created a working sculpture with a total reduction of 2.44×10^{20} to 1 or 244.14 quintillian to 1. As Arthur explains:

> With the motor turning at around 200 revolutions per minute, it will take well over two trillion years before the final gear can make but one turn. Consequently, it is possible to do anything at all with the final gear... even embed it in concrete...and the machine will run just fine.
>
> Arthur Ganson, *Machine with Concrete*, 1992

A mind-blowing example of a system producing a huge amount of torque, but very little speed!

Fig. 6.2   Arthur Ganson, Machine with Concrete, *1992.*

of the paddlewheel itself, in the same way as a longer oar is harder to row. So the reduction gear in the drive train should compensate for this and ensure the motor has the strength to paddle the boat forwards.

THE PADDLE-STEAMER ENGINE

The twin-cylinder oscillating cylinder engine uses several parts derived from the Pond Runner design, but they are derivatives, rather than direct copies. So the construction is explained in full in the text, rather than referring back to the earlier chapter, to avoid any confusion that might occur. This model also looks at the idea of using O-rings to help seal the pistons.

It is important to take a look through the drawings to note a couple of things. First, the two steam ports are different. Only the inlet port goes right though the frame: the exhaust port is drilled just halfway through and then meets another drilled hole coming in from the side of the frame.

Fig. 6.3 The complete paddle-steamer engine.

Getting these ports the right way round affects the direction of rotation of the engine, so it needs to be right, otherwise your boat will go backwards. Equally important is to check that the two engine frames are mirrors of each other, not the same part on both sides of the engine. Parts like this are sometimes called 'handed' parts. The parts are actually similar, apart from the port drillings, so you can make identical parts up to that point – but think hard when it comes to drilling the steam ports.

Second, the crank and main bearings are different to the Pond Runner. This is necessary because if we Loctite both crank discs to a single crank-shaft, we will never get the engine apart again for servicing and repair. So the crank is made in two halves, using a collar and two grub screws to hold everything together. This collar addresses another problem, which is that the axle on this engine is 4mm, and the Meccano sprocket for the power take-off is designed for imperial wire gauge size 8. No. 8 wire gauge is only fractionally over 4mm, but we can attach the sprocket to the crank collar, rather than use the original Meccano boss, to get everything running spot on.

Finally, note that the frame ports are not dimensioned – instead they are drilled using a jig. This method ensures that the ports are correctly positioned regardless of any accumulated inaccuracies that may have built up. Following the drilling of the ports in the frame, the inlet port is then used to locate the steam port in the cylinder. Again, this ensures that its position is exact.

THE FLYWHEEL

The flywheel is a job for the lathe and starts with a piece of iron or steel, or brass if you like. As a rule, it is best to turn the flywheel to size and then 'true' it up on a mandrel/arbor to get it running exactly.

To start, face one end of the bar and centre-drill, drill and ream it to a final size of 4mm. Add any shoulders or recesses you would like on this face, and then reverse it in the chuck and finish the second side.

Over on the drill press the flywheel can be drilled and threaded to take an M4 grub screw, after which the 4mm reamer should be pushed through the axle hole again, to clear away any burrs.

The next job is to machine an arbor to hold the flywheel. The arbor will be the same size as the axle, but the important thing is not to remove the arbor from the chuck until the job is finished, otherwise you will lose accuracy. Take a piece of scrap bar and place it in the three-jaw chuck with enough protruding to take the flywheel. Now turn a 4mm spigot, long enough for the flywheel, and thread the end portion with an M4 thread. Fit the flywheel and secure it with an M4 nut and the grub screw.

Now use light machining cuts to get the edge of the flywheel running true. The flywheel is only driven by the grip of the grub screw and the nut, so cuts must be light, and some oil may help. You can use the fine feed if your lathe has one, to get a nice finish on the rim. Reverse the flywheel on the arbor to machine the second side. The result should be a flywheel with very little run-out.

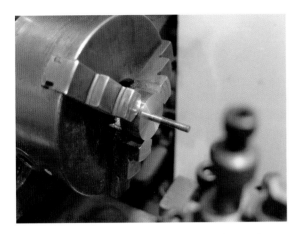

Fig. 6.4   A 4mm arbor to machine the flywheel rim. It is important that the part is not removed from the chuck at any point, or the true centre of the work will be lost.

Fig. 6.5   The flywheel being skimmed to run exactly true on the arbor. Light cuts must be used as the flywheel is only held to the axle with a grub screw and axle nut.

THE CYLINDERS

The cylinders are made before the pistons so that the pistons can be made to fit. The actual diameter of the cylinder bores is unimportant; more significant is that the bores should be parallel and smooth and perpendicular to the port face.

Each cylinder will need to be made in turn, and they are identical by design, and not handed as the frames.

To start a cylinder, cut and turn a piece of 16mm brass bar to length. Then using the milling machine or vertical slide in the lathe, machine a flat on one side, removing 2mm off the bar diameter. Also in this set-up, find the centreline of the part using an edge finder against the vice jaws, and measure from one end to drill and tap the cylinder pivot hole. Doing this in the same setting will ensure the hole is perpendicular to the flat previously machined. Before removing the part from the vice, add the shallow recess across the pivot section. This will remove the risk of any

Fig. 6.6   The cylinder flat and the pivot hole should be machined in one setting to ensure they are perpendicular.

Fig. 6.7   Adding a recess across the pivot hole is a worthwhile feature to help the cylinder sit squarely on the engine frame.

Fig. 6.8   The cylinder bore should be centre-drilled, drilled and reamed to final size. A reamer or a D-bit can be used to finish the hole. The position of the cylinder bore is not determined by measurement – it is given by the cylinder flat resting on one of the three-jaw chuck jaws.

Fig. 6.9   Machining marks can be polished out using a wooden dowel, turned to be a wringing fit in the cylinder, and some metal polish.

deformation around the pivot pin hole causing the cylinder to sit away from the frame.

Now place the part in the three-jaw chuck with the flat against one of the jaws, ensuring that at least 20mm of the part is sticking out. In this setting the cylinder bore can be centre-drilled, drilled 23mm deep and reamed to an 8mm bore.

Fig. 6.10   Lapping the cylinder port face is an important step to get a steam-tight joint. Fine wet'n'dry paper held to a flat glass plate is a good method to polish out the machining marks.

If a reamer is not available a D-bit can be made to finish the bore parallel and create a flat bottom to the hole. To finish, the outside of the cylinder can be reduced to 10mm diameter, along the 20mm length.

Now make a second cylinder following the same process.

To remove any machining marks in the bores, a hardwood lap can be turned in the lathe to be a wringing fit on the cylinder. Then, running the lathe slowly and with some metal polish, the bore can be polished to a smooth, bright finish. The port face must also be smooth, and this can be done by lapping the face on some fine wet'n'dry paper held on to a flat surface, such as a glass plate. Oil or water can be used to assist this process.

THE PISTONS

The pistons, piston rods and big ends are machined from a single piece. The only critical things are that the piston diameters are a sliding fit in the cylinder bores, and that the holes in the big ends are perpendicular to the piston axis.

As with the cylinders, each piston will be made in turn.

Start by placing a piece of brass in the three-jaw chuck with enough protruding for the whole

Fig. 6.11 Before machining the piston itself, some material is relieved beyond the piston, enough to allow a trial fit of the cylinder. For this reason, the material must stick out from the chuck equivalent to the cylinder bore length.

assembly. The piston will be on the outer end of the part, and will be the main part to get right. So undercut an area beyond the piston to a diameter of less than 8mm so we can work on the piston and trial fit the cylinder without anything getting in the way.

Reduce the piston diameter close to 8mm and then start trial fitting the cylinder until it is a tight fit. To reduce the piston from a tight fit to a sliding fit, a piece of fine wet'n'dry paper wrapped on a file can be used to polish the diameter. This will remove any machining marks and fractionally reduce the size. Proceed carefully and keep checking with the cylinder until you can slide the piston all the way down the cylinder. When the fit is fractionally too tight, stop using the paper and try some metal polish between the piston and cylinder, and work by hand to get a nice fit. When the cylinder is pulled from the piston it should make a nice 'pop' sound, indicating a gas-tight fit.

Adding a groove for an O-ring is optional but can significantly improve the piston seal. The groove dimensions will depend on a number of factors, but essentially it should be shallower than the O-ring cross-section to create a slight pinch and a good seal, but also slightly wider. The extra width is so that the groove can accommodate the expected 'swell' caused by the pinch from the shallow depth.

To cut the groove for the O-ring, grind a thin,

O-RINGS AND STEAM

O-rings can be made from a variety of materials. Nitrile, Viton, silicon, EPDM (ethylene propylene diene monomer) and neoprene are all commonly available. For steam engines the O-ring will need to withstand heat, oil and steam. The material most commonly used is Viton, and it is available in a range of sizes. However, silicon and Nitrile may also work. It is important to ensure the O-ring will not react with the steam oil, and a soak test with Viton, Nitrile and EPDM samples showed that the EPDM could swell when in contact with oil.

To use an O-ring as a piston seal, start by purchasing one with an outside diameter equal to the cylinder bore.

Fig. 6.12 The results of an oil soak test on three different O-ring materials. The ring marked 'E' for EPDM showed significant swelling. Nitrile and Viton rings were all right.

(continued)

(continued)

The dimensions for the groove in the piston need to be calculated to get the O-ring to work at its best. It is important to note that the following calculations are based on experimentation with model engines and differ to manufacturer's guidelines, which are usually based on applications where high friction is not such a concern. The numbers quoted below are derived from experiments by Tubal Cain and Mr Arnold Throp, and for a full understanding *The Model Engineer's Handbook* by Tubal Cain is a good reference. However, at the sizes we are working with here, some simplification is possible, and the following approach is suggested.

To use an O-ring to help seal a piston, start by purchasing one with an outside diameter equal to the cylinder bore. Next it is necessary to calculate the size of the groove in the piston. Although it is the piston that is being machined, in fact the calculations are based on the cylinder diameter and the cross-section of the O-ring. 'The groove in the piston should be wider than the O-ring cross-section diameter by about 1.3 times' (*Model Engineer's Handbook*, Tubal Cain).

Example:

A 10mm cylinder bore.

A 10mm Viton O-ring is shown to have a cross-sectional thickness of 1mm in the catalogue. So the width of the groove should be:

$$1.3 \times 1mm = 1.3mm$$

The diameter of the groove is not set by the piston diameter, but by the bore of the cylinder, and this time it is made undersized, to introduce a small amount of pinch to the O-ring. The idea is to get the ring to seal, but without too much friction. As a rule of thumb, you can make the groove 1.2 times smaller than the O-ring cross-section. So the depth of the groove (from the cylinder wall) is:

$$1mm \div 1.2 = 0.83mm$$

Following these rules, the piston groove should end up slightly shallow to help the O-ring seal but also slightly wide to allow it to swell outwards due to the 'pinch'.

Example of O-ring Fitting Tolerance

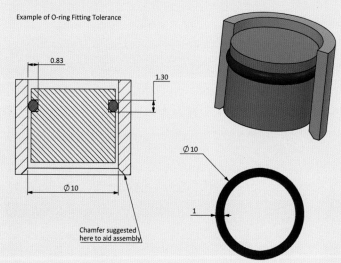

0.83

1.30

Ø 10

Ø 10

1

Chamfer suggested here to aid assembly

Fig. 6.13 Diagram showing the suggested clearances of an O-ring when used as a piston ring. These recommendations are different to manufacturers' suggestions because of the unique application to model steam engines.

Fig. 6.14 Checking the fit of an O-ring on the piston.

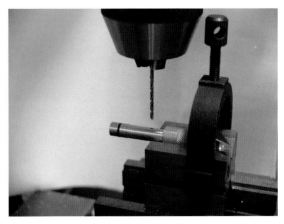

Fig. 6.15 Cross-drilling the piston rod for the crank pin. This is done before separating the component from the bar stock to make it easier to hold in the drill press.

sharp tool and proceed carefully with regular measuring and checking with the O-ring.

Now the working surface of the piston is complete, the remainder of the part can be reduced to create a connecting rod and big end. Before parting off the work, transfer over to the drill press and cross-drill the big end for the crank pin. A V-block is useful to ensure the workpiece is horizontal and secure; alternatively a vice with a parallel can be used. Take some time to ensure the part is drilled centrally.

To finish, return the bar to the lathe and part the component from the stock. The piston is now fin-ished and should make a healthy 'popping' noise when you pull it from the cylinder. The second piston should be made following a repeat of the process and using the other cylinder as a guide, in case they are slightly different diameters.

MAIN BEARINGS

The main bearings are a simple turning job, the only critical dimensions being the centre bore. The three mounting holes can be located with adequate accuracy using a small level on the

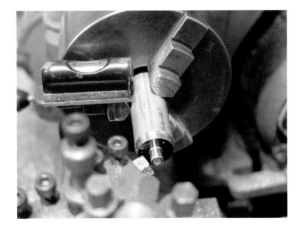

Fig. 6.16 An approximate method to mark out three mounting holes using a small level on the chuck jaws.

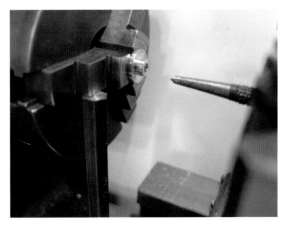

Fig. 6.17 Another method to position three mounting holes in the bearing flange using a hard stop.

chuck jaws, as shown in Fig. 6.16, or just a piece of bar the right length (Fig. 6.17) and marking with the lathe tool or a punch held in the tool post.

An oil hole is added between two of the mounting holes using the drill press and a centre-drill.

Two bearings will be needed, made to the same design.

CRANK DISCS

The crank discs start life as a piece of 16mm steel bar cut to 10mm long, with the end faces machined true. Two discs will be needed, made to the same design. To create the first one, place one of the parts in the three-jaw chuck and

$$Packing\ piece = 1.5 \times e - r + \left(0.5 \times \sqrt{(4r^2) - (3e^2) + (2ew \times \sqrt{3}) - w^2}\right)$$

where:
e = eccentric off-set
r = radius of workpiece
w = width of jaws

Fig. 6.18 shows the packing piece set up for drilling the off-set hole. The hole diameter needs to be an interference fit with a 2mm pin. If you have a number #47 drill in your drill box this would be perfect as it is 1.9939mm, giving a 6µm (micron) interference; alternatively a $^5/_{16}$in drill might be all right – at 1.9844mm it gives a 15µm interference with the crank pin.

Next the part can be held in the three-jaw chuck and the shoulder turned to length and diameter.

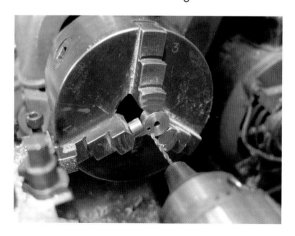

centre-drill, drill through and ream to 4mm diameter.

Before reducing the crank-disc length, it is better to drill the off-set hole for the crank pin so that the part can be held more securely in the chuck. The off-set hole can be made using the three-jaw chuck with a piece of packing against one of the jaws. As mentioned previously, this has to be done using some care and a slow speed to stay safe.

The height of the packing piece should be approximately 6.8mm tall, but it is worth checking this number for the lathe being used, which could have wider or narrower jaws. The formula is as follows:

The length is more important here – the diameter just needs to be less than the hole in the frame for a clearance fit. Finally, the part can be held in the three-jaw chuck by the boss, and then the crank disc reduced in thickness to 3mm.

The second crank disc can now be made using the same process and the same packing piece to create the off-set hole.

CRANK PINS

The crank pins are pieces of 2mm silver steel cut to 12mm long and trimmed on the lathe. On one edge a chamfer is added to assist its assembly into the crank disc.

AXLE

The axle is in two parts for assembly reasons. To help alignment, one axle part has a holed drilled in one end and the other has a short shouldered section to be a close fit in this hole. Both the drilled hole and the prong need to be dead on centre. A three-jaw chuck may not be accurate enough here. A collet chuck is one option, or just use the four-jaw chuck and clock it spot-on with your DTI.

Fig. 6.18 The three-jaw chuck can be used for off-set drilling by including a packing piece of the correct thickness against one of the jaws.

IMPROVING THREE-JAW CHUCK ACCURACY

If you don't have a four-jaw chuck or a collet to hold a round workpiece accurately, then you can improve the accuracy of your three-jaw by making a simple collet to go in it. To do this, turn a shouldered bush larger than the axle diameter, then drill and ream it to suit the workpiece. Mark where the jaw number one is on the part, then remove it from the chuck and saw through the side opposite where the jaw number one mark is. Then return to the chuck in the same orientation.

You should find that the workpiece runs very close to centre. In my old Myford lathe, the chuck run-out on a 10mm piece of bar was 0.08mm; with the collet modification, this was reduced to 0.02mm.

Fig. 6.19 *Creating a collet for the three-jaw chuck helps to reduce radial runout.*

CRANK COLLAR

Before making the collar, it is first necessary to remove the Meccano sprocket from its brass boss so we can use it as a gauge to machine a shoulder on the collar. Hold the part in the lathe by the boss, and then carefully machine off the swaged collar of the hub, until the sprocket can be removed. Now take a piece of 10mm brass

Fig. 6.20 *Machining a new bush for the primary drive sprocket. The sprocket was used as a guide to finish the shoulder.*

and machine a short shoulder on the end to fit snug in the sprocket. In the same setting, centre-drill, drill and ream a 4mm hole in the collar. Move the workpiece to the drill press or mill, to drill and tap the two 8BA grub screw holes; then return to the lathe and part the component from the workpiece. Finally, silver solder the Meccano sprocket on to the collar.

CRANK ASSEMBLY

A crank pin should be pushed into each crank disc using a vice or press. Take some time to ensure they are square, before pushing them home. If there is a problem with the pin being loose in the

Fig. 6.21 *Completed crank components, including the split main axle.*

crank disc, then Loctite retaining compound can be used to glue them in place. Now glue each crank disc to one part of the crankshaft axle.

DRILLING JIG

This simple but important part gives the best chance of having a working engine without any adjustment. Critical features are that the part must be 5mm wide, and the two holes drilled where shown and on the centreline. The top hole is tapped 8BA to match the pivot screw.

PIVOT SCREWS

These are a simple turning job, but hex bar is advised on this engine, as access will be tight in the finished model. Some $^3/_{16}$in hex is a good size, although anything close is fine, but it must be steel to be strong enough. Turn the small end first and add the 8BA thread. Next machine the long shoulder to 3mm diameter. Part off the component to finish.

If hex bar is not available, then round bar can be used with two spanner flats added with a file or the mill.

FRAMES

The frames are pieces of 4.75mm ($^3/_{16}$in) brass flat, 18mm wide and 60mm tall.

Fig. 6.22 Transfer-drilling the bearing holes to the frame. Check the orientation of the oil hole, which needs to be on the top side on the final assembly.

Remember: These parts are 'handed'. This really matters when you come to drill the port holes.

Also – not all the hole locations are dimensioned in the drawing – some are located using the drilling jig, or transfer-drilled from other parts.

To make a pair of handed frames proceed as follows:

Mark and drill the dimensioned holes in the drawing – specifically, all the holes on the centreline of the part and also the holes on the upper and lower edges. The holes for the bearing screws can be transfer drilled by fitting the bearing and drilling through and then tapping 8BA.

The port holes are drilled by using the drilling jig. The bearing must be installed at this point as the axle is used as a reference for the jig. Secure the jig at the pivot hole using the pivot screw and some washers. Then rotate the drilling jig until it hits the axle. The first small hole can now be drilled, but make sure you know if it needs to go right through or not. Note that only one of the port holes goes right through, and it matters which one to get the engine running in the correct direction. Once one hole is drilled, then rotate the jig all the way round until it rests on the other side of the axle and drill the second hole.

Now use the same drilling jig on the second frame and double check it is a mirror of the first frame.

To finish the frame, holes need to be drilled

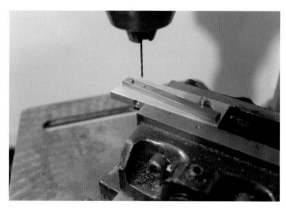

Fig. 6.23 Using the drilling jig against the axle to drill one port hole in the frame.

Fig. 6.24 *Using the drilling jig against the other side of the axle, to drill the second port hole in the frame.*

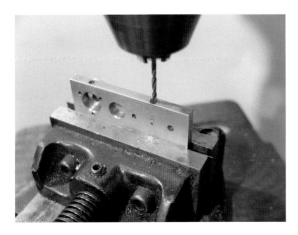

Fig. 6.25 *Drilling the steam exhaust connection into the side of the frame.*

and tapped for the support posts, and on the top edge, a counter-bored hole must be added for the steam exhaust.

SUPPORT POSTS

These are simple turning jobs, with an external 8BA thread on one end and an internal 8BA thread on the other. Turn and thread the external section first and then part off the bar stock slightly over-long. Then reverse the part in the chuck, face the end and centre-drill, drill and tap 8BA. Measure the length of the part, excluding

the external threaded section at the top, and then take this down to final size using the top slide on the lathe. Take some time to get all the lengths as similar as possible.

Note that it is important that all the unthreaded external sections are the same length so that the frames sit at the same height when assembled to the base.

THE ENGINE STAND-OFF

The engine stand-off holds the frames at the correct spacing, and also helps to pull them parallel so that the bearings are aligned. This part gives the opportunity to explore turning using the lathe tailstock as a support. The part is reduced in thickness along most of its length so that it clears the flywheel, whilst retaining a decent mating area on both ends to help everything stay square. Start by cutting a piece of 8mm bar and finish it to length on the lathe. The length is non-standard due to the thickness of the brass frames, but if you can hold this dimension, it makes marking out the base much easier.

Both ends should now be drilled and tapped with an 8BA thread, but when centre-drilling, make sure the drill goes in far enough to create a small conical shoulder with the larger part of the drill, as this will be used to engage with the tailstock centre.

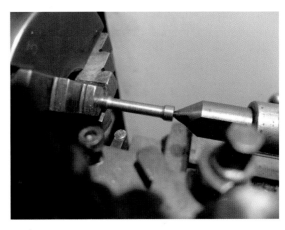

Fig. 6.26 *Turning the engine stand-off, using a fixed centre in the tailstock to support the workpiece.*

Once both ends have been drilled and tapped, hold the part just lightly in the chuck by the very end and bring up the tailstock with a fixed centre to engage in the hole on the outer end. This support will pull the part parallel and then the chuck can be tightened. Now oil the point on the fixed centre, engage it in the hole with light pressure, and lock the tailstock barrel in place. Now the part can be turned, either with a forming tool, which can cut both left and right, or with a combination of left- and right-handed tools to create the reduced section on the part.

ENGINE ASSEMBLY

To drill the steam port in the cylinder in precisely the correct place, assemble each half of the engine with its bearing, cylinder, piston and pivot pin. Then orientate the cylinder (by turning the crank) so that it is fully oscillated towards the inlet port. Next, use a 1mm drill through the inlet port to mark where the cylinder should be drilled. Finally, dismantle the engine and clean it thoroughly.

At this point it is possible to run the engines separately on compressed air, as two single-cylinder units. This is entirely optional, but it is a good test to perform before going further.

The primary task in assembling the twin-cylinder engine is getting the frames aligned, so

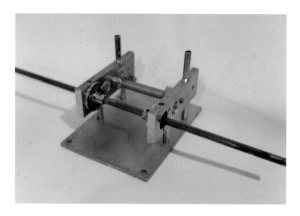

Fig. 6.28   Checking the bearing alignment with a 4mm silver steel rod during assembly of the fixed engine components.

there is no friction between the main bearings on the crank. The engine stand-off should hold the frames parallel, but this may not be adequate to get a running fit of the crank.

Start by assembling a bearing into each frame, ensuring the oil hole is correctly oriented. Next, assemble both engine frames and the central stand-off on the base, and pass a 4mm silver steel rod through one bearing and see if it lines up with the second one. In theory it should. The stand-off is designed to keep the frames parallel and aligned linearly; the base should then hold the frames rotationally aligned. If the 4mm rod spins freely, then you can continue the build, but if not, you'll need to make some adjustments to level things up. Experiment with slackening off each base screw and each bearing screw to find what eases the friction. Shims can be used under the support posts if needed. See if you can work out if the misalignment is angular or linear by having one engine frame loose to the base and biasing it slightly in all directions whilst turning the rod.

You can try to open out the mounting holes on one of the bearings, and also reduce the shoulder that locates in the frame. This will allow the bearing to 'float' to some degree, and may give enough adjustment to get the bearings lined up.

Fig. 6.27   Half the engine running on compressed air.

CONSTRAINTS, TOLERANCES AND FITS

Aligning the two halves of the paddle steamer engine is one of the trickiest parts of the build. Over-constrained assemblies can occur in a lot of places, and some are easier to solve than others. Two screw holes, for example, can be more easily aligned if the part to be clamped has slots rather than holes. This additional freedom of movement helps reduce the accuracy needed to get the parts to fit. An easy problem to solve.

One of the most difficult alignment problems to solve is that of coupling rods on steam loco-motives. Fig. 6.29 shows how a simple 0-4-0 locomotive can be modelled as a set of parallel rods. However, for the system to run without binding, the distance of the crank pin from the axle must be the same on all wheels, the coupling rod must be the same length as the axle spacing, and the crank pins must be perpendicular to the wheel.

The problem gets worse when the wheels on the other side of the loco are considered. The coupling rod for this pair of wheels needs to be 90 degrees from the first one. Now it becomes important that the angle between the crank pins on each axle is exactly the same. This is known as wheel quartering, and is one of the fundamental requirements in locomotive construction. In theory just having the correct dimensions would be sufficient to let the mechanism run smoothly, but in reality, tiny differences in parts due to tolerances of manufacture can give huge problems in the running.

Problems are further compounded if the chassis has more axles, and if the axles are sprung. Now, not only can the axles move up and down, but they can effectively twist, creating different distances and angles between wheel sets. When locomotive valve gear is modelled on CAD with perfect parts, the system will work, but the reality is different, and engineers must know about tolerances and limits and fits if they are to design something that can be manufactured and will work.

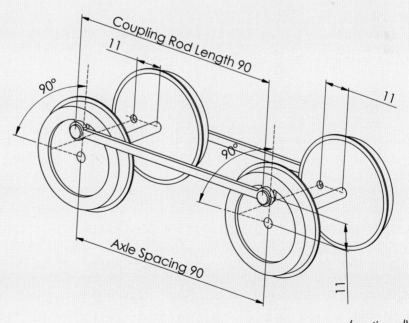

Fig. 6.29 Steam
locomotive coupling
rods.

(continued)

(continued)

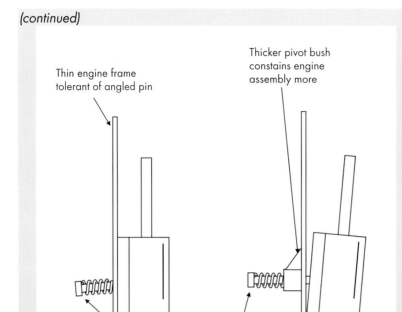

Thin engine frame tolerant of angled pin

Thicker pivot bush constains engine assembly more

Both cylinders have slightly non-square pivot pins

Fig. 6.30   Comparing two oscillating cylinder pivot bearings.

With problems of this type, it is important to focus on what is important in an assembly, and what will make the system work. Another example can be seen comparing oscillating engine designs in Fig. 6.30. The left image is a toy-like engine with a thin plate frame that takes the pivot pin. Even if the pin is not exactly perpendicular to the cylinder (as shown), the spring will still pull the port face of the cylinder flat to the frame, which is what matters for the engine to work.

The second design is nicer in many ways, with a larger pivot bearing area that is less likely to wear and looks a better solution – but now, the pivot pin angle to the port face is critical, because if this is not exactly 90 degrees then the port face will not be steam tight. The design has become more constrained and therefore difficult to manufacture – not impossible, and once sorted it will last longer than the toy engine – but the difficulty of manufacture needs to be balanced against the benefits.

Before assembling the rest of the engine, the inlet and exhaust pipes should be soft soldered to both frames. Assemble the frames on the base with the stand-off and axle as before, but this time add the connection pipes and steam inlet. Soft soldering these parts will mean the frames are now no longer movable, so it is important to get the axle running well before soldering.

When the engine has cooled, install both halves of the crank, including the flywheel and collar. Set the crank pins at 180 degrees by eye, and then the collar grub screws can be secured.

Add each piston and cylinder assembly, and secure with the pivot pins and springs. The whole engine can now be turned by hand to check for tight spots. Ensure the cylinders are not lifting from the frame at any point in the engine cycle.

If there are tight spots, try just one cylinder at a time to try to identify the cause. When trying the engine on compressed air, adding oil will help highlight any leaks. If one piston is tight, you could try lapping it into the cylinder with metal polish.

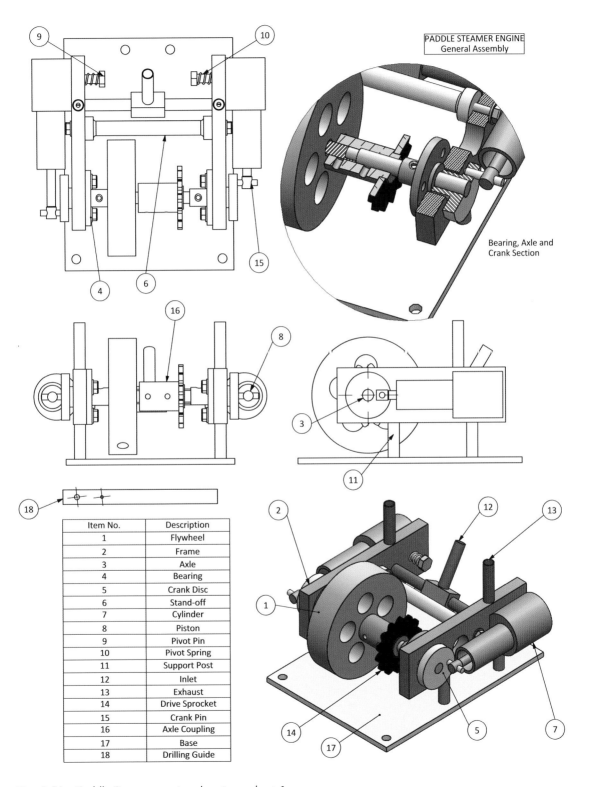

PADDLE STEAMER ENGINE
General Assembly

Bearing, Axle and
Crank Section

Item No.	Description
1	Flywheel
2	Frame
3	Axle
4	Bearing
5	Crank Disc
6	Stand-off
7	Cylinder
8	Piston
9	Pivot Pin
10	Pivot Spring
11	Support Post
12	Inlet
13	Exhaust
14	Drive Sprocket
15	Crank Pin
16	Axle Coupling
17	Base
18	Drilling Guide

Fig. 6.31   Paddle Steamer engine drawings, sheet 1.

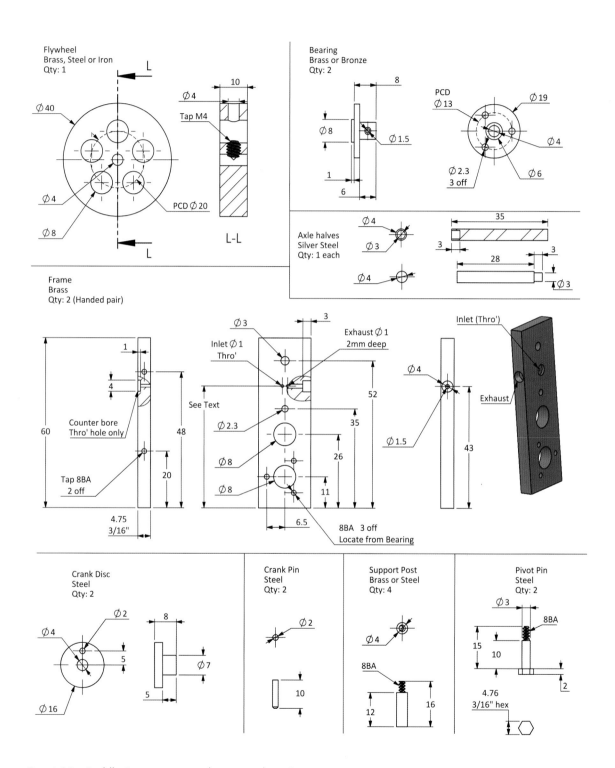

Fig. 6.32   Paddle Steamer engine drawings, sheet 2.

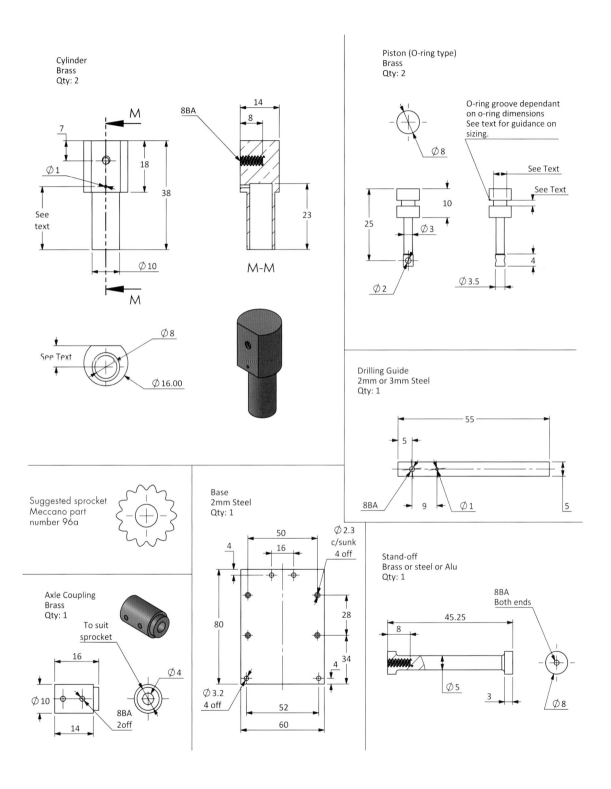

Fig. 6.33   Paddle Steamer engine drawings, sheet 3.

PADDLE-STEAMER HULL CONSTRUCTION

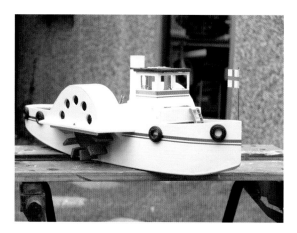

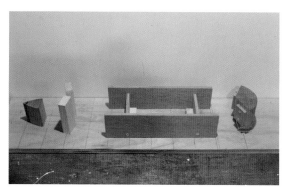

Fig. 6.35   Hull-forming jig made to the dimensions in the plans. The centre section should have parallel sides to assist in the attachment of the paddlewheels, and a flat bottom for the steam plant.

Fig. 6.34   Paddle Steamer hull and superstructure showing some of the simple details added, including trim stripes and car-tyre buffers.

The hull for the paddle steamer uses another construction technique. The sides of the hull are made first, formed from laminated thin ply against a former, so they are not tensioned in the final hull. This means we don't need the bottom of the hull to help hold them to shape, which means we can add the bottom later and curve it slightly to make the bow more streamlined and allow space for a rudder at the stern. The hull is sized such that a single sheet of 1,200 × 300mm sheet of modelling ply should be enough for the whole build.

FORMING JIG

The forming jig needs to be made first. This consists of some wooden blocks attached to a flat surface. The curve and the position of the wooden blocks is given by the plans. There are a couple of important points to take note of. First, the breast-hook at the front of the hull is 70mm tall, as this will be the final height of the deck from the keel: the breast-hook can therefore be used to support the deck at the bow.

Second, the transom is a curved block of wood made to the outer radius at the stern. This is 90mm tall and has two blocks secured to it, to support the deck. The blocks are, of course, 70mm from the keel to be level with the breast-hook deck support at the bow. These blocks are also positioned in from the outside edge by the thickness of three thin ply panels (3 × $^1/_{16}$in).

Three layers of $^1/_{16}$in ply can be used to make the hull sides, each part laminated to the next. One side should be assembled and clamped overnight before the bow can be sanded to final

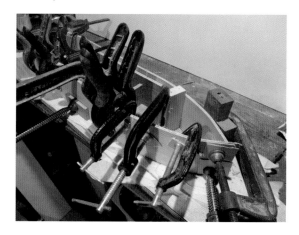

Fig. 6.36   Gluing and clamping the second side of the paddle-steamer hull. Each side was made from three lengths of $^1/_{16}$in ply laminated together.

Fig. 6.37 The hull sides removed from the forming jig.

Fig. 6.38 The bottom profile cut and sanded to shape. A flat section should be retained about the centre, enough to mount the steam plant.

shape and the second side added. Ensure that the clamps used bond the laminations together as well as hold the laminations to the jig.

When both sides are properly stuck, the hull can be removed from the jig and the keel profile marked on. This profile is very much a freehand curve, but ensure there is a flat section somewhere of at least 240mm for the steam plant. The hull underside can now be cut and sanded to shape.

The base of the hull is a piece of 6mm plywood clamped around the curve and glued into place. Kerfing cuts can be used if necessary, to get the wood to curve without splitting.

Finally, when the bottom of the hull is stuck fast, the top profile can be cut and sanded; but before we do this, trace the outside of the hull profile on to a piece of 6mm plywood to be used for the deck.

The suggested side profile is a gentle curve down from the bow to a depth of 12mm and then a straight line to the stern.

The deck is made in two parts, one panel up at

the bow, and then a separate piece at the stern where radio control equipment will be installed. There is an open section in the centre for access to the steam plant. For the bow deck, take the piece of 6mm plywood marked from the outside deck profile and use a woodworker's marking gauge, or just a nail in a block, to scribe an edge inside this line equal to the thickness of the hull side. Cut and sand to this line, and it should be a neat fit within the hull sides.

To support the deck, glue some woodstrips or off-cuts to both sides.

Fig. 6.39 As the deck outline was traced from the outside of the hull, a carpenter's marking gauge was used to mark a line off-set from the edge, to create a deck to fit inside the sides.

Fig. 6.40 Strips of scrapwood were added inside the hull sides to support the deck.

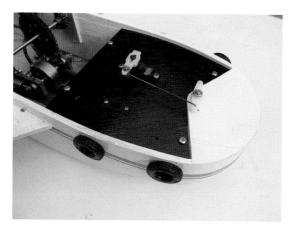

Fig. 6.41 Rear deck, rear bulkhead and control gear for the paddle steamer.

The rear deck is fitted along with a bulkhead in a position chosen by the builder, and somewhere to install the radio control equipment; both parts are cut and sanded to be a neat fit. The bulkhead should be glued in place, and the deck should be removable for fitting the control gear.

CONSIDERATIONS FOR PADDLEWHEEL DESIGN

The paddlewheels of the boat need to engage with the water without sitting too deep. A float

test is one way to see how deep the hull sits in the water, or you can use Simpson's rule on your plan drawing to calculate it. To perform a float test, load the hull with the steam plant fully fuelled, and mark where the waterline is with some sticky tape.

To match the paddle blades (actually called floats) to the boat we need to work out the diameter of the paddlewheel itself, as well as the number of floats and their area. All of this determines the float immersion, which is an important parameter to get the floats working at their best.

History tells us that the paddlewheel diameter needs to be maximized to get the most from it. We know that a float gives its greatest propulsion when its tangential velocity is parallel to the boat motion, and this proponent of the circle scribed by the floats is greater when the diameter is large.

To work out the paddlewheel diameter we need to know how high the axle is from the waterline. The waterline can be taken from your plans or your float test, and the highest sensible location for the axle is somewhere around the deck level. You can place the axle above the deck if you like, but be aware of how tall and top heavy the boat may become.

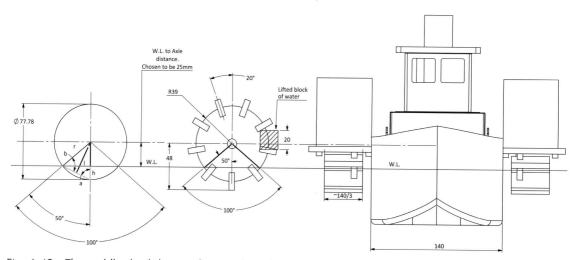

Fig. 6.42 The paddlewheel design, showing the axle-to-waterline distance, and other assumptions made to approximate the design.

In this case the most obvious position of the axle was found to be 25mm above the waterline, placing the axle just below the deck.

The other piece of information taken from the history books is that you don't want the immersed, swept arc of the paddle to be more than 100 degrees (*Hydrodynamics in Ship Design* (1957), Vol. 2, Ch. 71; H.E. Saunders). Above this value, plunging the wheel deeper to get a longer power stroke wastes energy lifting water up from the lake and pushing it down, creating noise and vibration in the process.

With these two numbers it should now be possible to use geometry to calculate the best swept radius for the floats.

Looking at Fig. 6.42 we can state:

r = Height of axle above waterline + h

To find *h*, first we need to find l, which is half the circle chord shown. We can calculate l using trigonometry because we know the angle at the top of the triangle is 50 degrees, and the vertical of the triangle is 25mm.

$$\text{Tan}50° = \frac{1}{25} \quad \therefore \text{l} = \text{Tan}50° \times 25 = 29.79\text{mm}$$

Now we can use trigonometry again to calculate the value of *h* because we can see from symmetry that angle *a* and *b* are equal, and we know that the interior angles of a triangle add up to 180 degrees:

$$180° - 50° = 130°$$
$$\frac{130°}{2} = 65°$$

So angle *a* is 65 degrees.

Now we can use the tan of this angle to find *h*:

$$\text{Tan}65° = \frac{29.79}{h} \quad \therefore h = \frac{29.79}{\text{Tan}65°} = 13.89\text{mm}$$

Going back to the first statement that the radius of the paddlewheel is:

r = Height of axle above waterline + h
∴ *r* = 25mm + 13.89mm = 38.89mm
Paddle wheel diameter is x 2, this = 2 x 38.89 = 77.78mm

This diameter indicates the arc scribed by the centre of the floats – but what dimensions should the floats be?

As a rule, sea-going vessels have narrower floats than calm-water vessels, because the roll of the ship is expected to be greater at sea, and wider floats do not provide an advantage if they are partly out of the water due to waves:

For sea going vessels the float width should be $^1/_3$ the boat beam.
Additionally, the float height is typically $^1/_3$ of the width.
(*Hydrodynamics in Ship Design* (1957), Vol. 2, Ch. 71; H.E. Saunders)

$$Float\ width = \frac{beam}{3} = \frac{140\text{mm}}{3} = 46.6\text{mm}$$

$$Float\ height = \frac{Float\ width}{3} = \frac{46.6}{3} = 15.5\text{mm}$$

This is a good starting point for the float dimensions, and gives a working area of:

$$46.6 \times 15.5 = 722.3\text{mm}^2$$

However, it is a fact that most boats have floats smaller than this, usually due to limitations in the environment such as the width of a harbour channel, or structural issues with the floats themselves causing them to deflect. So it wouldn't be out of place to do the same with our model. Less efficient, yes, but more in keeping with full-scale practice. So the width was reduced to 40mm, and consequently the height was increased to keep the same total area:

$$\frac{722.3\text{mm}^2}{40\text{mm}} = 18\text{mm}$$

Finally there is the question of how many floats

the wheel should have. Again there is a rule we can apply from historical information, which is that 'the length of the arc between the floats should be 1.5x the float height' (*Hydrodynamics in ship design* (1957), Vol. 2, Ch. 71; H.E. Saunders).

Arc length between floats = 1.5 × 18 = 27mm

This will now need adjusting to be an exact number of floats for the circumference:

Paddle wheel circumference = $2\pi r = 2\pi \times 38.89 = 244$mm

$$\frac{244}{27} = 9.05 \text{ floats or 9 whole floats}$$

Getting the correct number of floats ensures that more than one is in the water at any one time, creating a smoother propulsion force.

The paddlewheel definition is now complete:

Number of floats = 9
Angle between the floats = 40 degrees
Float dimension = 40mm wide and 18mm tall
Wheel diameter = 77.78mm
Height of the axle = 25mm above the waterline

This should give the required 100 degrees power stroke of each float in the water, without too much immersion.

If we know the area of the floats and the torque of our engine and the diameter of the paddlewheel, it should be possible to calculate the required reduction gear to be applied to the engine output. As with the propeller calculations,

it is difficult to work out the load on the paddle-wheels without knowing the boat velocity and hull resistance. However, we can reach an approxima-tion by looking at the water lifted by a single float.

The standard unit for torque is Nm, but in this small scale we can use mm for the length, as long as we are consistent:

- A single float area is 722.3mm².
- The density of water is 1000kg/m³, but the cuboid of water lifted has to be estimated, but could be reasonably set to 20mm tall, which is the approximate spacing to the next float (*refer back to Fig. 6.42*).
- The mass of the loaded floats can be multi-plied by gravity and the density of water to give a force.
- Water density is 1000kg/m³, which is 1 × 10^{-6}mm³ or $1e^{-6}$

∴ *Force on float = 722.3 × 20 × $1e^{-6}$ × 9.81 = 0.14N*

The radius of the paddlewheel is 38.89mm, and so the torque required to lift the loaded floats is:

Paddlewheel torque = 0.141 × 38.89 = 5.51Nmm

This is for a single float, but in reality there will be multiple floats in the water, probably at least

two each side, so it wouldn't be unreasonable to multiply this load by 4:

∴ *Total torque requirement = 4 × 5.51 = 22.04N*

Fig. 6.43   Paddle-steamer engine on the torque tester.

Checking the performance of the paddle-steamer engine on the torque brake from Chapter 3 provides some interesting data:

The power and speed curve at 30psi is shown below.

Maximum torque on 30psi was 20.09Nmm. During the test it was noted that the engine seemed happiest at about 1,400rpm. There was not too much vibration at this speed, and a reasonable

Engine torque spreadsheet

$$\text{Power} = (M_w - M_s) \times g \times r \times (2\pi \times (\text{rpm}/60))$$

Spring rate   0.0145 Kg/mm
Spring length   85 mm

PSI	Brake Mass (Kg)	Spring l (mm)	Spring Ext (mm)	Spring force (Kg)	$M_w - M_s$ (Kg)	G m/s	Radius (mm)	Torque (Nmm)	Time for 10 revs	RPM	Rads/s	Power (mW)
30	0	85	0	0	0	9.81	4	0	17.63	1939.875	203.1386	0
30	0.12	85.5	0.5	0.00725	0.11275	9.81	4	4.42431	18.56	1842.672	192.9597	853.7137
30	0.164	86.59	1.59	0.023055	0.140945	9.81	4	5.53068	18.87	1812.401	189.7898	1049.667
30	0.21	87.51	2.51	0.036395	0.173605	9.81	4	6.81226	21.42	1596.639	167.1957	1138.981
30	0.26	87.69	2.69	0.039005	0.220995	9.81	4	8.67184	22.47	1522.029	159.3829	1382.143
30	0.306	88.11	3.11	0.045095	0.260905	9.81	4	10.2379	22.94	1490.846	156.1174	1598.316
30	0.354	88.3	3.3	0.04785	0.30615	9.81	4	12.0133	24.81	1378.476	144.3504	1734.128
30	0.4	89.57	4.57	0.066265	0.333735	9.81	4	13.0958	26.06	1312.356	137.4264	1799.704
30	0.45	90.7	5.7	0.08265	0.36735	9.81	4	14.4148	28.99	1179.717	123.5368	1780.76
30	0.498	93.06	8.06	0.11687	0.38113	9.81	4	**14.9555**	28.83	1186.264	124.2224	1857.814
30	0.544	94.39	9.39	0.136155	0.407845	9.81	4	16.0038	31.38	1089.866	114.1279	1826.484
30	0.594	95.05	10.05	0.145725	0.448275	9.81	4	17.5903	34.28	997.6663	104.473	1837.712
30	0.64	97.99	12.99	0.188355	0.451645	9.81	4	17.7225	37.49	912.2433	95.52768	1692.994
30	0.686	99.21	14.21	0.206045	0.479955	9.81	4	18.8334	42.11	812.1586	85.04709	1601.729
30	0.736	100.44	15.44	0.22388	0.51212	9.81	4	20.0956	50.99	670.7197	70.23598	1411.433

Fig. 6.44   Torque curve for the paddle-steamer engine with the chosen operating point circled.

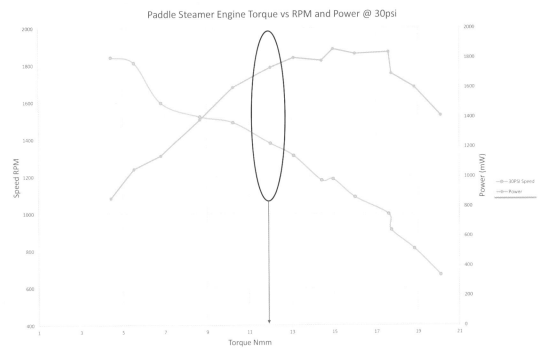

Paddle Steamer Engine Torque vs RPM and Power @ 30psi

torque output, so this was the chosen operating point for the engine. From the chart, this speed gave 11.5Nmm of torque.

This means the engine does not have enough torque to turn the paddlewheels. In any case, this is rather fast for a paddlewheel, and if the paddles were to turn at 1,400rpm, one could expect a high amount of spray and foam, which is all wasted energy. There will also be losses in the transmission system that we should make an allowance for.

If we introduce a reduction gear to the engine output, then we can slow down this speed and also gain an increase in torque, which will help the paddles to turn against the load.

To calculate a reduction gear, one approach is to consider scale speed. Scale speed is known to be the square route of the scale, multiplied by the speed or rpm. Our paddle steamer is not a scale model, but it is 600mm long, and full-scale, small paddle tugs would have been more like 20m long (20,000mm). This gives a scale of:

$$\frac{20000}{600} = 33.3 \therefore \text{ A scale of 1:33.3}$$

Full-size paddle-steamer wheels could reasonably be assumed to turn at about 40rpm:

$$\text{Scale rpm} = \sqrt{scale} \times rpm = \sqrt{33} \times 40 = 230rpm$$

$$\therefore Reduction\ gear = \frac{1400}{230} = 6.08 \text{ or roughly 6:1}$$

The primary Meccano gear is fourteen teeth, so the driven gear should be five times this, which is seventy teeth, to give the correct reduction gear. However, Meccano sprockets are only available in fourteen, eighteen, twenty-eight, thirty-six and fifty-six teeth versions. So a single-stage reduction gear will not work.

Also, talking practically, we need to get the chain drive to both paddlewheels. With a longer boat it may be possible to have a single shaft between the paddlewheels to keep them running

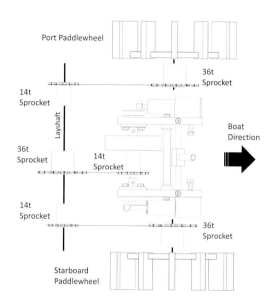

Fig. 6.45 Paddle-steamer transmission designed to give a torque increase of approximately 6×.

synchronously. However, in the short tug, the boiler is in the way. Therefore this model features independent drive to separate paddlewheel units, so each paddle is held in a housing with its own bearings and splash cover. A Meccano drive sprocket is then used to couple each wheel to a layshaft, with a third chain down to the primary drive on the crankshaft. This is shown schematically in Fig. 6.45.

This scheme provides the option to use a two-stage reduction gear, which will reduce the size of the large sprocket we need. This type of reduction gear is called a compound gear train, and with this system we can multiply two reductions together. Staying with the fourteen-tooth primary gear, we could link it to a thirty-six-tooth gear to give a reduction ratio of:

$$\frac{36}{14} = 2.57$$

Add a second reduction gear of the same ratio and we can get close to the 6.08:

$$\frac{36}{14} \times \frac{36}{14} = 2.57 \times 2.57 = 6.6$$

CHAINS AND EFFICIENCY

The target reduction is 6:1, meaning that for every turn of the paddlewheels, the engine will make four turns. This speed reduction will have an equivalent torque increase, so we can expect four times the torque from the engine with this gear. The result should be a set of paddlewheels running slowly, but with greater power, to move the boat forwards.

One reason to specify a chain drive over a belt drive is that the chain can be run with a lower tension without losing traction, and this means less radial loading on bearings, and less energy used to overcome friction in the system.

In full-size applications involving chains, the chain tension is maintained either by having an adjustable spacing between the sprocket axles, or by having a tensioner in the system. A sprung idler wheel can be used to maintain tension – the only requirement is that the idler wheel must be on the non-drive side of the chain. With any chain or belt system, the drive side will be doing all the work, and we can therefore expect this side to be under constant tension. This means that any slack in the drive chain will be on the non-drive side, and placing the idler wheel here will keep everything in check and prevent the chain rattling or jumping teeth.

A belt is another option, which gives a comparable drive system to the chain; however, a belt relies on friction between the pulley and the belt for transmission of motion, rather than positive engagement such as a chain and sprocket. As a result, a simple pulley system requires a higher tension to maintain traction. This tension loads the bearing shafts axially, making them harder to turn. Belts may also lose traction when wet or greasy.

A more advanced belt form is the V-belt, and this is a more powerful transmission. The V-belt (combined with a V-pulley) means the tension in the system pulls the belt tight into the pulley V, creating a tight 'wedge' action that dramatically increases the driving force between the pulley and belt for a given tension.

To create a transmission system with the lowest losses for the paddle steamer, a chain drive is proposed, running with no tensioners and therefore relying on the positive engagement of the chain and sprockets to maintain traction. This would be ill advised in full-size practice, but is perfectly acceptable here. Having said this, a slack chain must not be so loose that it falls off the sprockets completely.

THE MANUFACTURE OF PADDLES

The paddlewheels are discs of 6mm plywood, slotted to take 6mm ply paddles. Dimensions are given in the drawing. It goes without saying that these assemblies should be constructed with waterproof glue, and painted to protect them from their operating environment.

Fig. 6.46 Paddlewheel construction. Each paddlewheel can be made from a disc of 6mm plywood, notched to suit the floats. For gluing, the paddlewheel disc should be spaced off the reference surface by an off-cut of 6mm plywood.

Fig. 6.47 The two paddlewheels, painted and fitted with a Meccano bush wheel.

On the back of each paddlewheel a Meccano bush wheel is added, which will fit and grip the axle; the plate of the bush wheel is secured to the paddlewheel with some short wood screws.

PADDLEWHEEL COVERS AND SUPPORT FRAME

The inner and outer covers are made as a pair to ensure a matching profile. They can be clamped or screwed together, and if screwed, then positioning the screw locations where the large holes will (later) be cut is a good idea. Cut and sand the outer shape and drill for the bearing holes before separating the panels. The outer cover can then have the large holes cut with a hole saw or flat bit. The support frame for the wheel housings is a straightforward cutting and sanding job.

To assemble, choose a height for the paddlewheel axle based on the immersion calculations from earlier, and find the mid-position along the side of the boat. Drill a 10mm diameter clearance hole for the axle, and glue the inner cover in place. It is worth adding one or two screws or a couple of nuts and bolts to ensure this is properly secure. Add the support frame and outer cover together, and place a rod through the two bearing holes to ensure they are aligned whilst the glue dries.

PADDLEWHEELS FOR THE TWENTY-FIRST CENTURY

In times gone by when paddlewheels were the primary source of boat propulsion, a lot of innovation was seen with float design. Feathering mechanisms were commonplace. The feathering paddlewheel was patented in England in 1829 by Elijah Galloway, and subsequently improved by an engineer named William Morgan. In the feathering wheel, clever linkages would rotate each float about its horizontal axis during the wheel rotation to optimize how the float entered and left the water. There were experiments with different float shapes to try to reduce the amount of water lifted by the wheel, and side plates were added to prevent water spilling off the sides of the floats.

Although most paddle-powered boats are just seen as novelties these days, there is a school of thought that they might equal or even out-perform propellers in some scenarios. There is no doubt that a paddle boat can operate in much shallower waters than a screw-driven boat. Paddle-driven tugboats can also turn within their length by running the side wheels in different directions, something a screw-driven boat cannot do.

Furthermore, most paddle-design work was done before the advent of computer modelling of hydrodynamics, and materials have advanced immensely over the years. With this in mind, some engineers are starting to re-evaluate paddlewheel possibilities. Recent experiments with modern paddlewheel designs have shown comparable levels of efficiency and performance to a propeller. Their downside remains that they are handicapped in rough weather, but in shallow draughts and tight spaces they have advantages; so we might yet see them back on rivers and lakes in the future.

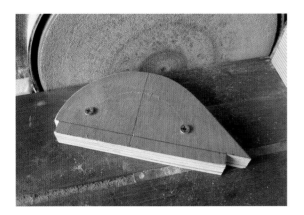

Fig. 6.48   Sanding a pair of wheel covers.

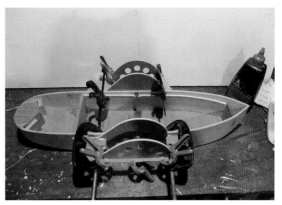

Fig. 6.49   The wheel side covers positioned and clamped for gluing. Note the metal rod being used to align the bearing holes.

The top of the splash cover is made from small strips of thin ply off-cuts glued and sanded to a neat finish with the side covers. The hull and splash covers are now ready for painting.

To fit the paddlewheels, place your chosen bearings in the two holes secured with a small dot of epoxy glue and with a 4mm axle passed between them to ensure alignment. These bearings will need to have an inner diameter of 4mm for the axle and an outer diameter of your choosing. Small bearings are available from many online bearing stores and also suppliers that sell parts for robot builds. The bearings used here were 9mm on the outside with a shoulder to help them sit square in the mounting hole.

When the glue is dry, hold the paddlewheel in the housing, push the axle into position from the inside, and secure the grub screw on the paddlewheel. Add the inside twenty-eight-tooth sprocket, and check that the wheel spins freely. Then do the same on the other side.

ENGINE INSTALLATION AND REDUCTION GEAR

A number of Meccano parts are used to create the transmission for the paddle steamer. All Meccano components are still available despite it being over 100 years old. If you require parts, then the list below is what you need to create a system like the one used here.

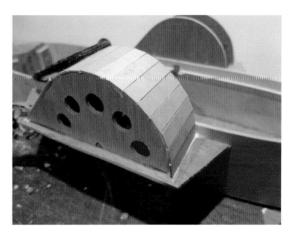

Fig. 6.50   Making the splash-cover top with strips of thin ply.

Fig. 6.51   Paddlewheel assembled in the cowling.

List of Parts Required

Part Number	Description	Quantity	Purpose
96a	14-tooth sprocket	3	Reduction transmission
95	36-tooth sprocket	3	Reduction transmission
94	Length of chain	~680mm (26.5in)	Reduction transmission
24	Bush wheel	2	Mount paddlewheel to axle

MECCANO AND THE FACTORY OF DREAMS

The 'Meccano' trademark was registered in 1907, but Frank Hornby's idea for a construction set began in 1898 when he started making toys for his son made from strips of metal bolted together. The breakthrough came when he realized that perforated strips enabled parts to be interchangeable, and allowed a builder to construct any model of their choosing.

Meccano kits had plate, girder and strip parts, plus axles, wheels, pulleys and gears, and of course nuts and bolts. In 1914 Hornby built his 'Factory of Dreams' on Binns Road in Liverpool, where it remained for the next sixty years.

Frank also launched a mechanics magazine, and funded build competitions for constructors to submit their most ambitious builds. Many of these large designs were later turned into leaflets to encourage other people to build them, selling more Meccano in the process. Along with Meccano, Hornby also produced several other highly successful toy lines, including clockwork trains, diecast Dinky toys, and the iconic Hornby 00 railway.

Common opinion amongst mechanical engineers is that the Meccano component system actually represents the DNA of modern mechanics, in the same way that atoms are the building blocks of science. For example, there is no differential gearbox in the Meccano range, but there are enough components to make one. It follows, therefore, that you should be able to make anything from Meccano. Over the years, builders have produced models of bridges, cranes, automobile chassis and trains. The selection of gears, although limited, allows a huge range of ratios, and the building of such things as working clocks and gearboxes. Most significantly, one of the earliest computers ever made was a difference engine made from Meccano components in 1937.

Fig. 6.52   Meccano set No. 4 and a model saloon car.

Fig. 6.53   The layshaft bearing support blocks.

Fig. 6.54   The layshaft and bearing blocks need careful positioning to get the chain tension correct. Chain tension should not be tight, as this will be too stiff to turn, but it should not be so loose that the chain can come off during running.

The steam plant should be placed in the hull to find a position where the burner tray is removable. The exact position is not critical, the only consideration being when we come to fit the funnel, as this needs to line up with the steam condenser.

The layshaft is a Meccano rod fitted with the three chosen sprockets to get the required final-drive ratio, and supported in bearings at both ends. The bearings rest in wooden blocks glued to the inside of the hull; the blocks are slotted to allow the layshaft to be removed for maintenance.

To position the bearing blocks, hold the layshaft and pull it to tension all the chains. Then just relax the tension a little so the system is easy to turn. This will then be the position to glue the bearing support blocks for the layshaft.

Once the layshaft is in, it should be possible to test the whole engine and transmission system on compressed air. If the chains are jumping off the sprockets, then check the alignment and tension. If all is well, then you can check the RPM of the

Fig. 6.55   Compressed-air test of the paddle-steamer engine and transmission system.

Fig. 6.56   The smokestack components, which are made from commercial 28mm plumbing fittings.

paddlewheels. The boat shown here had an output of 150rpm.

The superstructure is made from folded aluminium parts. Metal should be used because of the heat from the boiler nearby, and thin (0.5mm) aluminium is easy to work with. Mark the metal to the open profile given in the drawings, and then cut out with tin snips or old scissors. Make the fold using a bench vice, and check each fold is perpendicular to the edge with a square. The wheelhouse and the deck cover can be riveted together. The wheelhouse roof can be affixed with small nuts and bolts.

The smokestack is a 100mm length of 28mm plumbing copper. Using this material means it can be held to the deck cover with a plumbing union. You can machine the thread off the upper half of the union to disguise it a little, and you will also have to take the shoulder off the union nut so it can pull up tight to the aluminium plate.

The whole superstructure can be mounted on the front deck using small nuts and bolts. Before cutting the deck aperture over the boiler, place the housing over the boiler and line up the smokestack with the condenser. Then mark the deck for cutting.

Please follow the advice in Chapter 2 for the safe sailing of your paddle steamer at the lake.

Fig. 6.57   The Paddle Steamer out on the boating lake.

Paddle Steamer Hull Dimensions

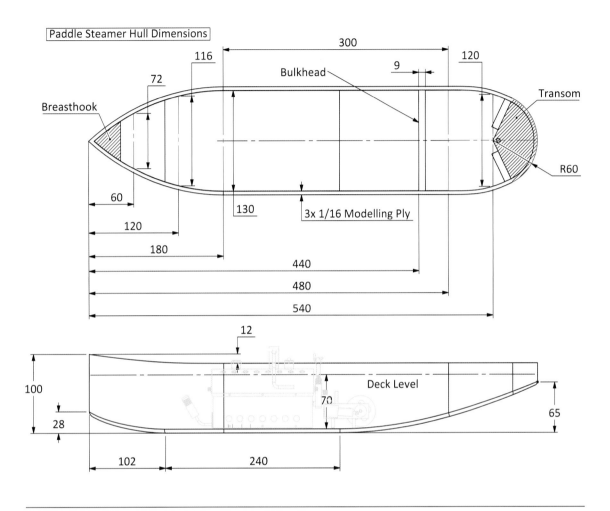

Suggested Forming Frame

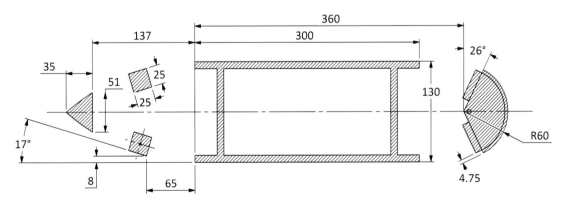

Fig. 6.58 Paddle Steamer boat drawings, sheet 1.

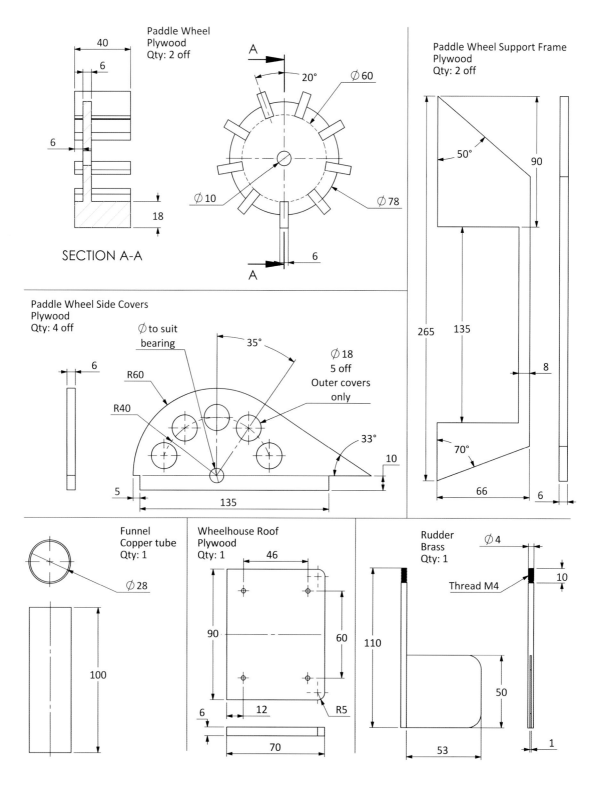

Fig. 6.59   Paddle Steamer boat drawings, sheet 2.

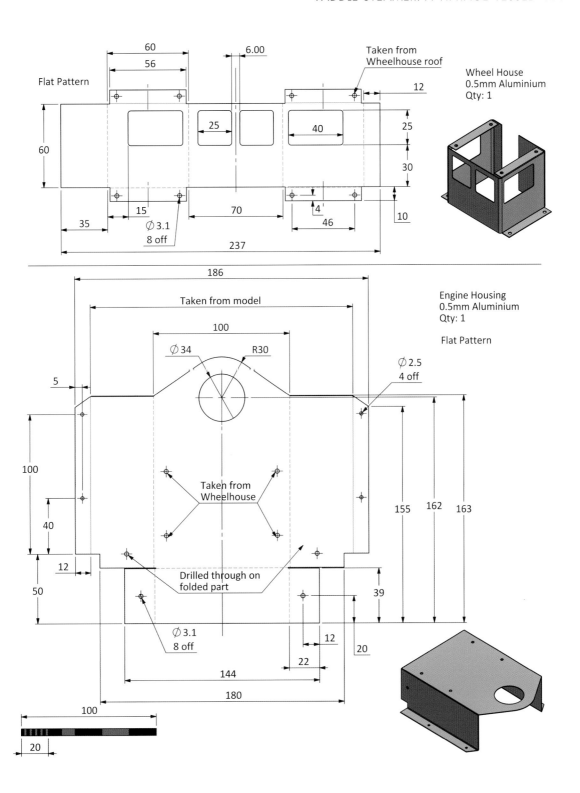

Fig. 6.60 Paddle Steamer boat drawings, sheet 3.

CHAPTER SEVEN

MORE IDEAS FOR MORE BOATS

It is to be hoped that this book has been informative to read, and you may even have made one of the models. If it has sparked an interest in model boats or model engineering, then this final chapter just throws up a few ideas for enhancements that you could make to your model or on a future build.

FURTHER REFINEMENTS

SCALE MODEL DETAILS

My preference is for a rugged working design rather than a lot of fine-scale detail, which is why I usually refer to my designs as steam toys, not models; but there is fun to be had adding scale details to your build. Some fittings you can easily make, such as handrails or masts, samson posts and portholes. Model shops sell all sorts of 'model chandlery' such as lifebuoys and rigging, vents and horns, which you can add if you like. If you have access to a 3D printer, the range of parts you could make is almost unlimited.

If you are artistic you could add 'distressing' to your model, such as rust or mould or even bullet

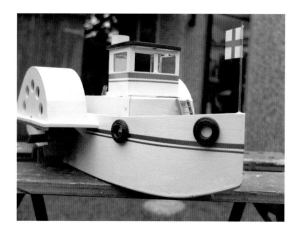

holes using paints. You can also draw planks on to the plywood parts with a straight edge and permanent pen, and then varnish over the ink to seal the design.

Model shops sell 'trim lines', which are long strips of self-adhesive vinyl. They can be used to create speed stripes, or just to add a contrasting line between painted panels.

On the subject of paint, white is the main colour for the majority of boats. Small modern boats are often white from top to bottom but with coloured stripes, and some have a darker colour below the waterline. If you are modelling a cargo ship, then the superstructure is typically white, but the hull may be blue, green or red. Battleships are, of course, grey all over. Vintage boats can also be white, but may also feature softer colours such as ivory or cream as the base coat, with brown accents with perhaps a splash of red. It is your model, so paint it as you wish.

REGULATOR CONTROL

There is no doubt that adding radio control to your regulator would give an extra level of functionality when at sea. However, be aware that the simple engines in this book don't have enough power strokes to self-start – they only run after a flick of the flywheel. So, if you are considering a variable regulator, it might be worth adding an 'idle' circuit that bypasses the main steam control. This way, when you shut the regulator, the engine will still run at a set minimum speed, so you are not marooned with a stalled engine.

Fig. 7.1   Trim lines can be used as speed stripes or to neaten the join between paint lines.

Alternatively, there have been implementations of a 'starting spring' system, which ensures the cylinder of an oscillating engine is always pulled across to the power stroke when stopped. The spring has to be strong enough to pull the cylinder, but it will also work against the engine when it is running so it must not be over-strong.

If you have ambitions for a fully self-starting engine, remember that each power stroke of a steam piston will cover about 90 degrees of crank rotation. So you will need four single-acting cylinders or two double-acting cylinders as a minimum, to ensure the engine will start from any position.

REVERSE GEAR

Going astern can be combined with the rudder to give full control of your boat, but like the regulator, your options depend on whether your engine is self-starting. If you have a self-starting engine, then reversing can be done by swapping the steam and exhaust ports on an oscillating cylinder, or by mechanical indexing of the valve gear on a slide-valve engine.

Another option is to make a variable pitch propeller. This would actually give you control over speed, direction and torque from a single system. Have a look at helicopter blade design, in particular the swash plates, to see how the pitch of a spinning blade can be adjusted. Boat propellers are smaller, but it has been done using a sliding control rod inside the main prop shaft.

Direction control can also be achieved with a style of tumbler reverse. Fig. 7.2 shows a twin flywheel on the output of a steam engine, with a friction drive that can contact either of the flywheels to take a positive drive to the propeller shaft. The output shaft direction can be swapped by moving the 'take-off' wheel from one side to the other. This system is suitable for a non-self-starting engine, as the engine itself doesn't change direction, just the output.

PERFORMANCE IMPROVEMENTS

The boats in this book work on modest pressures, and performance is therefore relaxed. If you are after more speed, then thinking about the system in terms of energy is a good approach. Processing more fuel in a given time, and getting more heat into the water will boost performance. Larger heating surfaces and higher pressures will also help, with the relevant adjustments made to maintain boiler safety.

Look at reducing friction wherever possible, and consider piston rings to produce a more powerful stroke. Pipe lagging, cylinder lagging and a superheater will help more energy reach the engine, and you could experiment with different fuels.

Fig. 7.3 Model steam-engine fuels. Modern methylated spirits can contain water, but bioethanol is purer and burns with a higher heat output. In the foreground is a can of Sterno fuel.

Fig. 7.2 Tumbler reverse gear idea using a single power take-off wheel to take transmission from one of two flywheels.

On the subject of fuels, methylated spirits (meths) is a long-held energy source for small steam plants. In bygone years meths was 100 per cent alcohol, but in recent years it has become diluted with water. It is also hydroscopic, so old fuel that has been stored may have an even higher water content. A good alternative is to use bioethanol. This is sold in hardware stores for flame-effect fires, and is purer than watered-down meths.

Many different meths burner designs have been produced over the years, but they can be broadly divided into simple 'wick' burners and 'vaporizing' burners. Wick burners are easy to make, and owners of Gauge 1 steam locomotives achieve astonishing performance from just two or three wicks connected to a fuel tank. However, these boilers are usually internally fired with a forced draught; a simple pot boiler will be much less effective. If you are building a wick burner, then avoid nylon or polymer-based string for the wick, which will just melt. Cotton string will work, but if the meths runs dry the cotton will burn away.

A good source of wick material is the ceramic fibre string sold to seal the doors of wood-burning stoves. It is available is different diameters and sold by the length. Another alternative is fibreglass, which can be found in old fire blankets and exhaust wrap for sports cars; but ceramic fibre is much more resistant to high temperatures (up to 1,260°C or 2,300°F). For reference, fibreglass can tolerate temperatures up to 550°C or 1,022°F, softening at about 840°C or 1,544°F.

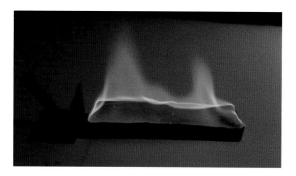

Fig. 7.4 Clean-burning Sterno fuel fire. Note the flame is largely blue and not too tall.

Experimenting with the length of the exposed section of the wick is needed to find the required flame without too much unburned vapour escaping. If your eyes are stinging when running the boiler, then it is a sign that the wicks need to be reduced. Generally, with meths, a small blue flame will give the best performance: if the flame is yellow then it is not burning cleanly. Figure 7.4 shows a nice blue flame from Sterno gel fuel, which is what you are aiming for.

Vaporizing burners take many different forms, but a simple box with a gauze top has a lot to recommend it. The box is filled with an absorbent wick material, which could be fibreglass or cloth, and filled until the meths just puddles at the top. When the meths is lit, the gauze will get warm and the boiling meths will produce a reliable flame. The size of the holes in the gauze is not important – instead it is the gauze area that regulates flame size. By adjusting the width, it should be possible to get a blue flame burning at the correct height for your boiler heating surface.

One benefit of this design is that the liquid fuel is held in the swab of material, so the risk of spillages is reduced. During use, expect the whole burner to get very hot, so the handle needs to be designed with this in mind.

If you do like to use meths to fire your boiler, be aware that it can spill easily, and it also burns clear, so pay close attention to what you are doing.

WORKING LIGHTS

Model railway lights, or LEDs (light-emitting diodes), can be used to add working lights to your model. Navigation lights should be red on the port side (left) and green on the starboard. Boats often have a spotlight pointing forwards on the foredeck, and another rearwards light shining down on the work area of the rear deck. Working lights add a whole new element to your boat when sailing at dusk.

LEDs need to come with a couple of warnings. First of all, they are polarity sensitive, meaning that they will only work with the current in the correct direction (this is exactly what a diode does). Conventionally, the longer leg on the diode will be the positive (also known as an anode). The anode should be connected to the positive of the power source.

LEDs need to be used with the correct voltage and current, which we can set with a resistor. Ohm's law tells us that voltage is equal to resistance multiplied by current:

$$V = I \times R$$

V = Voltage in volts
I = current in amps
R = resistance in ohms

To work out the resistor value, we need to know the voltage of our power source and the minimum and maximum operating voltages of our LED; also the expected voltage drop across our chosen LED and the maximum current, which is typically 20mA.

You can use a multimeter set to the diode setting to measure the minimum voltage for the LED. Make sure the red lead from the multimeter goes to the longer anode leg, and the black lead to the shorter cathode. The meter will display the minimum voltage, also known as the opening voltage, of the LED. A typical value would be 1.7v.

Typical Values of Different Colour LEDs

Colour	Forward Voltage @20mA
Red	2.0
Orange	2.2
Yellow	2.2
Green	3.2
Blue	3.2

The voltage drop across the LED will usually be about 2v. This is also known as the 'forward voltage', and should be given on the manufacturer's datasheet. Different colour LEDs will usually have different forward voltages: the table above gives typical values, but check if you can, because these may not be correct for your chosen LEDs.

With this information it should now be possible to calculate the required resistor. As a worked example, let's say we have a 3v battery powering a single red LED:

LED voltage drop = 2v
Max. current = 20mA

As we know, the LED will drop 2v out of the 3v from the battery, so we need the resistor to drop the remaining 1v. We also know the current in the whole circuit needs to be 20mA. Using Ohm's law we can calculate the required resistor:

$$R = \frac{V}{I} = \frac{1}{0.02} = 50\Omega$$

So a 50 Ohm resistor (or something close) would work well here. If an exact resistor cannot be found, then using the next nearest one of a higher value should give a satisfactory result. In this case it would be a 51Ω resistor.

The other check to make is the resistor power rating, which can be found using this formula:

Power = $I^2 \times R$

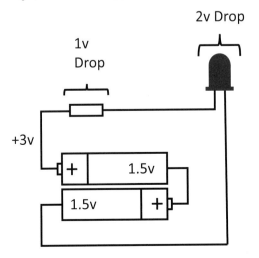

Fig. 7.5 Simple LED circuit.

In this example: Power = 0.022 × 50 = 0.2 Watts

Therefore, a 51Ω, ¼ Watt resistor will work for this circuit.

More complicated circuits are really beyond the scope of this book, but here is a second worked example using different colour LEDs. The different colour LEDs have been grouped so they can each have their own protection resistor.

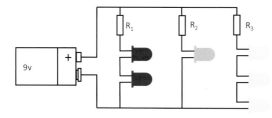

Fig. 7.6   Example of a circuit with multiple LEDs.

In any circuit, as long as you have the datasheet for the LEDs and you know your supply voltage, you should be able to calculate the correct resistor values.

BLUE TOOTH RADIO CONTROL

Blue tooth radio control is a whole other project on its own, but it is possible to control your boat from your mobile phone. This would save carrying the traditional radio gear to the lake side.

Gauge 1 locomotives are sometimes driven using nice palm-sized, compact handsets, which are more suited to live steam control than traditional 'two-stick' handsets.

If you are interested in programmable electronics, then modular kits such as the Arduino™ or RaspberryPi™ can be used to combine a blue tooth receiver with a servo output, to create the boat electronics to control the rudder. These systems require some programming skills but are highly adaptable, and can potentially give control to other onboard systems.

MORE ADVANCED ENGINEERING

With a larger build, you may be able to explore more advanced model engineering topics such as boiler feed pumps, automatic boiler control, gas firing and whistles. Boiler feed pumps, in particular, can extend running time significantly and remove any worry of the boiler running dry. Note that a boiler with a feed pump can be smaller and therefore raise steam more quickly, because it is constantly topped up when the system is running.

There are also many more engine configurations you could build, such as a slide valve steam engine, something with multiple cylinders perhaps, or maybe even a pair of engines driving twin propellers. You might like to scale up (or down) one of the designs in this book, or combine ideas from one engine with another to create your own configuration.

Worked Example using Different Colour LEDs

	Resistor 1	Resistor 2	Resistor 3
Supply voltage	9v	9v	9v
Total LED voltage drop	4v	3.2v	6.6v
Required resistor voltage drop	9v–4v=5v	9v–3.2v=5.8v	9v–6.6v=2.4v
Resistor value (R=V/I)	R=5/0.02=250Ω	R=5.8/0.02=290Ω	R=2.4/0.02=120Ω
Closest standard value	R=270Ω	R=300Ω	R=120Ω
Power (P=I²×R)	P=0.02²x270=0.1W	P=0.02²x300=0.12W	P=0.02²x120=0.05W

Boilers can achieve better efficiency if they are internally fired. There are other fuel options, and gas-firing or even coal boilers are possible. Perhaps you like one of the boiler designs here, but want to increase the heating surface using some of the other ideas from Chapter 4. You might want to add extra fittings, such as level gauges and pressure gauges. You could consider automatic boiler-control systems that have been developed in the past, ideal for a remote steam plant out on the water.

Or perhaps you prefer something different to a steam engine. An electric motor and clockwork motors are both options with different possibilities, in which case you might learn from the chapters on hull design, or adapt one of the given designs to your motor.

We should also mention Stirling engines, which are a very interesting type of heat engine well suited to model boating. If they are of interest, you could find out more and design one to power your boat.

Finally, hull forms are almost infinite in their possibilities. Single hull, catamaran and tri-hulls can be made, flat-bottoms, V or round cross-sections, with hard or rounded chines. Hull materials are often wood, but cardboard can be used for planking if properly sealed, and metal hulls have been made, often using biscuit-tin or drink-can material for the skin. You could design your own hull analytically, using the calculations detailed in this book, or just experiment with simple models made from plastic or card.

As is often said: 'Nothing new is learned without experimenting.' So don't be afraid of failure, and don't let comments from others put you off. Have a go, try new ideas, test things out, and enjoy your workshop time.

Bon voyage.

Fig. 7.7   Harbour Pilot departing the docks in 2022.

FURTHER READING AND INFORMATION

BOOKS

Bray, Stan, *Making Simple Model Steam Engines* (Crowood, 2005).
Bray, Stan, *Model Marine Steam* (Special Interest Model Books, 2006).
Cain, Tubal, *Building Simple Model Steam Engines* (Special Interest Model Books, 1998).
Cain, Tubal, *Model Engineer's Handbook* (Special Interest Model Books, 1998).
Darlington, Roy, *Stirling and Hot Air Engines* (Crowood, 2005). (This book has a fully detailed boat build as well as general information on Stirling engines.)
Harris, K.N., *Model Boilers and Boilermaking* (Tee Publishing, 2000).
Veenstra, André, *Handbook of Ship Modelling* (Argos Books, 1980).

SUPPLIERS

EKP Supplies
Unit A3
Brannam Court
Brannam Crescent
Roundswell Business Park
Barnstaple
Devon
EX31 3TD
Manufacturer and supplier of small fixings, steam fittings, soldering equipment and materials.
www.ekpsupplies.com

Just The Ticket Engineering Supplies
15 Hillside Drive
Salisbury
SP4 6LF
Model locomotive supplier but helpful in sourcing boiler materials and model engineering parts.
www.justtheticketsupplies.co.uk

Forest Classics
Woodedge Road
Off Ellwood Road
Milkwall
Coleford
Gloucestershire
GL16 7LF
Supplier of toy model steam engines and spares including safety valves, burners and fuel. They also sell an Edwardian paddle steamer kit.
www.forest-classics.co.uk

Link to .STL file for 3D printing of the final Harbour Pilot propeller
www.steves-workshop.co.uk/modelboats/pilot-prop.stl
(266KB)

INDEX